RECEPTION

Reception introduces students and academics alike to the study of the way in which texts are received by readers, viewers and audiences. Organized conceptually and thematically, this book provides a much-needed overview of the field, drawing on work in literary and cultural studies as well as Classics, Biblical studies, medievalism and the media history of the book. It provides new ways of understanding and configuring the relationships between the various terminologies and theories that comprise reception study, and suggests potential ways forward for study and research in the light of such new configurations. Written in a clear and accessible style, this is the ideal introduction to the study of reception.

Ika Willis is Senior Lecturer in English Literatures at the University of Wollongong in New South Wales, Australia.

THE NEW CRITICAL IDIOM

SERIES EDITOR: JOHN DRAKAKIS, UNIVERSITY OF STIRLING

The New Critical Idiom is an invaluable series of introductory guides to today's critical terminology. Each book:

- provides a handy, explanatory guide to the use (and abuse) of the term;
- offers an original and distinctive overview by a leading literary and cultural critic;
- relates the term to the larger field of cultural representation.

With a strong emphasis on clarity, lively debate, and the widest possible breadth of examples, *The New Critical Idiom* is an indispensable approach to key topics in literary studies.

Also available in this series:

Metre, Rhythm and Verse Form by Philip Hobsbaum
Mimesis by Matthew Potolsky
Modernism – third edition by Peter Childs
Myth – second edition by Laurence Coupe
Narrative – second edition by Paul Cobley
Parody by Simon Dentith
Pastoral by Terry Gifford
Performativity by James Loxley
The Postmodern by Simon Malpas
Realism by Pam Morris
Rhetoric by Jennifer Richards
Romance by Barbara Fuchs
Romanticism – second edition by Aidan Day
Science Fiction – second edition by Adam Roberts
Sexuality – second edition by Joseph Bristow
Spatiality by Robert T. Tally Jr
Stylistics by Richard Bradford
Subjectivity by Donald E. Hall
The Sublime – second edition by Philip Shaw
Temporalities by Russell West-Pavlov
Translation by Susan Bassnett
Travel Writing by Carl Thompson
The Unconscious by Antony Easthope

RECEPTION

Ika Willis

Routledge
Taylor & Francis Group
LONDON AND NEW YORK

First published 2018
by Routledge
2 Park Square, Milton Park, Abingdon, Oxon OX14 4RN

and by Routledge
711 Third Avenue, New York, NY 10017

Routledge is an imprint of the Taylor & Francis Group, an informa business

British Library Cataloguing-in-Publication Data
A catalogue record for this book is available from the British Library

Library of Congress Cataloging-in-Publication Data
Names: Willis, Ika, 1975- author.
Title: Reception/Ika Willis.
Description: Abingdon, Oxon; New York: Routledge, 2017. |
Series: The new critical idiom | Includes bibliographical references and index.
Identifiers: LCCN 2017022206 (print) | LCCN 2017035333 (ebook) |
ISBN 9781315666587 (ebook) | ISBN 9781138955097 (hardback: alk.paper) |
ISBN 9781138955103 (pbk.: alk.paper)Subjects: LCSH: Reader-response criticism. | Authors and readers. | Books and reading.
Classification: LCC PN98.R38 (ebook) | LCC PN98.R38 W54 2017 (print) |
DDC 801/.95–dc23
LC record available at https://lccn.loc.gov/2017022206

ISBN: 978-1-138-95509-7 (hbk)
ISBN: 978-1-138-95510-3 (pbk)
ISBN: 978-1-315-66658-7 (ebk)

Typeset in Times New Roman
by Sunrise Setting Ltd, Brixham, UK

For J,
la miglior lettrice

CONTENTS

Series editor's preface   viii
Acknowledgements   ix

Introduction: definitions, histories, objects   1

1 **Rewriting**   35

2 **Readers**   68

3 **Reading**   108

4 **Meaning**   142

5 **Conclusion**   166

Bibliography   171
Index   195

SERIES EDITOR'S PREFACE

The New Critical Idiom is a series of introductory books which seeks to extend the lexicon of literary terms, in order to address the radical changes which have taken place in the study of literature during the last decades of the twentieth century. The aim is to provide clear, well-illustrated accounts of the full range of terminology currently in use, and to evolve histories of its changing usage.

The current state of the discipline of literary studies is one where there is considerable debate concerning basic questions of terminology. This involves, among other things, the boundaries which distinguish the literary from the non-literary; the position of literature within the larger sphere of culture; the relationship between literatures of different cultures; and questions concerning the relation of literary to other cultural forms within the context of interdisciplinary studies.

It is clear that the field of literary criticism and theory is a dynamic and heterogeneous one. The present need is for individual volumes on terms which combine clarity of exposition with an adventurousness of perspective and a breadth of application. Each volume will contain as part of its apparatus some indication of the direction in which the definition of particular terms is likely to move, as well as expanding the disciplinary boundaries within which some of these terms have been traditionally contained. This will involve some re-situation of terms within the larger field of cultural representation, and will introduce examples from the area of film and the modern media in addition to examples from a variety of literary texts.

Acknowledgements

First of all, my thanks go to my colleagues and students at the University of Bristol (2005–2012), without whom I would not have become a receptionist. In Classics, Duncan Kennedy, Genevieve Liveley, Charles Martindale, Pantelis Michelakis and Ellen O'Gorman; in Theology, Jo Carruthers and John Lyons; in English, David Hopkins and Tom Sperlinger, for his work at the interface of English Literature and Community Engagement; and finally, all the students who took the MA in Reception and Critical Theory.

My colleagues and students at the University of Wollongong have continued to inform and challenge me since I moved here in 2013. Thanks in particular to Leigh Dale, Louise D'Arcens, Guy Davidson, Tanja Dreher, Joshua Lobb, Alison Moore, Lisa Slater and Sue Turnbull.

I am very grateful to the Arts Faculty at the University of Bristol and the Faculty of Law, Humanities and the Arts at the University of Wollongong for providing me with two periods of study leave: one to research and plan this book, and one to write it. At the University of Wollongong Library, the Collection Development, Resource Sharing and Liaison Service teams unstintingly provided support and help with tracking down research materials. Special thanks go to Afrodita Brbevski, Anne Brown, Fiona Carlisle, AJ Corradini and Leanne Webster.

Rita Felski, Alexis Lothian and John Lyons generously gave me access to unpublished and forthcoming work; Jenny Colgan supplied a page number for a reference to her own novel. Jenny Pausacker contributed an enormous amount of time and energy to this project in many ways, including scrupulous, wide-ranging research assistance, and compilation of the bibliography.

Readers bring texts alive, and I was lucky to have fifteen challenging and scrupulous readers to breathe life into my manuscript. In alphabetical order: Tom Clark, Rob Crowe, Leigh Dale, John Frow, Liz Gloyn, Michael Griffiths, Jason Grossman, James Machor, Imogen Mathew, Evan Milner, Ria Narai, Ellen O'Gorman, Jenny Pausacker, Laura Petersen, and Alex Wardop. My sixteenth reader was my editor, John Drakakis, his broad erudition and readerly sensitivity made an immeasurable contribution to the book.

Finally, extra thanks are due to Evan Milner, Michael Griffiths, Ellen O'Gorman, John Drakakis and Rob Crowe, for rescuing me from factual errors about the plot of the Rambo movies; Gary Oldman's glasses; the difference between the Elder and the Younger Senecas; Queenie Leavis's middle name; and the name of the street on which Neighbours is set. Any errors remaining are my own.

INTRODUCTION: DEFINITIONS, HISTORIES, OBJECTS

WHAT IS RECEPTION?

Reception involves looking at texts from the point of view of the readers, viewers, listeners, spectators and audiences who read, watch or listen to cultural productions, interpret them, and respond to them in a myriad of different ways. In this book, I use the word 'reception' to cover the following three areas: reception study, which analyses how readers and audiences interpret and use texts; reception history, which tracks the afterlives of texts and/or investigates the history of reading and the history of books; and reception theory, which explores the nature of interpretation, language and meaning itself.

In doing so, this book offers a new definition of reception. I redraw the boundaries of the broad and heterogeneous field(s) of enquiry covered by the term and reorganize the field around its central problems and questions. I sketch out a reception-informed critical practice which takes account of the inextricably intertwined relationship between texts and their interpreters, readers or receivers.

A reception-informed critical practice is rooted in one fundamental premise: the idea that all texts are designed for an audience, and only become meaningful when they are read, viewed or listened to. As the author and critic Ursula K. Le Guin puts it, 'The unread story is not a story; it is little black marks on wood pulp. The reader, reading it, makes it live: a live thing, a story' (1992 [1987]: 198). Or, as Terence Hawkes (1992: 2–3) says of Shakespeare, '"meaning". . . migrate[s] from the play itself to the material context in which it is performed . . . We use [his plays] to generate meaning. Shakespeare does not mean; we mean by Shakespeare'.

This premise places reception in an intriguing position vis-à-vis literary studies more broadly. If texts come into existence only when they are read, then without a reader we would not have a text to analyse: just 'little black marks on wood pulp'. Reception, as we shall see, is thus inseparable from the broader study of texts of all kinds. However, reception also challenges some widely held critical assumptions, transforming the way we think about texts in three key ways.

Firstly, by examining the real-life practices of historical and contemporary readers and audiences, reception study has produced findings which challenge received wisdom in literary history and textual theory. They make us rethink, for example, the way that identification works for cinema audiences (Barker 2005), or the way texts are grouped into genres (Lamond 2014). Secondly, by attending to the many different things that people *do* with texts, and to the afterlives of texts or the history of their effects, reception history greatly expands the field of possible objects of research. For example, Biblical scholars might find themselves tracking Biblical references by listening to pop songs or noting the stock numbers on military gunscopes (Roberts 2011: 1). Scholars of cinema might investigate the everyday lives of women in the 1950s, seeing how mundane actions, from brushing one's hair to walking downstairs, are saturated with memories and imitations of films (Stacey 2003 [1994]: 155). Thirdly and finally, reception theory challenges the idea that texts are self-contained and that we can 'lay claim to the discovery of [their] once-for-all "meaning"' (Hawkes 1992: 38). It involves us in big questions about the nature of interpretation, language and meaning, as well as questions about the relationship between texts and contexts.

'RECEPTION': THE WORD AND ITS USAGE

In current scholarly usage, 'reception' has both a broad and a narrow application. Most often, the term is used broadly to refer to an eclectic range of theoretical, critical and historical work on texts, readers and audiences, in a number of disciplines including media studies, cultural studies, literary studies, Classics and Biblical studies. Such work might include empirical research on the composition and preferences of media audiences; interview-based ethnographic research into the reading practices of romance fans; historical research into the ways in which past audiences and/or individual readers interpreted and evaluated particular texts or bodies of work; historical research into the economic and material systems for the production and distribution of physical books in a particular time and place; and textual analysis, tracing the ways in which a text seeks to generate particular meanings and effects through references to earlier texts, or tracking the afterlife of a text through its later interpretations, adaptations and appropriations.

Within this broad usage, different disciplines, sub-fields and schools employ the word 'reception' to refer to different methodologies and objects. What counts as reception in one field may not count as such in others. This means that the word is used inconsistently, in ways that can be confusing. For example, the Classical reception scholar Joanna Paul calls the film *O Brother, Where Art Thou?* 'a reception' of Homer's *Odyssey* (2007: 307), following common practice in her field. In media studies, however, the film itself would usually be called an adaptation of Homer's epic, while the word 'reception' would refer to an audience's interpretation of and responses to the film.

To complicate matters further, the word itself is not always used for analyses which nonetheless share a critical perspective, a theoretical approach, a research question or an object with work explicitly designated as 'reception'. For example, contemporary debates about what is sometimes called 'post-critical reading' rarely invoke the word 'reception', although these enquiries into ways of reading are necessarily involved in questions which have always been central to reception study and reception theory (Hensley 2015; Chew 2015). Similarly, work in media history and the history of the book which centres on the processes of text/audience or text/reader interaction often does not use the word 'reception', even though it tracks the impact of technological and material factors on audiences' perceptions and interpretations of texts (Littau 2006).

One strategy for dealing with this complexity is to employ the term 'reception' in a deliberately narrow sense, as opposed to the broad one sketched above. Some scholars have chosen to use the word 'reception', or sometimes 'reception aesthetics', in a highly circumscribed sense to specify one theoretical school, the Constance (or Konstanz) School, whose key members are Wolfgang Iser and Hans Robert Jauss. In this way, the name of 'reception' is reserved for a single coherent theoretical and methodological approach, to distinguish it from all the other ways of addressing the same questions and objects. Robert Holub (1984), the most vigorous advocate of this strategy, wants especially to differentiate Konstanz-School reception theory from work by a number of Anglophone critics from the 1970s and 1980s whose work was grouped together under the term 'reader-response criticism'.

It is true that there are important differences in critical perspective between the many schools and methodologies that make up reception study, theory and history. However, in my own attempt to produce a map of the field of reception, the strategy I use is the opposite of Holub's. This book covers work from multiple disciplines, and from a wide range of theoretical and critical frameworks, methodologies and objects of analysis. It also includes work that engages with the fundamental questions of reception but does not use the term itself. I take this approach because I believe that all the many heterogeneous disciplinary and theoretical approaches to reception have something to contribute to the study of texts, audiences and interpretation. Rather than choosing a single path, I aim to make visible as many as possible of the crisscrossing and divergent tracks that cross the field. For this reason, the style of the following chapters is quotation-heavy: each quotation should be seen as a signpost, signalling the start of a path which readers can then follow up.

This book draws on work in media and cultural studies as well as visual art and, occasionally, musicology, but it is primarily intended as an introduction to reception in the context of literary studies, including Biblical, Classical and medieval reception as well as historical and ethnographic work on the history of books and reading. This is partly because several useful media-oriented introductions to reception and audience studies already exist (Brooker and Jermyn 2003; Staiger 2005; Christie 2012). It is also because, as we will see later, verbal language has a privileged place in reception theory. The properties and characteristics of specifically verbal language have tended to serve as the model for sign systems or 'languages' in general, even those which do not use words as such, including the visual iconography of cinema and other visual art forms. As a result of the privileging of verbal language, many key theories, models and studies of reception are oriented around the analysis of literary texts.

The field of enquiry that I define as 'reception' overlaps with a number of other fields and terms, including hermeneutics, the study of interpretations, and reader-response or simply 'reading'. There are two main reasons for using the term 'reception'. The first reason is pragmatic: the word is currently being deployed by a majority of scholars to designate work on readers, reading practices and interpretation, across a number of disciplines. It is therefore already available and recognizable as a name for a cross-disciplinary field structured around a particular set of questions and problems. The second reason is theoretical: 'reception' carries a more capacious range of meanings than alternative terms, and frames the problem in a more useful way. 'Hermeneutics' has a specific and complex disciplinary history, bound up with the interpretation of Biblical and classical texts and with a particular strand of twentieth-century philosophical thought; it does not encompass the kind of empirical and historical research into readers and audiences which characterizes most work in literary reception study and reception history. 'Reading' suggests that processing alphabetic writing is *the* model for all interpretation, which is problematic, as we shall see below. 'Response' has a specifically intersubjective and ethical inflection. The term 'reception' instead refers to a whole range of receiving processes and embeds a communication metaphor into our way of thinking about the processes this book traces. This metaphor is a key element of the approach I adopt in dealing with this field.

At its simplest, the idea of 'reception' suggests a sender (an author), a message (a text) and a receiver (a reader), but it also implies that there must be a communications system which facilitates the sending and receiving of the message (Eco 1976: 32–47). Thinking about reception entails thinking about the system itself: about the people, processes and institutions involved in the production, transmission, distribution and circulation of messages and texts. Potentially, then, the term 'reception' suggests that the encounter between text and reader is mediated by contextual factors which enable and structure that encounter in the first place. The word thus directs our attention as literary critics not just to texts and readers, but to the factors influencing the ways in which texts and readers meet. For example, the Classical reception scholar Charles Martindale (1993: 8–9) argues that a historically accurate reconstruction of a performance of Early Music may be acoustically identical to a performance from the twelfth century, but it will be received differently by a twenty-first-century listener: if for no other reason, because it will be heard *as* a historically accurate reconstruction rather than as a piece of living contemporary culture.

Systems of communication and the acts of reception they enable are structured by multiple and multi-levelled actors and forces, drawn from many different domains of human experience and social life. Michael Warner refers to these structuring forces as 'constraints of circulation': the elements which determine how texts circulate, which readers they will reach and what might happen when they are received. These constraints, for him, are both material and internal. Material constraints include 'the means of production and distribution, the physical textual objects themselves, the social conditions of access to them', while internal ones include the 'forms of intelligibility' which determine the kind of reader that will be able to understand a given text (Warner 2002: 54–55).

To Warner's list, we might add cognitive and neurological factors, which are an increasing focus of research into reading and reception. Cognitive approaches use theory of mind (Zunshine 2010; 2012) or Text World Theory (Gavins 2007) to track the cognitive processes by which we relate to fictional characters or represent fictional worlds in our imaginations. Armstrong, meanwhile, shows through his work in neuroaesthetics and literature that even

> aspects of the [reading] experience that seem suspiciously fuzzy or even mystical to many tough-minded critics – for example, how reading entails filling in gaps left by the text or how literary works seem to be inhabited by a consciousness that comes alive when we read – turn out to have material foundations in the biology of brain processes.
>
> (2013: xiv)

In other words, the experimental findings of neuroscience in many cases confirm the accounts of reading given by reception theorists. The functions and capacities of the human brain underpin all acts of reading, not just on the level of pattern recognition and the decoding of alphabetic writing, but on the level of interpretation. This is not to say that our aesthetic and cognitive responses to texts are somehow pre-programmed and fixed at a biological level. Rather, the brain's 'wiring' works in complex relation to cultural and historical factors (Armstrong 2013: 14), and in any case varies according to an individual reader's history (73).

From the structure of human brains and the personal histories of individual readers to the material, economic and social structures which influence the production and distribution of texts, a vast number of interdependent factors are involved in acts of reception. The following chapters map the ways in which scholars think, and have thought, about the reader–text encounter and the structures of production, communication and reception which enable and mediate that encounter. The major ideas that this book deals with date from the last fifty years or so, beginning with the emergence in the 1960s of a constellation of ideas about the active power of readers, and more broadly about power itself.

However, it is not the case that, prior to 1960, literary critics and theorists ignored the existence of the reader and the effects of reading. Concern with the effects of literature on readers and audiences was central to European literary theory from classical Athens in the fifth century BCE until the eighteenth century, when the history of the reader took a different turn. The next sections of this introduction sketch a history of critical attention to the reader in Europe. It does not seek to be comprehensive, since the history of reading and the reader is well covered in several existing books (Manguel 1996; Raven, Small and Tadmor 1996; Finkelstein and McCleery 2002; 2012; Eliot and Rose 2009; Towheed, Crone and Halsey 2011). Instead, I draw out some specific aspects of the long history of reading and reception theory which provide a necessary background for the following chapters.

PREHISTORIES OF RECEPTION 1: CLASSICAL, MEDIEVAL, EARLY MODERN

When we talk about ancient Greek 'literature', using a name which in fact only comes into being much later to designate '"creative" or "imaginative" writing' (Widdowson 1999: 5), we primarily refer to poetry and drama. In ancient Greece, these works were performed for collective audiences, often in ceremonial or ritual contexts like religious/political festivals. Especially in the case of drama, notions of audience were bound up with notions of citizenship (Sommerstein 1993); in ancient Athens attendance at festivals was a civic duty. Theatregoing was thus one element in the production and maintenance of the identity of 'the citizen', a highly restricted category which did not include women, foreigners or slaves.

Because of the tight interconnections between citizenship and audience membership, much of ancient Greek literary theory debates the effects of literary performances on audiences, and whether these are positive or negative. The fourth-century BCE philosopher Plato 'object[ed] to poetry on the grounds that it excited the emotions, which ought to be kept under control' (Dorsch 1965: 17) and famously banished poets and singers from his ideal Republic. Unlike philosophers, Plato argues, poets are ignorant of the true nature of the phenomena they represent: their works are therefore necessarily untrue, and lead their audiences into error (Griswold 2016: n.p.). By contrast, Aristotle argues in his *Poetics* that poetry, and especially dramatic representation, has a cathartic effect on the emotions. The Greek word *catharsis* means 'purgation': theatregoing, it was suggested, released and purged potentially harmful emotions, and was ultimately beneficial to citizens.

Both Plato and Aristotle, however, saw the management of emotion as an important part of being a responsible citizen. Indeed, Augusto Boal (1985 [1974]: xiv) sees Aristotle as having devised 'the first, extremely powerful poetic-political system for intimidation of the spectator, for elimination of the "bad" or illegal tendencies of the audience'. Aristotelian catharsis thus produces an institution of spectatorship which functions to produce and/or reinforce a particular set of citizen behaviours centring on masculinity, rationality and the capacity to control one's emotions, appetites and body. Deeply embedded ideas about embodiment, emotion, cognition, reason, gender and citizenship continue to structure the way the West thinks about audiences, representation and reception to the present day.

Aristotle's *Poetics* circulated widely in Europe and the Middle East in the medieval period, in a version edited and translated into Latin by the

Andalusian-Arab philosopher Ibn Rushd (1126–1198), whose name is usually recorded in the West in its Latinized form, Averroes. Averroes's/ Ibn Rushd's highly influential edition focussed less on Aristotle's structural analysis of the plots of tragic drama, and more on its 'affective and audience-oriented' elements (Minnis and Scott 1988: 282). In the medieval and early modern period, then, Aristotle's thought joined with broader concerns about the moral and emotional effects of literature on audiences.

The other important Classical figure in this period was the Latin poet Horace (65–8 BCE). Horace's *Ars Poetica*, a poem which is also a work of poetic theory, stated that the function of poetry was to 'instruct and delight' its audience, a sentiment that 'was endlessly echoed and developed' by post-Classical critics (Dorsch 1965: 22). For example, Sir Philip Sidney's 1579 essay *An Apology for Poetry* or *The Defense of Poesy* claims that true poetry teaches its readers to take virtuous actions, and that the pleasurable aspects of its style are designed to compensate readers for the instructive truths that it embodies. True poets, Sidney (1973 [1595]: 102) wrote, aim 'both to delight and teach, and delight to move men to take that goodness in hand, which without delight they would fly as from a stranger; and teach to make them know that goodness whereunto they are moved'. In the seventeenth century Dryden (1964 [1668]: 128) stated, by contrast, that 'delight is the chief, if not the only end of poetry; instruction can be admitted but in the second place; for poesy only instructs as it delights'.

In general, medieval and early modern literary theory 'emphasized the relationship between the work of art and its audience – either how the literary work should be formed to "please and instruct" its audience or what that audience should be like in order to appreciate literature correctly' (Richter 2007: 2). Jane Tompkins (1980: 207) points out in an important essay, 'The Reader in History', that in both Classical and early modern theories 'literature is . . . defined as a shaper of public morals', so that 'its nature and value depend upon the kinds of effects it produces, effects that are equated . . . with moral behaviour and not with textual meaning'. Her essay clarifies the difference between notions of audience response in the pre-modern period and those in the present day. In the pre-modern period, 'response' was taken for granted as a key element of literary form and function, and understood in terms of moral behaviour. Conversely, recent reception and reader-response theories centre on meaning, not moral response, and ask 'whether response can be considered part of poetic meaning' at all (212). Tompkins shows that the question of whether or not it is legitimate for critics to consider audience responses to literature becomes meaningful only when literature comes to inhabit an autonomous aesthetic sphere, cut off from direct influence on political life and moral behaviour. More broadly, her essay shows that the ways in which critics, authors and audiences theorize reception and understand the effects of literature on them are deeply bound up with the place that literature holds at any given period within culture and society.

There are two important implications here. Firstly, although debates about literature from Plato to Dryden did centre on readers and their responses to the text, the responses considered significant were primarily moral and/or affective, rather than interpretative. In Tompkins' words, such critics were concerned with the moral behaviour of audiences, not with the textual meanings constructed by them. Drawing on and expanding Tompkins' viewpoint, Karin Littau argues that 'for the ancients, poetry's capacity for generating affect' was a key critical concern. 'Modern literary study', Littau (2006: 2–3) writes, 'tends to regard reading as a reducibly mental activity', while, by contrast, 'a tradition reaching back to antiquity . . . assumed that reading literature was not only about sense-making but also about sensation'. Modern literary theories think about reception in terms of cognition and interpretation: what meanings do readers find in texts? Earlier theories and approaches, meanwhile, focussed on the bodily, affective and moral dimensions of reception, which, as we saw in the discussion of Plato and Aristotle, were often seen as interconnected: what do texts do to readers' bodies, emotions and behaviours? And are their effects beneficial or harmful? We will return to the contemporary fixation on meaning, and the concomitant downgrading of the affective, moral and bodily aspects of reception, later in this chapter.

The other key implication of Tompkins' historical account is that theories of literature from the classical, medieval and early modern periods tended to regard the reader as passive in relation to the text. Contemporary theories see the reader as acting upon the raw material of the text to produce her own reading or interpretation of that text.

By contrast, in earlier accounts, it is texts which act, and readers who are acted upon. As Cathleen Bauschatz puts it,

> Platonic ideas on reading, from Plato himself to . . . the fifteenth and sixteenth centuries, stress if anything the reader's passivity. He is 'transformed' by the 'effects' of poetry, whether he will or no. The . . . Christian tradition, with its emphasis on the primacy of the Word, similarly places the reader or listener in a relatively subordinate position, while the text itself reaches out and converts or otherwise touches and changes him.
>
> (1980: 265–266)

Some pre-twentieth-century theorists, however, did credit the reader with a more active role in relation to the text. One of them was the French philosopher Montaigne (1533–1592), who compared reading to a game of tennis. Both reader and author must be 'actively involved . . . if the message (or ball) is to be transmitted and, more importantly, to be returned' (Bauschatz 1980: 264). Reading Montaigne, Bauschatz shows that historical periods are not uniform in their understanding and 'an oscillation between a belief in the text or author as dominant in the reading process and a view of the reader himself as creator of it is . . . a constant in the history of criticism' (289).

The contrast between pre-modern and contemporary theories of reception makes visible two axes which will be important throughout this book. The first axis involves a tension between the cognitive-interpretative and the ethical, emotional and/or embodied dimensions of the reception of texts. The question of 'meaning' has become dominant in twentieth-century criticism, and, as we shall see, reception is most often understood as an enquiry into the meanings that readers make out of texts, although other strands of thinking focus on modes of readerly response where meaning is not dominant: for example, bodily, affective or imaginative responses. The second axis involves the dynamic of relationship between readers and texts, often plotted in terms of activity and passivity, or, more broadly, agency, leading to the question of whether texts act on readers, or readers act on texts. Again, as we will see, different strands of reception take different positions on this question, but the question itself continues to structure work in the field.

PREHISTORIES OF RECEPTION 2: MODERNITY (1700–1900)

The eighteenth century is often seen as a major point of transition in reading practices from the early modern to the modern. It marks the culmination of a set of processes which began in the late medieval period, leading to the beginning of the forms of reading most characteristic of modernity (Wittmann 1999).

Firstly, the rise in silent reading in the fifteenth century led to a gradual 'privatization' of reading (Saenger 1997), intensified in the sixteenth century by the Protestant Reformation, a revolution which reshaped the thought and institutions of European Christianity. Protestants insisted that individual Christians must be allowed to read the Bible themselves, in their own languages, and permitted to interpret its meaning for themselves rather than having their interpretation of Scripture mediated and determined by the papal authority of the Catholic Church. Reformation ideals underpinned the distinctively modern sense of reading as an important locus of individual freedom and self-making (Simpson 2007).

A second process, which in some ways both facilitated and was counterbalanced by the first, was the gradual development of a system of mass communication and the emergence of a mass readership following the invention of the printing press in the fifteenth century, which meant that books no longer had to be individually hand-copied on parchment by scribes. As the production of books was mechanized, and the raw materials became cheaper, especially with the invention of paper, the sheer number of books in circulation in Europe and its colonies increased. Books were no longer necessarily luxury, one-off artefacts, scarce and expensive; they could be mass-produced. Other printed materials were produced and circulated, too, including political pamphlets, playbills, almanacs and other ephemera. Some scholars associate this technical change with a change in reading practices, from 'intensive', where people read one text (usually the Bible) repeatedly, to 'extensive', where people could read a larger number of texts more quickly, with less concentration on intensive rereading (Engelsing 1974; Brewer 1996).

There were more texts, and there were also more readers, as literacy itself spread beyond a small elite class in Europe (Vincent 2000). Print literacy was also a major factor in European colonialism, in ambivalent ways and in ways which played out differently in different local contexts. Firstly, print played an important part in the establishment of nationalism as a significant political force. Printed materials, including newspapers, were produced and circulated globally on transportation channels opened up by colonial projects. Through print-based practices such as reading the same edition of the same newspaper in widely separated geographical locations, readers were able to experience themselves as members of a new kind of dispersed collectivity, the 'imagined community' of the nation (Anderson 1983).

In addition, the new technologies of information storage and transmission associated with print were used by colonial administrators to track and control nations and populations, while the imposition of literacy was seen as a way of inculcating Christian beliefs and colonial ideologies in newly colonized peoples. At the same time, however, 'colonization does not imply a devouring march, where everything in [indigenous] cultures was suppressed by [European] pedagogical, religious, and administrative institutions'. The 'languages, literacies, memories, and spaces' of the colonized coexisted with those of the colonizers, although not on equal terms (Mignolo 2003: 2). Furthermore, print literacy could be, and was, appropriated, reconfigured, and used as a tool of resistance and a resource for identity formation by colonized peoples (Ghosh 2006). In Aotearoa/New Zealand, literacy was imposed on the Maori people (McKenzie 1984); in the US, by contrast, the acquisition of literacy by slaves was deeply feared by slave-owners. Slaves and owners alike understood literacy as a potentially powerful tool of emancipation from colonial control (Cornelius 1991; Jackson 2010: 260–261). Print literacy was thus bound up in complex and locally inflected ways with colonial power and resistance to that power.

Partly as a consequence of these two interrelated processes of privatization and colonialization, the eighteenth century saw a change in the ways in which authorship, literature and readership were conceived legally, economically and theoretically within Europe. In economic and legal terms, authors began to earn a living from the sale of their work, rather than from payments from patrons: the first copyright statute was passed in England in 1709 (Finkelstein and McCleery 2012: 63). Instead of writing for a circumscribed and known circle of readers, authors began to address a large, anonymous public, altering the relationship between author and reader and hence transforming the nature of literary reading. The Romantic movement redefined literature 'not as an activity deeply embedded in the social and political context of the day but as an autonomous and aesthetically driven pursuit' (Littau 2006: 19).

During the eighteenth and nineteenth centuries, a split developed and deepened between two forms of reading: those associated with 'high' culture, and those associated with mass culture. Critical attention to reading in this period was energized and structured by anxieties about the reading habits and materials available to mass audiences, in ways which continue to resonate in contemporary reception study. The anxiety was and is exacerbated by the fluidity and unenforceability of definitions of 'high' and 'mass' culture. John Guillory (1993: 24) has shown that the categories 'high' and 'mass', or 'serious' and 'popular', do not refer to fixed and stable corpuses of texts, but rather 'define *each other* in a system of literary production'. Shakespeare is a case in point: seen now as 'one of the barely accessible Classic Writers who [can] be approached only with great humility and even greater erudition' (Levine 1990 [1988]: 5), in the nineteenth-century US 'Shakespeare actually *was* popular entertainment' (4).

Although the contents of each category change across time, what remains constant, intensifying in the nineteenth century, is the perceived importance of reinforcing the boundary between categories and promoting 'serious' modes of reading and response to texts over popular ones. The influential British critic Matthew Arnold (1822–1888) was a passionate advocate for the importance of the form of reading associated with 'high' culture, which he simply called 'culture'. Arnold's terminology drew on the root meaning of the word 'culture', which is related to 'cultivation' and in the nineteenth century often referred to 'a process of human development' (Williams 1985: 87). In his best-known book, *Culture and Anarchy*, Arnold

recommend[ed] culture as the great help out of our present difficulties; culture being a pursuit of our total perfection by means of getting to know, on all the matters which most concern us, the best which has been thought and said in the world.

(2006 [1869]: 5)

At the same time, in the United States, as Joan Rubin (1992) has shown, the pursuit of high culture was similarly seen both as a pathway to self-improvement for individuals and as crucial to the success of democracy, shaping the tastes and moral sensibilities of citizens. Inseparable from the attempt to cultivate a taste for 'great literature' among the reading public, however, was a fear that mass reading practices, inculcated by popular culture, would inevitably lead to the misinterpretation or devaluation of such texts (Dowling 1996). The US poet and critic James Russell Lowell argued in 1893 that although printing had 'democratized information', the over-availability of cheap reading material had caused the 'strenuous habit of thinking' to be replaced by 'a loose indolence of reading which relaxes the muscular fibers of the mind' (cited in Rubin 1992: 18–19).

Modern anxieties about good versus bad reading were clearly associated with class and race, but were also strongly gendered. The eighteenth and nineteenth centuries saw a massive rise both in female readers and in female authors: women's work, both as readers and authors, was often seen as a threat to literary standards, good taste and high culture. Nathaniel Hawthorne, symptomatically, complained that female authors have corrupted the 'public taste':

> America is now wholly given over to a d---d mob of scribbling women, and I should have no chance of success while the public taste is occupied with their trash – and should be ashamed of myself if I did succeed.
>
> (1987 [1855]: 304)

As Andreas Huyssen (1986: 191) has shown, in the mid-to-late nineteenth century, a discourse emerged which 'consistently and obsessively gender[ed] mass culture and the masses as feminine, while high culture, whether traditional or modern, clearly remain[ed] the privileged realm of male activities'.

The key forces in the modern construction of reading and the reader are, firstly, the privatization of reading, and the notion of reading as culture, self-culture or self-making; and secondly, the division between 'good' and 'bad' forms of reading, and the way these map on to gender, class and race. As we will see throughout this book, these ideas continue to structure both critical and popular notions of audience and reception down to the present day.

PREHISTORIES OF RECEPTION 3: C.1920–1960

In the first half of the twentieth century, two parallel strands of critical thought were precursors to the emergence of reception and reader-response criticism in the 1960s–1980s. One, associated particularly with scholarship in Eastern Europe but also a small number of critics in the UK and US, insisted that it is not possible to understand a literary work without reference to a reader and the reading process. The other school of thought, increasingly dominant in the Anglophone world over this period, focussed on the literary work of art itself and, in some cases, explicitly ruled out reference to readers. Confusingly, the term 'formalist' has commonly been used to describe both traditions.

In Eastern Europe from the 1910s to the 1930s, the interrelated critical schools known as the Russian Formalists and the Prague Structuralists began to investigate questions about literary language and meaning. The Russian Formalist critic and linguist Roman Jakobson argued throughout his career that literary and poetic effects could and must be analysed with the tools of linguistics. He stated in his book *Modern Russian Poetry* in 1921 that 'the subject of literary scholarship is not literature . . . but literariness' (cited in Erlich 1980: 172). In a 1958 essay, 'Linguistics and Poetics', he calls 'literariness' 'the poetic function of language', which is not confined to a particular subset of texts or utterances (poems); instead, it is one of six linguistic functions which, in varying proportions, may be seen to be present in all 'verbal communication' (Jakobson 1987 [1958]: 69). Thus, Jakobson claimed, 'the *poetic* function of language . . . cannot be productively studied out of touch with the general problems of language', while at the same time, 'the scrutiny of language requires a thorough consideration of its poetic function' (69). Ultimately, he concluded, citing John Hollander, 'there seems to be no reason for trying to separate the literary from the overall linguistic' (93).

Meanwhile, the Prague structuralist Felix Vodička (1982 [1941]: 110) argued in 1941 in his essay 'The Concretization of the Literary Work: Problems of the Reception of Neruda's Works' that the work of art is 'a sign whose meaning and aesthetic value are comprehensible only on the basis of the literary conventions of a specific period'. A text has meaning only in relation to extratextual conventions, which determine the way in which it is read. The term Vodička used in his title, 'concretization', was taken from the Polish philosopher Roman Ingarden (1974 [1931]: 252), who demonstrated in *The Literary Work of Art* that works of art contain 'spots of indeterminacy' and that the meaning of a work of art is 'concretized' or 'realized' by a reader who fills in those spots in concrete ways.

The work of the Russian Formalists and Prague Structuralists in the 1920s and 1930s was not translated into English until the 1970s or later, and thus did not have a direct influence on scholarship in the UK and US at the time it was written. Nonetheless, their emphasis on the fundamentally linguistic nature of literature, and especially on the role of the reader, was mirrored by some Anglophone critics in the 1920s and 1930s. The very influential British critic I. A. Richards (2001 [1929]), in *Practical Criticism*, wrote what could be read (but was not) as a manifesto for reception and reader-response criticism:

> The *original* difficulty of all reading, the problem of *making out the meaning*, is our obvious starting-point. The answers to those apparently simple questions: 'What is a meaning?' 'What are we doing when we endeavour to make it out?' '*What* is it we are making out?' are the master-keys to all the problems of criticism.
>
> (2001 [1929]: 174)

Richards emphasized reading and meaning as central to the problems of literary criticism. Ten years later, in the US, Louise Rosenblatt (1938: 59) proposed a 'transactional' theory of literature which similarly centred on reading and the reader. In *Literature as Exploration*, she wrote that 'the reader's role is an active, not a passive one'. Therefore, in studying literature, we cannot attend only to the text, but must 'centre [our] attention' on the 'interaction between the reader and the book' (33). Interactivity is crucial to Rosenblatt's model: for her, 'meaning is not "in" the text, nor is it "in" the reader, but rather involves a range of unique factors that contribute to create a full, responsible, sensitive encounter' (Federico 2016: 19).

At the same time, however, another critical tradition was developing in the Anglophone world, one which looked away both from the problem of meaning and from readers and reading. Beginning with the emergence of formalism (with a small 'f') in the 1920s (Davis and

Womack 2002: 53), this approach culminated in the US with the New Criticism of the 1940s and 1950s.

A formalist approach, in this sense, understands literary works in terms of their formal properties and analyses the techniques which give those works their particular shape or form. The New Critics codified principles for the formal analysis of literature, for example in a well-known pair of essays by Wimsatt and Beardsley (1954), 'The Intentional Fallacy' and 'The Affective Fallacy'. The intentional fallacy, which led critics to analyse poetry in terms of its author's intentions, produced 'a confusion between the poem and its origins'; the affective fallacy, which involved analysis of the effects of poetry on a reader, introduced 'a confusion between the poem and its *results*'. Both fallacies, Wimsatt and Beardsley (1954: 21) claimed, 'have actually led away from criticism and from poetry'. The New Criticism thus deliberately turned away from both author and reader to focus on the poem, understood as a bounded, self-contained, autonomous object. This approach placed authorial intention, social context, the reader, the reading process and the problem of meaning outside the remit of literary criticism.

Meanwhile, in the UK, the period from the 1920s to the 1940s saw 'a "critical revolution" that, within twenty years, transformed the academic study of literature and raised it to a new prominence within the national culture' (Mulhern 1979: 19). This revolution was led by two critics and disciples of I. A. Richards, F. R. and Q. D. Leavis. As suggested by the titles of two of F. R. Leavis's best-known works, *The Great Tradition* and *Mass Civilisation and Minority Culture*, the Leavisite revolution involved the study of 'great' works in order to protect a minority high culture against the degradations of mass civilization, themselves enumerated in Q. D. Leavis's 1932 book, *Fiction and the Reading Public*, in which she compared the reading of popular fiction to an addiction to narcotics (Leavis 2011 [1932]: 14). Leavis explicitly saw himself as reviving Matthew Arnold's project of promoting 'culture' as 'the great help out of our present difficulties' (Baldick 1983: 163, 196). In the twentieth century, however, this project involved an emphasis on the technical skills of practical criticism and close reading, which were seen as more rigorous or even 'scientific' than previous approaches to literary texts and therefore served as a key 'symbol of the intellectual professionalism to which the [Leavises'] generation aspired' (Mulhern 1979: 28), as the study of 'English Literature' became institutionalized through changes in university and school curricula (Longhurst 1982).

THE BIRTH OF THE READER: 1960–1990

In the 1960s–1980s, a new generation of critics began to turn their attention to the dimensions of literature that Leavisite scholarship and New Criticism had neglected, especially the question of reading practices. In literary and cultural studies, the period was one of intense theoretical enquiry into the conditions of textual production and interpretation in which critical analysis was entangled with larger political interventions into intellectual practice. Rather than being an autonomous, bounded object defined by its formal characteristics, the text began to be understood as plural and open, constituted by relationships with external domains such as the pre-existing systems of language and genre; the rules for interpretation that it shares (or does not share) with its readers; the contexts of its production, circulation and reception; and the specific properties of the media and communications technologies through which texts are accessed. This period, then, saw multiple interventions into theories of interpretation and reading, whose impact still structures reception study, history and theory as currently practised. In mapping out the theoretical underpinnings of reception, we will often find ourselves returning to the ideas introduced below, as well as to the ways in which later scholars have developed or challenged those ideas, from the 1990s to the present day.

Starting in the 1960s, the New Critical model of the autonomous text came under attack from five directions, all of which helped to shape the current theoretical landscape of reception. Firstly, the material properties of texts, and the technologies which produce and circulate them, began to be the object of significant critical attention. Rather than simply being seen as an inert vehicle carrying literary meaning, the printed book and other media forms became objects of interest in their own right. Secondly, reader-response criticism and Konstanz-School reception brought 'the reader' into the foreground of literary-critical theory and practice. Thirdly, politicized modes of literary criticism, especially feminist and black thought, demonstrated that the analysis of texts is not a question of neutral expertise or 'competence', as it had been for the New Critics, but politically and ideologically situated. Fourthly, Marxist theories of interpretation offered new frameworks for understanding the relationship between texts and their social contexts of production and reception. And fifthly, the idea of textuality itself was radically expanded as a result of the so-called 'linguistic turn', a shift in philosophy and critical theory influenced in complex ways by structuralist and, more consequentially, post-structuralist theories of language (Colebrook 2014 [2010]). As a result of the linguistic turn, the boundaries of the New Critics' autonomous text were exploded, and more and more aspects of human life and interaction began to be understood through theories of language and communication.

These five areas of thought were profoundly interrelated: scholars working in each one influenced and were influenced by scholars working in the others. Moreover, within each of the five areas I list, a number of very different critical approaches and theoretical frameworks could be found. The following sections should therefore not be seen as descriptions of coherent and self-contained schools or theories, but as a provisional and relatively conventional way of organizing some of the most important theoretical innovations of the 1960s–1980s.

THE MEDIA HISTORY OF THE BOOK

For a number of reasons, including the spread and popularization of television and the beginning of the computer revolution, the 1960s were experienced as a significant break in the history of Western communication. As a result, critical attention began to turn to the historical, material and technological aspects of reading.

Scholars like Marshall McLuhan (1964) and Walter Ong (1982) argued for a very broad three-phase understanding of the history of communications technology. The first phase was the shift from orality to literacy; the second, from manuscript to print; and the third, from print to electronic technologies for storing and disseminating information. Friedrich Kittler's 1985 book *Discourse Networks* (in German, *Aufschreibesysteme*, literally 'notation systems') added a fourth transition that took place around 1900, when film and phonographic technologies became capable of recording reality directly without our 'notation systems' having to involve transcription into alphabetic writing.

New technologies, according to these media historians, are not just new ways of storing and transmitting 'content', but have important consequences for social organization and even human consciousness. Ong (1982: 77) writes that 'more than any other single invention, writing has transformed human consciousness', while McLuhan's (1964) *The Gutenberg Galaxy* and Elizabeth Eisenstein's (1979) *The Printing Press as an Agent of Change* made the case that print technologies created new forms of culture, knowledge and consciousness in the West. Benedict Anderson (1983) extends Eisenstein's argument even further in *Imagined Communities*, coining the term 'print-capitalism' to characterize the technological-economic system which underpinned Western social organization and made possible the foundation of the nation state in the eighteenth and nineteenth centuries.

These scholars made two important contributions to the field of reception, which will be examined further in Chapter Three. Firstly, they showed that the technological and material aspects of reading cannot be readily separated from the interpretative aspects, as the book is indissociably both 'physical object' and 'expressive form' (McKenzie 1984: 334–335). Secondly, and relatedly, these theorists and writers began to elaborate an expanded notion of 'technology' and its relationship to social forms, skills and protocols. Indeed, the textual bibliographer and historian of printing D. F. McKenzie (1984: 336–338) defined literacy itself as a technology made up of multiple knowledges, skills and cultural assumptions.

At the start of this introduction I suggested that the term 'reception' encodes a communications metaphor, so that the encounter between text and reader takes place within a historically and culturally specific system of communication. An expanded sense of technology provides one important framework for understanding that system, and the material and social forms through which texts are produced and circulated.

READER-RESPONSE CRITICISM

New Critics believed that a poem 'should not mean, but be' (Wimsatt and Beardsley 1954: 4): but in order to understand what a poem *is*, these same critics had at times to posit the existence of a reader on whom certain formal properties of the text such as irony or ambiguity were designed to have effects. The 'turn to the reader' (Freund 1987: 2) and the rise of reader-response criticism were thus in part attempts to solve problems which arose from formalist approaches.

'Reader-response criticism' is one of several umbrella terms used to cover a range of methodologies and theories developed in Europe and the Anglophone world in the 1960s–1970s in particular. Susan Suleiman (1980: 6), for example, listed 'six varieties of (or approaches to) audience-oriented criticism', including the 'hermeneutic' or 'phenomenological' approaches of the Konstanz School, in her introduction to *The Reader in the Text*.

Suleiman's six 'varieties' ranged from highly theoretical and abstract models of reading to empirical methods for investigating readers. At the theoretical end of the spectrum, scholars like Wolfgang Iser and Gerald Prince invoked an abstract or ideal 'reader' to explain the way a text or textual system functions to produce meaning, while at the empirical end, sociological and ethnographic methods were used to investigate the behaviour of real readers. The difference can be seen in approaches to books with ambiguous endings, like Sarah Waters's (2009) *The Little Stranger*, which invites 'the reader' to make up her own mind about who or what is the source of the apparently supernatural manifestations which have occurred throughout the novel. This reader is an abstraction, however: as empirical methods have shown, a real reader might stop reading Waters's novel in the middle, and thus never reach the point in the text where 'the reader' has to make a decision.

Reader-response criticism also covered a range of critical aims and objectives. Some scholars, like Hans Robert Jauss and Stanley Fish, aimed to establish more adequate interpretative methods for literary critics, based on a better understanding of interpretation itself. Others attempted to theorize the subjective responses of 'ordinary' readers. Norman Holland (1968), for example, developed the idea that the meanings readers find in texts are determined not by the properties of the text but by readers' own psychological inclinations. Holland's deterministic and strongly psychoanalytic approach has not itself had much impact on contemporary reception theory, but as Suleiman (1980: 31) points out, work on this end of the spectrum was important in reminding us that 'reading is not only an institutionalized and interpersonal phenomenon, but one that involves daydreaming, private delusions and fantasies'.

In general, reader-response criticism foregrounded the communicative aspects of texts which the New Critics sought to minimize, and turned attention to 'the significant role of the reader in the interpretive process and in the construction of meaning' (Davis and Womack 2002: 53). Attention to the reader, especially to non-professional readers, had a democratizing edge. The French critic Roland Barthes' influential 1968 essay, 'The Death of the Author', together with a series of related works from the same period, argued for a move away from the author's intention towards the reader's interpretation as the place where meaning is made. This new 'theory of the text extend[ed] to infinity the freedoms of the reader' (Barthes 1981 [1973]: 42), and reading began to be seen as a productive, even creative activity, with the reader playing an active role in, and ultimately in control of, the generation of meaning (Barthes 1989a [1970]; 1989b [1971]). The text is not 'closed' by an appeal to authorial intention, but opened up by and for the reader's productive play.

FEMINIST, BLACK AND POSTCOLONIAL CRITICISM

A third set of important transformations in the way we think about texts and interpretation came in this period from feminist, black and postcolonial literary criticism and theory. Scholars in all these fields worked to articulate or recover the perspective of marginalized and/or oppressed readers. Their work focussed attention on the political and social aspects of interpretation, and the ways in which interpretation is not simply a matter of technical expertise, but always bound up with power and resistance.

Second-wave feminism was an intellectual and activist movement in the 1960s and 1970s which built on the 'first wave' of activism around voting rights for women in the nineteenth century. In the second wave, reading and interpretation became highly politicized activities, as feminist attention expanded from the legal and economic spheres to encompass the cultural, social and interpersonal.

Feminism made two key points about literature and interpretation. Firstly, literature is seen not as an autonomous realm of the aesthetic, as it was for the Romantics, but as part of a broader social and ideological system which functions to maintain the authority of patriarchy. One of the earliest key texts of second-wave feminism, Kate Millett's (1977 [1970]) *Sexual Politics*, made its groundbreaking argument that sex and gender should be seen as political and social categories, not biological ones, in large part through a reading of literary texts. Millett showed how literary representations of women function politically to legitimate and normalize a patriarchal and sexist system. She read twentieth-century literature as equivalent to the 'explanatory myth[s]' through which traditional cultures articulate and justify misogyny; literary texts, she argued, similarly function as 'highly influential ethical justifications of things as they are' (Millett 1977 [1970]: 51). Accordingly, she read D. H. Lawrence's (1995 [1926]) novel *The Plumed Serpent*, for example, as an expression of Lawrence's 'phallic sect' which ultimately seeks to show that 'the salvation of the world lies in a reassertion of virility which will also make it possible for women to fulfil their true nature as passive objects and perfect subjects to masculine rule' (285).

Secondly, and relatedly, feminist literary critics argued that the interpretative norms we apply to literary texts are not neutral, but gendered. Aesthetic value and canonical status are routinely attributed to texts from a standpoint which is presented as neutral, but which is in fact specifically masculine and patriarchal.

Similar points were made in the context of race by black/African-American literary critics like Henry Louis Gates Jr (1992a [1985]: 69), who showed that interpretative systems 'are not "universal", "color-blind", or "apolitical", or "neutral"'. Like feminists, black literary critics attend to the ways in which different groups read differently, and to the histories of reading. Looking 'from margin to centre', in the words of the subtitle to a 1984 book by the black feminist bell hooks, they drew attention to the coexistence of multiple ways of reading, as well as to the hierarchies that centre and legitimate certain ways of reading while marginalizing others, hierarchies which are complicit with broader ideological factors and structures of oppression.

Postcolonial literary criticism analyses the ways in which European colonialism has structured reading regimes and practices, both within Europe and in its colonies and former colonies. Like feminist and black criticism, it insists on the situatedness of reading, and on the way that literary texts are implicated in broader colonial discourses. Thus for postcolonial critics, 'not only are literary texts useful for analysing colonial discourse, but the tools of literary analysis can also be used for understanding the other "texts" of empire' (Loomba 2005: 72).

As well as attending to the ways in which interpretative norms are bound up with social power relations and oppressive hierarchies, all three of these strands of thought also framed reading, rereading and rewriting as important acts of political resistance. The poet and critic Adrienne Rich (1972) advocated a feminist practice of reinterpreting or 're-visioning' existing texts, while Gates Jr (1992b [1990]: 32) stressed the importance of 'critical revaluation and . . . reclamation through revision' to the black literary tradition: for example, Aimé Césaire's *A Tempest* (1965) rewrites *The Tempest* in order to critique Shakespeare's representation of the indigenous inhabitants of the island on which the play is set. The notion of critical revision and reinterpretation has a special place in postcolonial literary studies, where the literature produced by writers from colonized or formerly colonized peoples is seen as 'writing back' to Empire (Rushdie 1982; Ashcroft, Griffiths and Tiffin 1989). Postcolonial writers have reinterpreted and reinscribed classical and European canonical literary texts in various ways, including 'reading for contrapuntal meanings of colonial texts; cultural translations and transmissions of classic works; [and] creative and critical acts of rewriting that [led] to the formation of an alternative canon for a postcolonial . . . age' (Mukherjee 2014: 113).

MARXIST CRITICISM AND THEORY

Marxist theories of culture in this period reformulated Marx's model of ideology, or the 'base/superstructure' model, and generated new ways of understanding cultural production and reception in the light of the changes in capitalist social and economic organization that had taken place since Marx's works were published.

Within orthodox Marxist economic theory, 'culture . . . is supposed to be epiphenomenal, a region of experience and expression basically derived from economic imperatives' (Agger 1992: 41). Cultural productions function ideologically to express the values of the dominant class. They inculcate false beliefs in their readers or listeners which may run counter to those readers' actual economic and political interests, and which work to prevent them from taking action to change the system.

Later Marxists reformulated Marx's notion of ideology, regarding culture as 'a realm of theoretical and political autonomy', 'both a region of domination and a crucial political battleground in the struggle for socialism' (Agger 1992: 43–44). The Italian Marxist Antonio

Gramsci developed the notion of 'hegemony', arguing that cultural works did not simply express the values of the dominant classes, but functioned in a more complex way to secure consent for domination among the dominated classes. Meanwhile, the French Marxists Louis Althusser, Etienne Balibar and Pierre Macherey argued that cultural productions express not the values of the dominant group, but the contradictions and incoherences of the total cultural system at a given moment. Read 'symptomatically', then, cultural productions can provide evidence of the internal contradictions of capitalism, and hence serve as valuable resources for struggle and resistance to hegemony. The British Marxist Terry Eagleton (1981) developed these insights into a methodology of 'reading against the grain'.

In these strands of Marxist cultural theory, all cultural productions are ambivalent. They attempt to secure the consent of the dominated, but they also express the contradictions of their time, and serve as resources for resistance. This applies to both 'high' and 'low' culture, although perhaps in different ways (Agger 1992: 81). This is an important contribution of Marxist theory, because it counters the Arnoldian/ Leavisite position that high culture is beneficial to individuals and society while mass culture is actively harmful.

Finally, Marxist theories of culture emphasize the institutional and cultural contexts within which texts are circulated and received. The German Marxist Theodor Adorno (2001 [1938]: 41) argued that there are more possibilities for resistant listening in Beethoven than in jazz, but that these possibilities may themselves be neutralized by the institutions of concert-going in late capitalism (38). Where the institution of the Athenian drama, for Boal, functioned as a 'system for intimidation of the spectator', the capitalist institution of the market, for Adorno, commodifies music and turns it into just another article to be purchased and consumed, rather than a cultural resource for thinking and resistance.

THE 'LINGUISTIC TURN'

The fifth and final strand of thought to be traced through the 1960s–1980s is a series of interrelated theoretical and political innovations which wove through almost all the disciplines of the Humanities. Associated in particular with semiotics, structuralism/post-structuralism and deconstruction, this moment of cross-disciplinary theoretical innovation is often called the 'linguistic turn' (Colebrook 2014 [2010]).

The theory of language which underpinned the linguistic turn was derived from the account provided by the Swiss linguist Ferdinand de Saussure in his book *A Course in General Linguistics*, posthumously published in 1916. Saussure's work took some decades to have an impact beyond linguistics, and it was transformed as it was taken up in the fields of literary and critical theory in the context of post-structuralism and semiotics.

Saussure's approach to linguistics shifted the study of language from a diachronic to a synchronic axis. Instead of tracing words back to their roots and looking at the historical development of grammars over time, as was usual, he insisted that languages should be analysed in the specific form they take at particular moments of their history. This synchronic approach enabled him to develop a model of language which exposed the unified system that underpins each linguistic act.

Saussure (2013 [1916]: 77) defined the basic unit of linguistic analysis as the *sign*, a 'two-sided. . . entity' consisting of a signifier and a signified. The signifier is the material aspect of the sign; the signified is its conceptual aspect, or meaning. What binds signifier and signified together into a single sign is not a physical law or a logical connection, but simply the conventions of a language, by which users have to abide if they wish to be understood. The radical implication of this model is that signs only have meaning within a given language, or sign system. Saussure writes that

> it is a great mistake to consider a sign as nothing more than the combination of a certain sound and a certain concept. To think of a sign as nothing more would be to isolate it from the system to which it belongs . . . The system as a united whole is the starting point.
>
> (133)

Saussure's theory of language will be explored further in Chapter Four, but here I want to draw attention to two points that are important for the linguistic turn. The first is the idea of language as a 'system', a 'united whole', which means that analysing any particular utterance or text requires paying attention to the underlying rules of the whole system. The second is the fact that Saussure's model of language could be generalized beyond what linguists call 'natural' languages like French or Hindi, to 'sign systems' in general. Indeed, Saussure described himself as a semiologist, or student of signs (from the Greek *semeion*, sign), and is regarded as one of the founders of the field of semiology or, as it is more often called, semiotics. He believed that language is the richest and most exemplary kind of sign system, but that all other sign systems behave in the same way (Fabb 1988).

The new discipline of semiotics gave researchers new tools for understanding how texts function to produce meanings. A semiotic approach sees all kinds of 'texts', in all kinds of media, as deploying organized systems of signs which, like languages, associate particular visual or aural signifiers with particular signifieds. Thus the cinema scholar Christian Metz (1974) used semiotics to analyse the 'language of film', while Barthes (1990 [1973]) analysed *The Fashion System*, discovering the underlying codes used to generate particular meanings in fashion photography. The musicologist Susan McClary (1994: 211) insisted that classical music is not 'sublimely meaningless'; it does not 'escape social signification', but instead acts on us through its deployment of particular codes, including gendered codes.

McClary's reference to 'social signification' alerts us to the other major consequence of the 'linguistic turn', which was a vast expansion of the field of textuality, reading and interpretation. Fashion magazines, films and musical compositions are 'texts' in a fairly narrow sense, in that they are self-contained artworks; but semiotics was also used to understand all kinds of cultural phenomena as 'texts' in the sense that they draw on organized systems of signs. The structuralist anthropologist Claude Lévi-Strauss used Saussurean tools to analyse myths as a coherent system of signification, which can be broken down into its constituent elements or 'signs' and whose rules can be analysed like those of a language. Eventually, all cultural activity, everyday life, and experience itself came to be understood in terms of 'symbolic communication'. Language and semiotics became the structuring framework for all kinds of social and cultural analysis, as described by Jean-Marie Benoist in 1975:

> semiotics of the unconscious for [the psychoanalyst Jacques] Lacan, semiotics of the codes of kinship and myth for [the

anthropologist Claude] Lévi-Strauss, semiotics of the relations and contraditions in society for [the Marxist Louis] Althusser, semiotics of literature for [the literary scholars Roland] Barthes and [Gérard] Genette, and a semiotics of historical discourse and documents for [the theorist Michel] Foucault.

(Benoist 1975: 16, translated and cited in Culler 1981 [1977]: 33)

The expansion of the field of textuality had a politicized edge, made visible, for example, when semiotics collided with Marxist theory in the work of the Birmingham Centre for Contemporary Cultural Studies (CCCS) in the UK in the 1960s and 1970s. The Centre was founded by Richard Hoggart (1958 [1957]: 341), whose 1957 book *The Uses of Literacy* analysed working-class culture in Britain, focussing both on the potentially harmful impact of 'mass-produced sex-and-violence novel[s]' and on the 'resilience' of working-class people, who were able to 'react positively to ... the useful possibilities of cheap mass-production' (330). In the 1960s and 1970s, members of the CCCS included the highly influential scholars Stuart Hall, Dick Hebdige and Angela McRobbie. Combining aspects of the Marxist traditions described above with British work on popular culture and with work from the field of semiotics, their work went beyond the analysis of 'texts' in the sense of self-contained artworks. The CCCS sociologists Dick Hebdige (1979) (in *Subcultures or the Meaning of Style*) and, later, Paul Willis (1990) (in *Common Culture: Symbolic Work at Play in the Everyday Cultures of the Young*) analysed youth subcultures, asking what punks and Teddy boys 'do with' the 'raw material of social ... existence' (Hebdige 1979: 80), and finding answers in terms of the 'symbolic work' and 'meanings' produced by subcultural codes and behaviours.

The centrality of *meaning* to models of textuality and reception has been noted and, to some extent, critiqued since the 1970s, when the reader-response critic Stanley Fish (1980a: 355) wrote that 'like it or not, interpretation is the only game in town'. However, meaning remains the dominant category through which we approach the text–reader encounter. Because verbal language was the exemplary sign system for Saussure, 'reading' has become a primary metaphor and framework for reception but 'reading' is used to designate the processes by which audiences receive all kinds of texts, not just written ones. Thus viewers read visual art, for example in Bal's (2006 [1991]) influential book *Reading Rembrandt*, as well as films and music.

There are drawbacks and limitations to this generalized use of 'reading' as *the* model for the process by which audiences receive texts. Most significantly, attending to the meaning-bearing properties of texts and the processes by which meaning is decoded risks drawing attention away from the aesthetic dimensions of reception: the pleasure that we take in beauty, for example. As we shall see in Chapters Two and Three, aesthetic response has often been folded into the question of meaning. For example, the cognitive critic Lisa Zunshine (2010: 195) argues that 'sociocognitive satisfaction . . . underlies aesthetic pleasure'; 'she implies that you're kidding yourself if you think you *don't* read fiction because it gives an intense and pleasurable "workout" for your cognitive adaptations' (Federico 2016: 104).

The semiotic approach may also lead us to overlook the specific material and perceptual qualities of artworks. Listening to music is a very different experience from looking at sculpture, which is very different from reading a verbal text. By understanding all these different kinds of artwork in terms of 'language', the semiotic approach risks flattening out the differences between them – including, ironically, the qualities specific to reading itself. It also risks missing the aspects of the reception of a text which cannot be described in terms of language and meaning.

The limitations and problems of the semiotic approach will be further explored in Chapters Two and Three. For the most part, however, this book necessarily reflects the centrality of this approach to reception, not least in the terminology it uses. Despite the reservations just stated, I follow convention in using the terms 'reading' and 'readers' inclusively, to cover receivers of texts in any medium; similarly 'writing' and 'rewriting' include the writing or rewriting of texts in non-verbal media, for example book-to-film adaptation. This is partly because, for simplicity, I avoid listing 'readers, viewers, spectators, listeners, and audiences' every time, but also because the terminology accurately reflects the centrality of literary texts to this book, which is, as mentioned above, primarily intended as an introduction to *literary* reception. Thus 'readers' in the narrow sense feature more often than viewers, listeners and audiences.

FROM RECEPTION AND ITS HISTORIES TO RECEPTION AND ITS OBJECTS

Even the brief history sketched above shows that a broad range of approaches, disciplines, and political and critical orientations have contributed to the field of reception. Complex institutional, disciplinary and national histories have meant that communication between different areas or schools is patchy and unreliable at best, and as a result different schools of reception have often developed in relative isolation from one another, unaware of complementary, contradictory or overlapping theoretical possibilities being developed nearby.

As a result, although this Introduction is intended to orient the reader to some of the ways in which the theoretical terrain has already been mapped and named, I have not structured the rest of the book around named schools, disciplines or approaches. My primary aim is to open up dialogue and interplay between scholars and schools, instead of deepening divisions by insisting on the strict categorization of approaches by school, discipline or philosophical tradition. Taxonomic approaches and techniques also risk overvaluing philosophical consistency, when in practice a great deal of very valuable critical work has been done by scholars appropriating tools and techniques from schools which can be shown to be fundamentally incompatible. For example, Martindale's work in reception theory draws on both Hans-Georg Gadamer and Jacques Derrida, despite the widely held view that their theories are radically irreconcilable (Martindale 1993; Derrida and Gadamer 1989; Littau 2006: 105). Finally, given the complex history of reception scholarship, a taxonomic approach would risk producing false distinctions between different approaches, based in contingent institutional, disciplinary and national-historical factors rather than in any real theoretical or conceptual differences.

The following chapters are instead organized around the different entities that reception, as currently practised, takes as its objects of critical attention: rewritings and textual afterlives; readers; reading systems and practices; and meaning itself. The chapters move from the most concretely and immediately available object to the most abstract and complex one. Each chapter provides a detailed discussion of a number of the most interesting or generative critical and theoretical approaches to these objects over the last fifty or sixty years, with a range of examples from different historical periods, genres and media.

Chapter One introduces critical theories and practices for the study of texts which draw on, appropriate, allude to or rewrite earlier texts. Looking at what I call 'text-to-text theories of reception', the chapter covers practices of rewriting including translation, performance and adaptation. It explores theories of creative imitation and the role of transformative rewriting or remix in literary creativity. It examines the factors which influence rewriting practices, including poetic norms and ideology, and presents a range of critical perspectives on the way in which later rewritings interpret, illuminate, critique or simplify earlier texts. The chapter concludes with an investigation of the notion of tradition and literary history from the point of view of reception.

Chapter Two moves from text-to-text reception to text-to-reader reception, looking at theories and models which understand readers as the site where textual meaning is realized and/or where the effects of a text are registered affectively and ethically. Like the texts which are the subject of Chapter One, readers are relatively accessible to analysis. Their readings, however, understood as internal cognitive, affective and/or interpretative processes, are not accessible in themselves, but must be mediated and represented in some way, usually through a written or oral account: a journal, a book review, a conversation in a book group, an interview. As such, readers, the readings they produce and the effects that texts have on them require more complex and less purely literary types of analysis.

In Chapter Two, I cover a range of models of the text-to-reader dynamic, ranging from the text-dominant to the reader-dominant. The chapter opens by distinguishing the 'implied reader', the addressee of the text whose characteristics can be inferred from textual evidence, from the 'real reader', the real-life person who picks up a book or watches a film. It discusses the ways in which real and implied readers interact, before moving on to cover historical and ethnographic methods for the study of real readers. Demonstrating that the readings of real readers are sometimes influenced more by other readers than by the text, the chapter ends by looking at reader-to-reader dynamics, and introducing the idea of 'not reading' as a modality of reading.

Reading, the subject of Chapter Three, is even more complex and manifold than readers, because it is a generalized sociocultural system. Reading, in this sense, refers to the socially, culturally and historically specific system of signification and meaning which must be in place before an individual reader can learn to read. This chapter surveys approaches which enable us to analyse not individual or collective readers, but historically and culturally specific reading practices: the rules, conventions, strategies, institutions, ideologies and laws which govern interpretative practices in specific historical and cultural contexts. It introduces the ways in which critics have mapped the institutional and sociocultural processes which shape the reading practices of readers, including conventions, genres, frames, technologies and protocols. It ends by investigating literacy itself, sometimes thought of as the most fundamental level of reading.

Chapter Four looks at the way that reception theorizes language and meaning itself. It introduces the ways in which critics have mapped the linguistic, semiotic, textual and historical structures which enable and shape the reading practices of readers, and gives four reasons why reception is a necessary part of the study of texts. The first reason is the instability of the text, which is a specific kind of object, one which is co-produced by its interpreters. The second is the inaccessibility of fixed literal meaning outside or prior to interpretation. The third is the dialogic nature of interpretation and the inextricability of the interpreter from the text. The fourth is the polysemic nature of linguistic meaning, which can only be fixed or determined by appealing to extratextual authority.

The fifth chapter concludes by extending the ideas covered in the first four to tease out the implications of reception theory for our understanding of the nature of the literary text and the reading experience, and what this means for our practice as self-aware readers.

These chapters are interrelated, and the examples and approaches covered in each chapter comment on, critique and complement each other. For example, the idea of a 'transformative rewriting' in Chapter One is interwoven with the idea of a 'resistant reader' in Chapter Two; with the ideas about historical, cultural and institutional norms of reading in Chapter Three; and with the ideas about the conditions of possibility of linguistic or semiotic interpretation itself in Chapter Four. In practice, all acts of reception are forms of interpretation (Chapter Four), conditioned by historically and culturally specific systems of reading (Chapter Three), learned and practised by individual readers in complex relations to other readers (Chapter Two) and producing a specific interpretation or reading which is most visible in the form of a new text (Chapter One). Separating out the stages of reception in this way is not meant to suggest the hermetic and self-contained nature of each stage, but, on the contrary, to encourage communication between the approaches discussed in each chapter in order to enable thinking about the ways in which they interrelate.

My approach here follows the model of Robert Darnton in 'What Is The History of Books?' Darnton argues that book history is a complex and heterogeneous field:

> Books . . . refuse to be contained within the confines of a single discipline when treated as objects of study. Neither history nor literature nor economics nor sociology nor bibliography can do justice to all the aspects of the life of a book.
>
> (Darnton 1982: 81)

Because of the unwieldy complexity of the real-life processes by which books are produced, distributed and received, individual researchers and works will usually have to focus on just one aspect of the life of a book in any given case: 'but', Darnton writes, 'the parts do not take on their full significance unless they are related to the whole' (67).

Exactly the same goes for acts of reception. What happens when we read a book, watch a film or listen to a piece of music is too complex to be captured by a single theory or within a single discipline. Each of the four 'objects' I have listed here is just one part of the whole complex process of reception. In this book, I aim to draw out the significance of those parts in relation to the whole.

1

REWRITING

This chapter focusses on what I call text-to-text approaches to reception. It covers theories and methods of reception which take as their object of analysis not readers or audiences directly, but instead the texts which readers/authors generate in response to other texts.

The divide between text-to-text approaches and text-to-reader approaches is one of the deep divisions in terminology and methodology that, as we saw in the Introduction, characterize the field of reception as it currently stands. In many disciplines, notably media and film studies but also including traditional literary studies, reception is understood as a text-to-reader relationship: it is a process that takes place in readers or audiences. Text-to-text approaches, by contrast, are central in Classical and Biblical reception; in medievalism; and in the strand of fan studies which focusses on creative production. In these disciplines, reception scholars usually work not on audiences, but on texts which have been created in response to earlier texts. These responding texts are then seen as the place where the process of reception happens.

Thus, work on film in Classical reception studies usually analyses the films themselves as the locus of reception; it 'tends to overlook the end user, the person watching the film in the cinema or at home'

(Potter 2009: 220). Similarly, in Biblical reception studies of popular music, 'the primary units of study are songs': texts, not listeners (Abraham 2015: 248). For example, the Biblical reception scholar William John Lyons (2015a: 225) finds in Depeche Mode's 2005 song 'John the Revelator' a polemical interpretation of the apostle John as a 'liar, thief, [and] tyrant'. Lyons shows how the Depeche Mode song borrows elements from a traditional gospel song of the same name, 'using both its title and its call and response structure to good effect' (225), but ultimately presenting a very different interpretation of the Book of Revelation. His approach, however, cannot tell us how Depeche Mode's listeners understand or relate to 'John the Revelator' itself (Abraham 2015: 250–252). Are they persuaded by the song's interpretation of Revelation? Are they even aware that the song *is* an interpretation of Revelation, or do they just like to dance to it? To understand how listeners receive texts, we need different methodologies, some of which will be covered in the next two chapters of this book.

In media studies the word 'reception' is usually used to refer to text-to-reader processes. This discipline does provide useful tools for studying text-to-text reception, but it uses different terminology to do so, most notably terms such as 'adaptation' or 'remix'. In literary studies, the phenomenon that I am calling text-to-text reception has also been discussed in terms of intertextuality, translation, performance and tradition. This chapter will introduce and explain all these terms.

Firstly, however, I need to define the phenomenon itself. What is it that theorists describe by so many different names? Broadly, text-to-text reception scholars study texts that adapt, appropriate, allude to, continue, critique, comment on, translate, revise or reframe other, existing texts. In this chapter, for simplicity and consistency, I will use the term 'rewriting' for all these texts and processes, although I use it in a broad sense to include rewritings which do not take primarily written form, such as film adaptations and visual art.

Some examples of rewriting might be: ancient Greek tragedy's retellings of myth in the fifth century BCE, including stories from Homer's *The Iliad* and *The Odyssey*, composed two centuries previously (Davidson 1994); medieval rewritings and continuations of Classical texts, including a new ending to Virgil's first-century Latin epic the *Aeneid* written by Maffeo Vegio in the fifteenth century (Kallendorf 1984; Rogerson 2013), or William Henryson's sixteenth-century additions to

Chaucer's fourteenth-century poem, *Troilus and Criseyde* (Storm 1993); nineteenth-century retellings of Bible stories for children (England 2015); contemporary fan fiction, which tells new stories about existing characters set in the fictional universes of media texts (Penley 1991); and machinima, an art form which uses graphic software engines to create new video works out of existing video games (Ito 2011).

Widely disparate in historical and cultural context, genre, mode and medium, these texts have only one thing in common. That is the condition of being 'in the second degree', a term coined by Gérard Genette (1997a [1982]: 1) for all texts which are 'in a relationship, whether obvious or concealed, with other texts'. We can think of these second-degree texts as *receiving* earlier texts: taking those texts into themselves, interpreting them, and/or making use of them for their own purposes.

Textual reception, or rewriting, thus covers many different kinds of texts and also many different modes of relationship between texts. Rewriting can be partial, as when one text quotes or refers to another in passing, or total, as when one text translates or adapts the whole of an 'original'. It can remain within the same mode or medium, as with the blues, pop and hip-hop genre of 'answer songs', which directly respond to other artists' songs. One example is Roxanne Shanté's 'Roxanne's Revenge', a song from the point of view of the woman described in U.T.F.O's 1984 hit 'Roxanne, Roxanne' and the first of over a hundred songs in the so-called 'Roxanne Wars'. Rewriting can also change medium, as with adaptations from book to graphic novel, graphic novel to film, or film to stage musical. It can be fictional, as when a fan writes a new story set in an existing universe, or non-fictional, as when a scholar explicates her interpretation of an existing text in the form of a commentary (Hawkes 1992: 31–39).

Rewritings can also take a range of different attitudes, or what Genette calls 'moods', in relation to the texts they rewrite: in Genette's (1997a: 28) terms, they may be playful, satirical or serious. A rewriting may parody another text or pay homage to it; it may critique it, or claim it as an authenticating or legitimating predecessor; it may use it as a model of excellence, or try to outdo it, as in the rhetorical technique of *aemulatio* in Roman and Renaissance poetry or the increasingly spectacular action sequences in the *Die Hard* sequels. Finally, what is taken over from one text to another in rewriting varies too. Rewritings may quote sections of other texts verbatim or in paraphrase; retell their stories; insert their characters into other stories and universes; or imitate the style, mode or structure of an earlier text.

Text-to-text reception thus covers a vast area. In fact, as we shall see later in this chapter, some critics believe that no text can be produced or received outside the network of relationships to other texts in which it is enmeshed. Framing the relationship between texts as one of *reception*, however, gives us a specific set of questions and approaches with which to start making sense of this vast and disparate set of texts and textual networks. If we think about a rewriting text as receiving another text, we will ask questions about how the later text interprets the earlier one. We will also ask questions about the nature of reception as a process, based on what we see happening in these text-to-text receptions.

This chapter will first of all introduce some of the basic principles underlying the study of text-to-text, as opposed to text-to-reader, reception. It will then go on to explore some of the models of reception which underpin these principles, and investigate the theoretical questions they open up and address. We will look at reception as intertextuality; as creation; as interpretation; and as 'writing back'. Next, we will explore the related notion of tradition, which is an important way of thinking about the broader system of communication which structures relations between texts. That system of communication is both intertextual and extratextual, and the chapter concludes with a brief discussion of reception beyond the text.

TEXT-TO-TEXT RECEPTION: TRANSFORMATION AND CONTINUITY

Text-to-text approaches to reception proceed, as I have indicated, on the basis that texts, rather than audiences, are the place where reception happens. John Frow (2008: 26) makes the case that studying rewritings, 'taking new production as a stand-in for reception', enables us to 'focus on relatively objective transformations which can be taken as correlates for a process of reception that can otherwise be reconstructed only with great difficulty and in ways that are methodologically cumbersome'.

Frow's point here is that text-to-text approaches to reception are both less methodologically complex and more secure in their use of evidence than text-to-reader approaches. By looking at a 'new production', a text that rewrites an earlier text, we can bypass the attempt to reconstruct the complex processes involved in text-to-reader reception. These processes are not directly available to observation, because they take place inside a reader's mind and body, and must be represented in some form before we can access them. In text-to-text approaches to reception, however, we can look directly at a text and see how it 'registers either transformation or continuity' in comparison to the text it rewrites. It prompts questions such as: what has the new text kept the same as the old one? What has it changed?

Any text which draws on or receives an earlier text 'works by selection', as the Classical scholar Gian Biagio Conte puts it. Textual reception is not a passive process of repetition or copying, but an active process of selection, intervention, interpretation and reworking. A receiving text 'realign[s] along its own axis the features of the [earlier text] that are pertinent to it, activating some of them and disregarding others' (Conte 1986 [1980]: 133). Thus, in studying text-to-text reception, we observe how a text has selected and reorganized aspects of an earlier text: which elements it has activated, and which it has disregarded. Conte is writing about the Latin poet Virgil's use of the Orpheus myth in his *Georgics* (29 BCE). The same principles can be used to analyse contemporary modes of rewriting. One example which makes the processes of selection and realignment very visible is the phenomenon of the fan edit. Fans use video editing software to edit movies, selecting out elements from the original film and rearranging or realigning them according to the tastes and preferences of the fan editor and their intended audiences. The new text can then be analysed through direct comparison to the original. It functions as what Frow calls a 'stand-in' for the complex processes of reception and adaptation through which the fan edit is produced. Thus, for example, in 2000, Mike J. Nicholls circulated *The Phantom Edit*, a popular fan edit of George Lucas's *Star Wars* film *The Phantom Menace*, which activated or emphasized some aspects of the film and disregarded others: most conspicuously, his version completely deleted the character Jar Jar Binks, who was hated by many *Star Wars* fans.

In more subtle ways, texts may signal both transformation and continuity, similarity and difference, in their relationship to earlier texts. For example, the 2011 film *Tinker Tailor Soldier Spy*, based on a 1974 novel by John Le Carré, opens with the lead character, George Smiley, played by Gary Oldman, at an optician's. Smiley/Oldman exchanges a pair of wire-framed glasses for a pair with large, square, tortoiseshell-style frames, very similar to those worn by Alec Guinness in his iconic performance of the same role in the 1979 BBC television adaptation. The scene signals a blend of continuity and transformation: Oldman wears Guinness's glasses. The 2011 film thus shows an awareness that Oldman's performance will inevitably be compared to Guinness's, and sets up a comparison between itself and the BBC version which centres on the performance of the male lead. The optician scene does not significantly advance the narrative of the film or Smiley's characterization. Its function is solely to communicate something about the relationship between the present film and the earlier adaptation. As Harold Bloom (1975: 108) claims, 'meaning is always wandering around between texts'.

RECEPTION AS INTERTEXTUALITY

The state of the 'between-ness' of meaning is often called 'intertextuality'. The prefix 'inter' is a Latin preposition which simply means 'between'. The term itself was coined in French by Julia Kristeva in 1968, when she showed that any text is 'a permutation of texts; an intertextuality [*intertextualité*]' (Kristeva 1980 [1968]: 36). Texts are not created out of nothing, but from already existing texts and discourses. Neatly enough, Julie Sanders explains this idea in her book *Adaptation and Appropriation* by quoting and adding to Graham Allen's book *Intertextuality*. Allen (2000: 1) writes that literary texts 'are built from systems, codes and traditions established by previous works of literature'; Sanders adds that they are also built from those 'derived from companion art forms' such as 'art, music, drama [and] dance' in 'an ever-expanding network of textual relations' (Sanders 2006: 3).

If meaning wanders around between texts, we understand texts in part through comparing them to others. When texts refer specifically and openly to a particular earlier text, as with the 2011 version of *Tinker Tailor Soldier Spy*, the process of comparison involves a kind of double vision or layered reading. We understand the meaning of Gary Oldman's glasses only by recalling Alec Guiness's, and thus, in a sense, reading both texts simultaneously. As a 'second-degree' text,

Tinker Tailor Soldier Spy has a palimpsestuous quality, to use a term taken from the title of Genette's book *Palimpsests: Literature in the Second Degree*. A palimpsest is a page, usually from a vellum manuscript, which has been written on once, then erased and reused for a new text. The original writing remains detectable and partially legible beneath the new words. Adaptations and other forms of rewriting are indeed 'inherently "palimpsestuous" works, haunted at all times by their adapted texts' (Hutcheon 2006: 6).

Even works which are not openly and intentionally palimpsestuous in this way, however, can be understood as intertextual in a broader sense. All texts necessarily situate themselves within a literary system both by referring to an earlier model, suggesting a relationship of sameness or repetition, and comparing themselves to that model, suggesting difference. Thus, 'intertextuality creates meaning in texts through a dialectic between sameness and difference' (Fowler 2000 [1997]: 121), and texts are produced and read 'within a matrix of possibilities constituted by earlier texts' (Fowler 2000: 117).

Don Fowler's theory of intertextuality builds on that of Conte, who demonstrates that interplay between texts is not just a quirky feature of some particularly self-conscious or second-degree texts, but an irreducible part of the way in which we read and interpret *all* literary texts. On this view, literary texts are inextricably part of a system or a matrix of possibilities, rather than isolated, self-contained entities. Literary texts cannot be purely new or entirely original; indeed, 'a work that had only original elements would be doomed to incomprehensibility' (Conte 1986: 91). Authors do not create out of nothing, but 'realize, transform or transpose' – that is, actively receive and rework – material which already exists within the system in which they write. Literary texts are original, then, insofar as they creatively rework or transform the possibilities that have been set up for them by past texts and contexts: creativity becomes a matter of transformative imitation.

RECEPTION AS CREATION

In a four-part Web series from 2011, the filmmaker Kirby Ferguson states that 'everything is a remix'; the 'basic elements of creativity' are copying, transforming and combining. He both implicitly and explicitly counters those who believe that remixing, borrowing or imitating earlier artworks is a form of copying or plagiarism, a derivative act devoid of originality and creative merit. Linda Hutcheon (2006: 33) similarly argues for the creativity of adaptation, defining adaptation as 'a creative and interpretive transposition of a recognizable other work or works' and writing that it is '*a process of creation*' and 'a derivation that is not derivative – a work that is second without being secondary' (8–9). Indeed, as Hutcheon also points out, adaptations are legally differentiated from straightforward plagiarism or theft of intellectual property on the basis that they 'recast' or 'transform' the adapted text. The category of 'transformative use' of a text has protected legal status (9).

The notion of transformative use has been taken up vigorously by the fan-run Organization for Transformative Works (OTW). Like adaptations, the creative works of fans, including fan fiction, fan art and fan vids, have often been seen as derivative and without merit. Established in 2007, the OTW advocates a different view of fanworks, adopting from legal discourse a terminology and a framework within which creativity and/or originality reside not so much in invention as in transformation. In the words of its mission statement, the OTW 'believe[s] that fanworks are transformative and that transformative works are legitimate', and 'envision[s] a future in which all fannish works are recognized as legal and transformative and are accepted as a legitimate creative activity' (n.d.).

These defences of the legitimacy and creativity of transformative work or remix are historically specific. They arise from a view of creativity and originality grounded in a particular cultural, economic and legal context and framed in terms of copyright law, itself a relatively recent development in terms of the history of human creativity (Finkelstein and McCleery 2012). The idea that imitation can be creative has a very long history, and was in fact dominant in Western literature before the advent of the Romantic conception of 'genius' in the eighteenth century. Prior to the Romantics, the idea that transformative work was creative would not have had to be defended, simply because imitation and transformation were fundamental to the concept of creativity.

In thinking about the creativity of adaptation, Hutcheon uses the notion of *Creative Imitation*, borrowing this 'triumphant oxymoron' (Hinds 1998: 18) from the title of a 1979 book on Latin literature. The thesis of the book is that '*Imitatio* is neither plagiarism nor a flaw in the constitution of Latin literature. It is a dynamic law of its existence' (West and Woodman 1979: ix, cited in Hutcheon 2006: 20).

In the classical, medieval and early modern periods, imitation was at the heart of theories of creativity and embedded in educational systems. Students learned to read and to write by imitating the models set down by the great *auctores* (authors/authorities). Michael Leff summarizes *imitatio* as a teaching practice by saying '*[I]mitatio* was not the mere repetition or mechanistic reproduction of something found in an existing text. It was instead a complex process that allowed [texts] to serve as resources for invention' (Leff 1997: 97). The practice, codified by Quintilian in the first century CE, survived in Europe into the eighteenth century and was certainly flourishing in Shakespeare's time, as Sanders points out: 'Shakespeare's age had a far more open approach to literary borrowing and imitation than the modern era of copyright and property law encourages or even allows. Imitation was learned and practised in schools and continued into adult writing careers' (Sanders 2006: 47).

Imitatio involves both continuity and transformation. The Roman writer Seneca the Younger, in the eighty-fourth *Moral Letter to Lucilius*, makes several distinctions between good and bad imitation, writing, for example: 'I would have you resemble [the person you are imitating] as a child resembles his father, and not as a picture resembles its original; for a picture is a lifeless thing' (Seneca 1920 [c 65 BCE] 281). For classical, medieval and Renaissance writers and readers, imitation was not lifeless copying, borrowing, stealing or gathering materials from others; instead, it was a process of digestion, transformation, combination and affiliation, as authors made new texts not out of nothing, or out of direct observation of the world around them, but out of the materials afforded them by the literary system. As Simon Gaunt and Sarah Kay explain, writing about medieval France, 'the aesthetics of writing in the Middle Ages entail some form of *re*writing. This phenomenon [is] a specifically medieval form of what Modern critics call "intertextuality"'. They point to the example of Villon's *Testament* (c. 1461–146), which not only reworks previous texts but also 'explicitly acknowledges its own susceptibility to reworking at the hands of others, positioning itself thereby in a dynamic, constantly evolving process of textual transformation' (Gaunt and Kay 2008: 6–7).

On this model, everything is indeed a remix. All new creation involves a degree of reworking of existing forms and material, and all texts are, to some extent, receptions of earlier texts. This is an important reminder that we cannot draw a firm or stable distinction between 'second-degree' and 'first-degree' texts. Even Homer's *Iliad*, often designated the earliest work of Western literature and the origin of the classical tradition, reworks existing material. Laura Slatkin (1991: 114) has shown how Homer's poem uses a pattern of references to the myth of Thetis, the mother of the hero Achilles, to locate the narrative against a broader mythological backdrop. She concludes that 'fundamental to the poetics of compositions like the *Iliad* . . . is a process of selection, combination, and adaptation'. Reception is creative, rather than purely derivative; active, rather than passive. Text-to-text reception involves an active process of interpretation and intervention; the transformative reception of earlier texts and models is a fundamental aspect of creativity.

RECEPTION AS INTERPRETATION 1: TRANSLATION AND PERFORMANCE

Models of text-to-text reception regard writing and reading, creation and interpretation, as intertwined. As André Carrington (2016: 9) puts it, 'Every interpretive act is an act of authorship, and every act of authorship is an act of interpretation'. The consumption of a text is also an act of production: the production of an interpretation. Two textual forms which involve the literal production of new texts as interpretations of old ones have also been used as metaphors for textual reception in general: these are translation and performance.

Susan Sontag (1966: 15) writes that 'the task of interpretation is virtually one of translation', while Janice Radway (1987 [1984]: 9) argues that reading always involves 'the activity of translation'. George Steiner (1975: 28) elaborates the idea that 'whenever we read or hear any language-statement from the past, be it Leviticus or last year's bestseller, we translate. Reader, actor, editor are translators of language out of time'. Steiner is referring to what the linguist Roman Jakobson called 'intralinguistic translation', when a text is reworded within the same language, as in the cases of parody, satire and modernization. Jakobson also recognized two other kinds of translation (Bassnett 2014: 6–8): interlinguistic, or translation proper, when a text is reworded in a different language; and intersemiotic translation, when the content of a text is 'translated' into a different sign system altogether, as in book-to-film adaptation or, more quirkily, the 'Dance your PhD' contest, where since

2007 postgraduates in the sciences have been challenged to represent their research findings for a general audience through the medium of dance. The 2014 winner, Uma Nagendra, for instance, choreographed a group of trapeze artists to explain the effects of tornadoes on soil in forests (Bohannon 2014).

Broadly conceived, then, translation offers a way of understanding and modelling the complex combination of transformation and continuity that characterizes text-to-text reception. We will see several examples of interlinguistic translation later in this chapter, but many of the examples of rewriting covered here could also be seen as intralinguistic or intersemiotic translation.

Another practice where interpretation and authorship are closely related is performance. Stagings of plays, especially well-known plays from past historical periods such as Greek tragedy or Shakespeare, can transform the works, producing 'new' texts out of old ones. Martin Fortier (2002: 138) shows that 'a radical staging changes the meaning of the work even when the words remain relatively the same', citing Peter Brook's controversial 1970 production of *A Midsummer Night's Dream* which led critics to posit a difference between 'Brook's *Dream* and Shakespeare's' (Fortier 2002: 148, citing Selbourne 1982: 7). Similarly, an arrangement or cover version of a popular song can change its significance, mood and/or tone, without altering the lyrics or melody. Cyndi Lauper's upbeat 1983 pop hit 'Girls Just Wanna Have Fun' becomes melancholy and wistful in Greg Laswell's minor-key cover version, used in the film *Confessions of a Shopaholic* (2009).

The performance history of a play or piece of music can thus provide a rich archive of text-to-text reception, showing how textual and contextual features intersect and interact at the moment of reception to produce a new interpretation (Macintosh, Kenwood and Wrobel 2016). Furthermore, performance provides a useful metaphor for textual reception and reading in general. Umberto Eco argues that 'every reception of a work of art is both an *interpretation* and a *performance* of it' (Eco 1979a [1959]: 49). The Classical reception scholar Charles Martindale develops the analogy of musical performance to describe the process of reading:

> a musical work only becomes such when it is realized in a performance (whether this is a public performance, or a private

> reading of the score 'in the mind's ear'). Every performance is different from every other performance . . . So too with a verbal text. A set of signs becomes a poem when it is realized by a reader, who thus acts as a 'performer'.
>
> (1993: 17–18)

Translation and performance are thus both examples of and metaphors for text-to-text reception, as the process involves both authorship and interpretation.

RECEPTION AS INTERPRETATION 2: INTERPRETERS

Translations and performances bring existing texts into new contexts. Like other forms of rewriting, they work by selection and realignment. Thinking about rewritings in terms of translation and performance can help us to understand the principles of selection and realignment that guide rewriters' decisions.

In other words, by analysing the specific way in which a rewriting 'translates' or 'performs' an earlier text, we can learn something about the interpretative strategies and priorities of the receiving text or culture. This notion is fundamental to the field of medievalism, defined as the reception of the medieval in post-medieval texts and cultures. 'Medievalism', Louise D'Arcens writes,

> discloses as much, or indeed in many cases more, about the time and place in which it has been produced as it does about medieval Europe . . . The medieval period . . . has long provided a reservoir of images and ideas which, in expressing modern ideas about the past, are in fact closely engaged in defining what it is to be modern.
>
> (2016: 6)

Writing about the past, then, may be a way of articulating ideas about the present. In *Translation, Rewriting and the Manipulation of Literary Fame*, André Lefevere demonstrates that rewritings of earlier texts are structured by the priorities and concerns of the rewriter, and by their broader cultural and historical context. He identifies two axes that we can use to analyse the way in which a rewriting represents or receives an earlier text: the 'dominant poetics' of the receiving culture, and its ideology (Lefevere 1992: 13).

In terms of poetics, we might look at the history of English translations of Homer's epic poem the *Odyssey*. Although ancient Greek poetry does not rhyme, translators of Homer into English verse tended to use rhyme, especially prior to the eighteenth century, because rhyme was an important feature of the English poetic system. When E. V. Rieu translated the *Odyssey* for the Penguin Classics series in 1946, however, he rendered it as prose, not poetry. Since the novel was the dominant form for long narratives in twentieth-century Britain, as hexameter verse had been in archaic Greece, Rieu felt that prose better represented the *Odyssey* in the dominant literary system of his own receiving culture (Rieu 1946: 17–18; Schein 2016: 181).

The second axis of rewriting that Lefevere isolates, ideology, is well illustrated by the translation history of the Bible. As mentioned in the Introduction, translation was a central feature of the theological disputes involved in the English Reformation in the sixteenth century, out of which the English Protestant Church emerged. The Catholic Church maintained that the Latin translation of the Bible was the only acceptable version, and it was up to the Church to determine the correct interpretation of Scripture. The making, circulation and reading of English translations of the Bible were forbidden. Meanwhile, the emergent Protestant movement insisted that individual Christians should be allowed to read Scripture for themselves and interpret it on its own terms with the help of the Holy Spirit, rather than being guided by the institution of the Church.

In this context, what might otherwise have appeared to be relatively minor linguistic issues of translation became extremely fraught, as questions of terminology were entangled with questions of religious practice, institutional authority and the salvation or damnation of the soul. One example was the translation of the Latin term *penitentia*, 'repentance' or 'penance'. The Protestant William Tyndale translates the word as 'repentance'; the Catholic Thomas More insists that this is linguistically and religiously incorrect, and that the only correct translation is 'penance'. The latter word, in the usage of the time, referred not only to the inward feeling of 'repentance' but also, as More wrote, to 'every part of the sacrament of penance, confession of mouth, contrition of heart, and satisfaction by good deeds' (1532, cited in Simpson 2007: 75). As James Simpson writes:

> The profound significance of the translation issue is . . . clear: one of the sacraments of the Church is, for More, threatened by any variation from 'penitence'. Discussion of philology, or the meaning of words, takes us quickly into nonphilological territory, because so much is at stake in the choice of one translation over another.
>
> (2007: 75–76)

Translations are not purely linguistic phenomena: as receptions or rewritings of texts, they are shaped by ideology.

Lefevere's book is mainly about non-fictional modes of rewriting, which position themselves to some extent as delivering an accurate or fair representation of an earlier text: he covers translation, historiography, anthologizing, literary criticism and editing. These texts may be particularly revealing because they often profess a kind of neutrality or transparency with respect to the earlier text. Thus the changes that are made can tell us a lot about the poetic and ideological priorities, and the interpretative strategies, of the receiving culture.

RECEPTION AS INTERPRETATION 3: EXEMPLARY OR MONSTROUS, HIGH OR LOW

So far, we have mainly analysed written receptions as interpretations in terms of their authorship: that is, as transformatively original texts which use an earlier text as raw material for creative expression and which thus tell us about the interpreters' priorities. However, if these texts really are interpretations, then we can also see them as telling us something about the texts being interpreted.

Using later texts to shed light on earlier ones is common in two particular circumstances: firstly, when the earlier texts are very old and have canonical status, either as literary classics or as Scripture; and secondly, when the later texts are seen as actively critiquing or 'writing back' to the earlier texts. 'Writing back' is covered in the next section of this chapter but, first, we will explore rewritings as interpretations of canonical texts.

In both Classical and Biblical studies, some scholars believe that the task of the interpreter of ancient texts is to reconstruct their original context, and to disregard as far as possible any later interpretations, including those which arise from the interpreter's own historical position. Later interpretations are understood as anachronism, bias or distortion. The classical scholar Richard Jenkyns (1989: 26), for example, sees the reception history of a work as the slow accretion of wrong interpretations, or 'the barnacles of later tradition and interpretation', which 'we need to scrape away . . . if we are to see [the work] in [its] true shape'.

In opposition to Jenkyns, the influential Classical reception theorists Charles Martindale and David Hopkins believe that later texts can help us interpret earlier ones. In the introduction to their *Oxford History of Classical Reception in English Literature*, they explain that one of their aims is to 'explor[e] the ways in which classical texts have been remade and refashioned by English writers in ways that might cast (now, as well as then) as much light on the originals as on their English "derivatives"' (Hopkins and Martindale 2012: x). Similarly, in *Reception Theory and Biblical Hermeneutics*, David Parris (2009: xv–xvi) makes the point that 'the reception history of the text . . . helps us to learn from previous interpretations' (cf. Carruthers, Knight and Tate 2014: 86). For Classical and Biblical reception scholars, past interpretations of texts, and past readers, are relevant and helpful in our own approach to those texts. Just as we might turn to a contemporary critic, reviewer, scholar or commentator for insight into a text, we can also turn to the readers and interpreters of the past.

This position counters the view that past interpretations were incorrect or distorting, and that the critical and interpretative tools and systems of the present day are necessarily superior to them. It involves a kind of resistance to 'paronthocentrism' or 'present-centredness', a term coined by Mieke Bal (2006 [1991]: 19) to critique interpretations of artworks that take present-day concerns as real or universal rather than historically situated. Taking our present-day ideological and poetic concerns for granted as natural, correct or inevitable, Bal argues, 'undermines the possibility of understanding the present's historical other: the past'. Instead, we can learn something about ancient texts by seeing what past readers found in them, and how those texts responded to concerns and interpretative strategies other than our own. As Giulia

Sissa (2016: 205) puts it, we can 'trust in the profound intelligence of past readers ... Their insight is not merely a matter of curiosity in reception studies but an inspiring source of relevant questions and exemplary interpretations'.

The idea that past readers are a source of 'exemplary interpretations' ultimately relies on a theory of reception and interpretation elaborated by the German critic Hans Robert Jauss. Jauss (1982: 59) advocates a way of reading texts based on an 'aesthetic of reception', and claims that the meaning of a text 'is extracted only during the progressive process of its reception'. Jauss draws here on the notion of *Wirkungsgeschichte*, 'effective history' or 'history of effects' (Evans 2014: 2–8), a term developed by the philosopher Hans-Georg Gadamer, to focus attention on the afterlife of a text, or the history of effects that it has had as it is read and reread across time. For Gadamer and Jauss, the history of a text's effects is an important element in its meaning and aesthetic function: 'the understanding of the first reader will be sustained and enriched in a chain of receptions from generation to generation' (Jauss 1982: 20). Elsewhere, Jauss calls this 'chain' a 'summit-dialogue of authors', as Parris explains:

> The [summits], or high points [of reception], represent the more significant interpreters because of the impact they had on their contemporaries, the influence they had on later readers, or their innovative interpretation that was retrospectively recognized into the canon of exemplary commentators.
>
> (2009: 217)

Reception scholars take different attitudes to the question of which commentators are 'exemplary', and what they are examples of. Some critics working on the afterlife of Biblical or classical texts, like Parris, work to reconstruct a 'canon of exemplary commentators', whose insights into the original text are in some sense correct, and therefore useful and relevant to present-day readers and scholars in developing their own interpretations. As we have seen, this is not necessarily a conservative position, and can even be seen as a mode of resistance to paronthocentrism.

However, other scholars, like Antoinette Wire and Yvonne Sherwood, reject the 'canon of commentators' approach and the hierarchical ranking of interpretations that it necessarily involves. Wire (1990: 11) argues in her book *The Corinthian Women Prophets* that 'voices from outside the canon may speak with authority', while Sherwood (2000: 208) in *A Biblical Text and its Afterlives: The Survival of Jonah in Western Culture* states her intention to 'pay attention to all mutations of the biblical in Culture, including those that the Mainstream may well regard as monstrous or deviant' (capitalization original). Robert Evans (2014: 276) summarizes the value of such approaches as 'the recovery of neglected or subversive reception', arguing that non-mainstream, monstrous or deviant receptions may still be interesting or valuable. These receptions are 'examples' of actually existing historical interpretations, which are regarded as interesting in their own right, rather than as 'exemplary' in the sense of providing models for contemporary interpreters to follow.

A third position is taken by scholars who believe that it is, in fact, deviant interpretations, not 'Mainstream' ones, which drive and structure literary history. Thus, in his influential book, *The Anxiety of Influence*, Bloom (1973) believes that the texts which comprise the literary tradition or the Western canon can all be described, in a quasi-Oedipal drama, as 'strong misreadings': these are literary texts which productively 'misread' or reinterpret an earlier, patriarchal, text in ways that are generative, producing new possibilities for literature. Genette (1997a: 117) takes a similar line, writing that Marcel Proust's 'vision' of the earlier French writer Gustave Flaubert is valuable precisely because it is 'a "distorting" vision'. 'Only non-artists have a "correct" vision', he continues, 'but that correctness is sterile' – that is, 'correct' interpretation adds nothing to our understanding of a text.

Another, very different, critical tradition puts a high value on deviant interpretations of texts: fan studies, particularly the study of the creative practice of fans, including the production of fan fiction and fan vids. In the early 1990s, two scholars, Constance Penley and Henry Jenkins, took up ideas from the French sociologist de Certeau's (1984 [1980]) *The Practice of Everyday Life* and applied them to fannish creative forms. Penley (1991: 139) uses de Certeau's notion of 'tactics', 'guerilla actions . . . not designed primarily to help users take over the system but to seize every opportunity to turn to their own ends forces that systematically exclude or marginalize them'. Meanwhile, Jenkins (1992: 26) draws on de Certeau's model of reading as 'poaching' or 'bricolage', a process whereby 'readers fragment texts and reassemble the broken shards according to their own blueprints, salvaging bits and pieces of the found material in making sense of their own social experience'. Fanworks are examples of 'locations where popular meanings are produced outside of official interpretive practice' (26); fan fiction reinterprets and critiques media texts. For example, Jenkins provides a detailed close reading of a 1988 *Star Trek* fan novel entitled *The Weight* by Leslie Fish, which 'focuses attention . . . on the sexist treatment of women within the original episodes' (192).

Another example of fannish reconfiguration is Flummery's 'Handle-bars', a video artwork or 'vid' (Coppa 2008). The vid's visual track is comprised of clips from the second, third and fourth seasons of the BBC's rebooted *Doctor Who* (2005–2010), centring on the Tenth Doctor, played by David Tennant, and set to the song 'Handlebars' by Flobots. The song's lyrics gradually segue from what appears to be a celebratory mood of pleasure in boyish showing-off ('I can ride my bike with no handlebars'), into an expression of fascist mascu-linity rooted in dominance and violence: 'I can rule a country with a microphone . . . I can end a planet in a holocaust'. The visual clips mirror the lyrics' development as we move from the Doctor in playful mood, swinging on an office chair or joyfully hugging his Compan-ions, to clips documenting his increasing abuses of power, from his behind-the-scenes manipulation of British electoral politics, through the cruel and unusual punishment of individual criminals, to the vio-lent destruction of entire alien races. Flummery's vid thus makes vis-ible a particular, and politicized, interpretation of the Tenth Doctor's character arc.

Receptions as 'distorting visions' tend to be seen as valuable espe-cially because, or when, they 'offer a revised point of view from the "original"' . . . voicing the silenced and marginalized' (Sanders 2006: 19). However, as Sanders goes on to point out, rewriting 'can also consti-tute a simpler attempt to make texts "relevant" or easily comprehensi-ble to new audiences and readerships via the processes of proximation and updating' (19).

The distinction Sanders draws between what she calls 'revisionary' and 'proximating' adaptations correlates with the 'split' that Lefevere (1992: 3) points out between '"high" and "low" rewriting'. 'Low' rewrit-ing, including the production of anthologies, translations, reviews, edi-tions, popular abridgements, reference works, reader's guides, summaries and study notes, tends to involve proximation and updating. One example is Shmoop's (2014) YouTube video '*A Midsummer Night's Dream* Summary', which opens with Puck saying: 'I have the best job. How awesome is it to be a professional troublemaker for Oberon, the King of the Fairies. I mean, I get paid to mess with the villagers'. This rewriting diverges widely from Shakespeare's text and brings Puck into the present day both in terms of his language and in terms of his 'professional' status. Shmoop's tagline is 'We speak student', framing the video as a form of intralinguistic translation from Shakespeare's English to 'student' English.

Lefevere rightly claims that 'most professional readers . . . tend to treat ["low" rewriting] with a certain disdain', even though such works 'have become the lifeline that more and more tenuously links "high" literature to the non-professional reader'. He argues that 'the non-professional reader increasingly does not read literature as written by its writers, but as rewritten by its rewriters' (Lefevere 1992: 4), and

> since non-professional readers of literature are, at present, exposed to literature more often by rewritings than by means of writings, and since rewritings can be shown to have a not negligible impact on the evolution of literatures in the past, the study of rewritings should no longer be neglected.
>
> (7)

Similarly, in the context of Biblical reception, the Introduction to the *Oxford Handbook to the Reception History of the Bible* states:

> The goal of reception history is not to recover the original meaning of a text or to establish an authoritative reading . . . but rather involves examining the readings that have been attached to a given text or object and saying something salient about the social role of that text or object. That some of these readings may be dangerous, destructive, logically incoherent, even morally repellent, does not permit the ethically responsible reception historian to reject them out of hand, or, which is worse, to pretend that they do not follow the grain of the text.
>
> (Roberts 2011: 2–3)

Tony Bennett (1983: 8) writes that 'meanings are meanings; and marginalized, subordinate, quirky, fantastic, or quixotic ones are just as real, just as ontologically secure, just as much wrapped up in the living social destinies of texts as are dominant ones'. In this model of reception history, all the meanings that have been found in texts are historically real and worthy of study.

WRITING BACK

Lefevere points out that 'low' rewritings have tended not to receive much scholarly attention. Rewritings which critique earlier texts, offering political or ethical commentary on them, have attracted the most intensive scholarly and critical attention. As Sanders demonstrates, twentieth- and twenty-first-century literary critics tend to read rewritings in terms of their ethical, political or theoretical orientations, rather than, say, their 'stylistic achievements', which would have attracted more attention in earlier periods. For contemporary writers and critics, however,

> when assigning a political or ethical commitment to acts of literary appropriation such as ... postcolonial rewritings of canonical texts ... we acknowledge that stylistic imitation is neither the essence nor sole purpose of the approach to the source text, even though it may be a defining feature.
>
> (2006: 5)

Such texts fall into a category named 'transposition' by Genette. These are rewritings which openly transform, rather than simply imitate, earlier texts, and which do so in a serious mode, rather than a playful or satirical one (Genette 1997a: 28–29). For Genette, transposition is 'the most important of all hypertextual practices' (212), 'by far the richest in technical operations and in literary applications' (30): his evaluation is reflected in the critical emphasis on transposition over other forms of hypertextuality.

Literature, as we have seen in this chapter, is made from literature; writers take earlier writers as models to imitate and transform, and literary texts become legible against the background of a whole literary system. But what happens when the literary system in which one writes is not one's own: when the dominant poetics and ideology of that system do not accommodate the position from which a writer would want to write? For example, what happens to a woman writer in a male system, a black writer in a white system, a queer writer in a heteronormative system, or someone from a colonized culture writing within the literary system of the colonizers?

In 1972, the poet and feminist critic Adrienne Rich (1972: 18) wrote that 're-vision – the act of looking back, of seeing with fresh eyes, of entering an old text from a new critical direction – is for us [women] more than a chapter in cultural history: it is an act of survival'. 'Writing', she said, 'is re-naming' (23), and, as the feminist theologian Mary Daly (1973: 8) wrote the following year, 'women have had the power of *naming* stolen from us'. Alicia Ostriker (1985 [1981]: 318) argues for a feminist practice of rewriting as stealing back the power of naming, as women writers become 'thieves of language', reinscribing and resignifying the words, images, character, stories and myths of patriarchal culture. When a woman receives and reworks them, 'the old stories are changed, changed utterly, by female knowledge of female experience, so that they can no longer stand as foundations of collective male fantasy. Instead . . . they are corrections'.

Feminist rewritings of fairy-tales, like those of Angela Carter (1995 [1979]), exemplify the practice of re-entering, re-visioning, changing and correcting old stories in the light of 'female knowledge of female experience'. Another example might be Dorothy Parker's short poem 'Penelope', which rewrites Homer's *Odyssey*, 'entering it from a new critical direction', and realigns the story so that it centres on a contrast between masculine and feminine activities and values.

The poem consists of two stanzas, one describing Odysseus's activities as he 'ride[s] the silver sea', and one Penelope's, as she 'sit[s] at home, and rock[s]'. Where Odysseus's stanza depicts a timeless epic heroism, Penelope's is subtly anachronistic: she 'sip[s her] tea', for example. This realigns the poem around the present-day concerns and activities of women, and insists on a continuity between past and present. The structure of the poem, moreover, gives equal weight and significance to Odysseus's activities and to Penelope's, but the last line runs: 'They will call him brave'. Parker thus suggests that the emotional discipline and endurance required of Penelope in her long wait for her husband's return is as 'brave' as Odysseus's more active and traditionally heroic exploits.

The poem exemplifies Ostriker's (1985: 330) argument that women's revisionist mythmaking

> involve[s] revaluations of social, political and philosophical values, particularly those most enshrined in occidental literature, such as the glorification of conquest and the belief that the cosmos is – must be – hierarchically ordered with earth and body on the bottom and mind and spirit on the top.

We may also see Parker's poem as making possible, or contributing to, a reinterpretation of the *Odyssey* itself. As many scholars have noted, Homer uses many of the same epithets for Odysseus and Penelope throughout his epic, including *schetlios/schetlia* ('ruthless') and *ekhephron* ('cool-headed'), and Winkler's (1990) interpretation of the *Odyssey* shows that it represents the wife and the husband as equals. In the light of Parker's poem, we may be more attuned to the ways in which the *Odyssey* itself suggests an equivalence between Odysseus's accomplishments in the masculine sphere and Penelope's in the feminine.

Black writers and writers from colonized countries have also 'had the power of naming stolen' from them, and revisionary rewriting is an important strategy for these authors too. The editors of the volume *The Postcolonial Jane Austen* see their task as 'recuperating and reinstalling Austen in our world' (Mukherjee 2014: 119, citing Park and Rajan 2000: 3). Just as Parker reinstalls Homer in *her* world, one where women are brave and their activities are significant, so the postcolonial readers and rewriters of Austen set her in the context of the real concerns and questions of a postcolonial world, rather than consigning her to a fantasized history where everyone is white. Importantly, as You-me Park and Rajeswari Rajan state, this move can be 'recuperative' rather than, or as well as, critical.

The foundational postcolonial critic Edward Said takes a similar line to Park and Rajan's in a discussion of the global settings of Dickens's *Great Expectations*, which include Australia and 'the Orient'. He writes that the critic's task is 'to describe [the novel] as pertaining to Indians *and* Britishers, Algerians *and* French, Westerners *and* Africans, Asians, Latin Americans, and Australians despite the horrors, the bloodshed, and the vengeful bitterness' (Said 1993: xxii). Ankhi Mukherjee (2014: 117, citing Said 1993: xxii) describes Said's move as 'a humanist renegotiation of the common history' which seeks to reverse 'the "insidious and fundamentally unjust" separation of Europeans and natives under imperialism'. 'Postcolonial rewriting' is thus 'a detangling and undoing of the accreted values . . . of the Western canon' (Mukherjee 2014: 117), or, in Gayatri Spivak's (1990: 228) words, a process of 'reversing, displacing, and seizing the apparatus of value-coding'.

The process of 'reversing and displacing' in postcolonial writing was described by Salman Rushdie as a form of 'writing back' in a 1982 essay, 'The Empire Writes Back with a Vengeance'. Rushdie's idea, as well as his title, was taken up by Ashcroft, Griffiths and Tiffin (1989) in their book *The Empire Writes Back: Theory and Practice in Post-Colonial Literature*. The book reads a number of influential postcolonial texts as critical rewritings of Western classics, opening those texts onto the concerns of colonized subjects and demonstrating the ways in which they attempted to marginalize or silence the experiences, histories and forms of consciousness of the colonized. Such texts are examples of what Genette (1997a: 214) calls 'thematic transposition', 'in which transformation of meaning is manifestly, indeed officially, part of the purpose'. Many of them also employ 'transfocalization' (287–293), rewriting the events of a narrative from a different perspective. For example, Jean Rhys, a white West Indian-born writer, rewrote Charlotte Brontë's *Jane Eyre* in her *Wide Sargasso Sea*. Rhys's novel is told from the point of view of Bertha Antoinetta Mason, Edward Rochester's 'mad wife', who is portrayed as little better than an animal in Brontë's text and whose narrative function is solely to delay Jane's marriage to Rochester. Harking back to Mary Daly on 'the power of naming', Rhys literally renames Bertha, calling her Antoinette Cosway. Through a process of transfocalization, *Wide Sargasso Sea* critiques *Jane Eyre's* refusal of subjectivity to Bertha, although, as Spivak (1984) has pointed out, Rhys's novel also repeats some of Brontë's imperialist moves.

'Writing back' has been seen as an important literary, political and ethical strategy for postcolonial writers because, as colonized people, their encounters with the canonical texts of Western literature were part of their experience of colonial oppression itself, as Gauri Viswanathan has shown in detail in the context of English literary studies in India (Viswanathan 1989). The West Indian writer Derek Walcott engages with these ideas in his epic poem *Omeros*, which involves a sustained dialogue with Homer's *Iliad* as it tells the story of two fishermen from St Lucia, Achille and Hector, and their rivalry over a woman, Helen. As the poem explains, the names of the characters connect them transtemporally to the leading Greek and Trojan warriors in the *Iliad*, Achilles and Hector, and to Helen of Troy, the woman whose abduction by the Trojan prince Paris caused the Trojan War. Their names are thus a literary parallel, suggesting a relationship of analogy between Homer's world and the world of late-twentieth-century St Lucian fishermen. At the same time, however, their names are also a historical marker of slavery. It was common for European slave-owners to give their slaves Classical names. The presence of these Homeric names in Walcott's St Lucia is therefore not simply a neutral or quaint analogy, but a direct historical consequence of slavery, and of the massive and traumatic break in kin networks and cultural continuity perpetrated by the slave trade. In a dream-vision, Achille confronts his African ancestors and has to confess that he does not know what his own name means, to which his father responds:

> . . . if you're content with not knowing what our names mean,
>
> then I am not Afolabe, your father, and you look through my body as the light looks through a leaf. I am not here or a shadow. And you, nameless son, are only the ghost
>
> of a name.

> (25.3. 54–58)

Omeros consistently plays on the tension between two different historical models of relationship between Homeric Greece and late-twentieth-century St Lucia: a direct analogy, or a relationship predicated on the history of slavery and colonialism. The tension is registered in the two contrasted figures of Homer, or Omeros, who appear in the poem: a white 'marble Homer', who represents the Western canon and its transmission along the networks of imperialism, and a black 'ebony' Omeros, analogous to another character in the poem, the contemporary black oral poet and storyteller Seven Seas. Walcott suggests that the 'marble Homer', Homer as 'Western' classic, is just one among many possible appropriations of Homer's works and their meanings. And of course the English claim that Homer is the ancestor of 'English' literature is itself an act of appropriation. Omeros, Walcott shows, is open to reappropriation by anyone, and here he reappropriates him for the West Indies.

Rewriting, or 'Signifyin(g)', has also been important in African-American writing, as the critic and theorist Henry Louis Gates Jr (1989) shows in *The Signifying Monkey*. Gates Jr examines the figure of the Signifying Monkey, a trickster figure from African-American oral/mythic tradition, derived ultimately from Yoruba mythology. He finds that 'the Monkey's language of Signifyin(g) functions as a metaphor for formal revision, or intertextuality, within the Afro-American literary tradition' (xxi). In African-American vernacular, to Signify, or to 'signify upon' something, is like improvisation in jazz: it is to create a variation on a theme, to repeat something with a difference. 'Black texts Signify upon other black texts in the tradition by engaging in . . . formal critiques of language use, of rhetorical strategy. Literary Signification, then, is similar to parody and pastiche' (xxvii).

Signification for Gates Jr is in part a solution to a particular problem faced by African-American writers. 'Black writers . . . learn to write by reading literature, especially the canonical texts of the Western tradition' (xxii). But as Gates Jr (2003 [1989]: 113) points out elsewhere, 'unlike almost every other literary tradition, the Afro-American literary tradition was generated as a response to eighteenth- and nineteenth-century allegations that persons of African descent did not, and could not, create literature'. Black writing thus stands in a particularly charged relationship to 'the literary tradition', and Signification is part of its solution to this problem.

African-American texts Signify upon the texts of the Western tradition, repeating them with a difference; they also Signify upon other African-American texts. Gates Jr's (1989: xxviii) reading of Alice Walker's *The Color Purple* as a rewriting of Zora Neale Hurston's *Their Eyes Were Watching God* shows that 'acts of formal revision can be loving acts of bonding' as well as critique, and he sees the black tradition as constituted by such acts.

RECEPTION AS TRADITION

In the previous two sections, the term 'tradition' has begun to emerge as an important one for thinking about text-to-text reception. The word derives from a Latin word meaning 'handing over' or 'handing on', and the idea of a 'black tradition', a 'women's tradition', the 'Classical tradition', or 'the literary tradition', suggests that ideas, styles and conventions are handed on from text to text within specific communities through time.

'Tradition' can be understood, then, as a name for the organized system of texts, genres, models and modes against which we read individual texts. As we saw above, Conte defined intertextuality as 'the condition of literary readability', writing that 'the sense and structure of a work can be grasped only with reference to other models hewn from a long series of texts of which they are, in some way, the variant form' (1986: 29). Similarly, Bloom (1975: 32) claims that 'if one tries to write, or to teach, or to think, or even to read without the sense of a tradition . . . nothing at all happens, just nothing'. We necessarily write and read within a tradition, a series of texts which form the matrix of possibilities against which we understand new texts as repeating and transforming earlier texts and conventions.

This is the model used by both Showalter (1985 [1981]; 2009) in her work on the female literary tradition, and by Gates Jr in his work on the black literary tradition. Showalter (2009: xvii) writes that 'the female tradition in American literature is not the result of biology, anatomy, or psychology. It comes from . . . literary influence rather than essential sexual difference'. Similarly, for Gates Jr (1992b [1990]: 39) the black tradition is 'not defined by a pseudo-science of racial biology, or a mystically shared essence called blackness, but by the repetition and revision of shared themes, topoi, and tropes'.

On this model, traditions are intertextually constituted: they are made by writers and structured by 'literary influence' or 'formal relationships . . . among texts' which revise and rewrite each other in a networked structure. This notion of tradition is often associated with a highly influential 1919 essay by T. S. Eliot, 'Tradition and the Individual Talent'. In it Eliot writes of 'our tendency to insist, when we praise a poet, upon those aspects of his work in which he least resembles anyone else', and counters that

> No poet, no artist of any art, has his complete meaning alone.
> His significance, his appreciation is the appreciation of his

relation to the dead poets and artists. You cannot value him alone; you must set him, for contrast and comparison, among the dead.

(1975 [1919]: 37–38)

Eliot goes on to elaborate a theory of tradition as 'a simultaneous order', in which 'the whole of the literature of Europe from Homer . . . has a simultaneous existence and composes a simultaneous order' (38). Indeed, if a tradition is the system of texts within which a new work is produced and read, then all those traditional texts must be present and readable at the moment when that new work is written and read. Homer's epics were composed two and a half thousand years ago, but the *Iliad* is on my bookshelf now, in 2017, next to works from many other historical periods.

This raises two important questions. The first is to do with temporality: the notion of tradition as a 'simultaneous order', characterized by a complex coexistence of pastness and presence, challenges ideas about linear time and historical context. The second question is to do with transmission. The *Iliad* is in my bookcase now, but the *Aithiopis*, another archaic Greek epic poem dealing with the Trojan War, is not. We know of its existence through a tiny number of fragmentary quotations, references and summaries in other texts, but no full text of the poem survives. Not all of the past maintains a presence in the now, and so, we may ask, what factors determine the transmission, survival and reception of past texts?

TEMPORALITY

When we encounter texts, in the moment of our reading, they become part of our present day, whenever they were originally written. Reading texts from the past thus inevitably involves a kind of anachronism. Trained in 'historical consciousness', Western scholars have tended to downplay the anachronistic dynamic involved in reading and have sought instead to interpret texts by placing them in their historical context, as Dipesh Chakrabarty points out:

Historical [consciousness] . . . is produced by our capacity to see something that is contemporaneous with us . . . as a relic of another time or place. The person gifted with historical consciousness sees these objects as things that once belonged

> to their historical context and now exist in the observer's time
> as a 'bit' of that past . . . If such an object continues to have
> effects on the present, then the historically minded person
> sees that as the effect of the past.
>
> (2000: 238–239)

Thinking about texts from the point of view of reception, however, involves rethinking the notion of historical context and linear time that underlies the model Chakrabarty sketches here.

One way of doing so is simply reversing the direction of causality that normatively underlies the notion of 'tradition', in which the past has effects on the present. Bal (2006 [1991]: 1) does just this in her book *Quoting Caravaggio*, which traces how the work of the late-sixteenth/early-seventeenth-century painter has been 'quoted' in twentieth-century visual and performance art. The book opens with the words: 'Quoting Caravaggio changes his work forever'. For Bal, it is the later work which has effects on the earlier one. As we have seen, artistic receptions of a work can change our perception of an earlier work, but Bal takes the idea further, arguing that later artworks actually create the earlier ones that they quote or rework:

> Art is inevitably engaged with what came before it, and that
> engagement is an active reworking. It specifies what and how
> our gaze sees. Hence, the work performed by later images
> obliterates older images as they were before that interven-
> tion and creates new versions of old images instead.
>
> (1)

We do not have to see earlier artworks as the 'source' from which later artworks derive, or as a 'bit' of the past which survives into the present. Rather, we can use contemporary artworks to illuminate past artworks, by allowing ourselves to be guided by the visionary and interpretative work of those new artworks.

Other work on text-to-text reception does not see the present as altering or determining the past, but sees the two as entangled, focussing on what Rita Felski (2011: 579) calls 'the coevalness and connectedness of past and present'. In particular, work on the entangled temporalities of reception is being done in queer studies, in relation to a project dubbed 'queer unhistoricism' by Valerie Traub (2013). Beginning with the work of Carolyn Dinshaw (1999: 142), who perceived queer histories as 'affective relations across time', 'queer unhistoricists . . . seek to productively disturb schemas of development and progress by pitching sexual and temporal dissonance against sexual and temporal normativities' (Matzner 2016: 181). Queer unhistoricism, like Chakrabarty's critique of historicism, sees anachronism as productive and interesting, rather than as a failure of historical consciousness. It attempts to account for the affective dimensions of reception: the desire to connect with the past, to use its difference from the present as a resource to imagine other ways of being, and, through identification and desire, to forge communities and relationships across the boundary between the living and the dead. In Dinshaw's (1999: 142) words, it 'recognizes the historical past as a vibrant and heterogeneous source of self-fashioning as well as community building'.

Where Bal sees the past as the product of the present's gaze, so that text-to-text receptions create the texts they read, Dinshaw sees the past as an important resource for present-day affects and actions. Queer unhistoricism involves the active reception and reworking of the past, realigning past texts in relation to present concerns and future prospects. It puts past and present in contact with each other, in what Dinshaw calls the 'queer touch across time' (21).

TRANSMISSION

The notion of the active reception of the past, and the role of the present in touching, recovering or rescuing that past, brings us to the second question raised by Eliot's theory of tradition: the question of transmission. In Richard Brodhead's words, 'no past lives without cultural mediation. The past . . . does not survive by its own intrinsic power' (Brodhead 1986: 6). Rather, the past survives only if it is preserved or recovered by the activities of people in the present. In the case of 'the classical tradition', the vast majority of texts from antiquity have not been preserved: the work of the female poet Sappho survives only in fragments, and many other works, like the *Aithiopis*, have been lost completely. Moreover, during the 'Dark Ages' Europeans stopped working to preserve classical texts, and many works of classical literature, philosophy, medicine and science only survive now because they were actively received, preserved, edited and translated by Arabic and Syrian scholars like Averroes/Ibn Rushd (Reynolds and Wilson 2013: 44–79). To this extent the 'European' tradition is by no means continuous or entirely European.

Intertextual theories of tradition like Eliot's do not account for the extratextual, historical/cultural factors which influence the availability of a tradition. Eliot breezily refers to 'the whole of the literature of Europe from Homer', but in practice, there are significant constraints on the material that can possibly be included within 'the whole'. For one thing, a single human lifetime is only enough to read a tiny proportion of the literature that already exists (Zaid 2003: 22); also, very few texts from any given historical period and/or culture remain in print or are otherwise easily accessible to readers in the present day.

Franco Moretti (2005) uses 'natural selection' to model the process of textual survival, arguing that the 'fittest' texts survive, the ones which are best adapted to cross into new environments. Thirty years earlier, the Marxist literary critic Raymond Williams (1977: 115) advanced a very different understanding of the role of selection in literary traditions, writing: 'what we have to see is not just "a tradition", but a *selective tradition*: an intentionally selective version of a shaping past and a pre-shaped present'. 'Any tradition', he continues, 'is . . . an aspect of *contemporary* social and cultural organization, in the interest of the dominance of a particular class. It is a version of the past which is intended to connect with and ratify the present' (116).

The process of the selection of texts to form a 'tradition' is a crucial aspect of textual reception. Selection is, in practice, mediated through multiple cultural institutions, including education and publishing, and these institutions can often be shown to be working 'in the interest of the dominance of a particular class' or group, as Williams argues. Jane Tompkins (1984: 618), similarly, writes that 'the literary works that now make up the canon do so because the groups that have an investment in them are culturally the most influential'. She demonstrates this through an analysis of the historical process of reception of two authors working at the same time: Nathaniel Hawthorne, the author of *The Scarlet Letter*, now considered a classic nineteenth-century author, and Susan Warner, the author of the sentimental novel *The Wide, Wide World*, who at the time of Tompkins' essay was out of print and hardly remembered. Tompkins shows that Hawthorne's work survived and Warner's did not because Hawthorne's work was *made to fit*, not because it was inherently 'fitter'. Contemporary critics of both authors considered them to be of comparable quality, and valued those aspects of their texts that were the most similar. After the Civil War, however, very different aspects of Hawthorne's work were seen as valuable, while Warner's work 'ceased to [be] take[n] seriously as literature':

> Under the pressure of new conditions, Warner's work, like Hawthorne's, came to be redefined. The circumstances that create an author's literary reputation were of the same kind in either case – that is, they consisted of the writer's relation to centers of cultural domination, social and professional connections, blood relations, friendships, publishing history, and so on – but in Warner's case the circumstances were negative rather than positive.
>
> (1984: 637)

Traditions are produced not just by intertextual relations, but by social, institutional and economic factors working in a complex relationship with the textual.

Studying the reception history of a text, then, does not only involve intertextual relations or the comparison of an earlier text to a later text: it can also involve historical and archival work, as scholars study the social, cultural and economic factors which influence the survival of a text. Texts are 'received' through creative interpretation, as they are rewritten, adapted and performed, but there is also a more material dimension to their reception, as they are (or are not) re-edited, reprinted and recirculated.

BEYOND THE TEXT

The complex relationship between the textual and the 'real world' is also registered in the way that the 'afterlife', reception, or *Wirkunggeschichte*, of a text can be observed in many contexts other than the literary. Jonathan Roberts writes that

> the reception of the Bible comprises every single act or word of interpretation of that book (or books) over the course of three millennia. It includes everything from Jesus reading Isaiah,

or Augustine reading Romans, to a Sunday-school nativity play, or the appearance of '2COR4:6' as a stock number on military gunscopes.

(2011: 1)

Texts can be 'received' by being rewritten, adapted or performed, but they can also circulate in culture through material objects, like military gunscopes, or bodily practices of imitation and copying; for example, Jackie Stacey's (2003 [1994]: 155) interviews with women cinema-goers from the 1940s and 1950s reveal stories about women brushing their hair to look like Bette Davis in *Dark Victory* or 'descending the cinema staircase like a Hollywood heroine'. Ellen Kirkpatrick's work on cosplay, where fans dress up as fictional characters from media texts, sees it as a mode of embodied reception and an interpretative act. This element of interpretation is, for Kirkpatrick (2014), particularly clear in the case of superhero cosplay, where heroes themselves 'dress up' in costume in the texts being imitated by cosplayers.

We might understand such practices of reception in terms of what Daniel T. Kline calls 'participatory medievalism', which he defines as

a spectrum of active, embodied encounter that carries participants into created medieval worlds with differing degrees of immersion, yielding the sense of participating in, and even inhabiting, a neomedieval fictional world.

(2016: 76)

Such active, embodied encounters include live-action role-play, medieval re-enactment and Renaissance/Medieval Fairs – activities and experiences which often fall outside the boundary of the narrowly textual. These encounters highlight the ways in which texts are received, read, imitated and transformed by interpreters in manifold media and modes, from literary or filmic adaptations to various forms of performance practice, from the staging of a Shakespeare play to cosplay at fan conventions or costume parties. In all these activities, interpretation and the production of new texts cohabit: reading and (re)writing are intertwined with one another, and interpretation is a productive and creative act, not simply a passive act of receiving or correctly decoding a message.

In the next chapter, we move from text-to-text reception to text-to-reader reception. We will look at readers themselves, and the methodologies that scholars have used to understand how readers interpret texts. As noted, this always involves some degree of textual analysis, since the internal act of reading must be represented before it can be seen and analysed, so the next chapter overlaps to some extent with this one. However, the emphasis shifts from the analysis of interpretations as texts, to their analysis as evidence for the internal activities of readers.

2

READERS

Chapter One focussed on text-to-text approaches to reception, the 'relatively objective transformations' (Frow 2008: 26) which take place when one text rewrites another by means of allusion, quotation, imitation, adaptation, performance or translation. However, text-to-text approaches ultimately ground their arguments in readers and reading. The idea of intertextuality has to posit the existence of a reader, someone who is capable of perceiving, organizing and interpreting relations between texts. Even Gian Biagio Conte, a strict proponent of the text-to-text approach to reception, as we saw in Chapter One, introduces a reader to his definition of intertextuality: 'A text can be read only in connection with, and in opposition to, other texts. These texts form a grid through which the text is perceived according to the expectations of a reader capable of organizing its sense' (1986: 29).

While the New Critics 'tended to treat the . . . literary work . . . as if it existed as an object, like a machine, whose parts can be analyzed without reference either to the maker or to the observer (or reader)' (Rosenblatt 1995: 267), reception-oriented critics would argue that, because literary texts are designed to be read, they are necessarily addressed to a reader, and this reader is part of their design. In other words, as the semiotician and literary critic Umberto Eco puts it in a book that analyses *The Role of the Reader*, 'the reader as an active principal of interpretation is part of the . . . generative process of the text' (Eco 1979b: 4).

One way of thinking about the reader, then, is as a feature of the text; and one thing that we can observe about a text is the kind of reader to whom it is addressed. For example, Melissa Lucashenko's (2013: 1) *Mullumbimby* opens with the line: 'It is a truth universally acknowledged, reflected Jo, that a teenager armed with a Nikko pen is a pain in the fucking neck'. We can infer that Lucashenko expects her reader to have read Jane Austen's *Pride and Prejudice* or, at least, to be familiar with its famous opening line, which has travelled far and had a rich cultural afterlife on its own (Garber 2003: 204–206). The presence of a glossary at the end of the book, on the other hand, suggests that the reader of *Mullumbimby* is not expected to know dialect words from Aboriginal English, Bundjalung or Yugambeh. From this and other features of the novel, such as its tone, its pattern of emphasis, the details that it explains and the ones it takes for granted, we can build up a fairly detailed picture of the kind of reader the novel is addressing.

Of course it is possible that a different kind of person might read Lucashenko's book: one who does know Bundjalung, Yugambeh and Aboriginal English, for example, and does not know *Pride and Prejudice*'s opening line. Real-life readers may be very different from the readers expected or addressed by texts, and may do unexpected or unpredictable things with texts. They may skim and skip (Benwell, Procter and Robinson 2011: 93), or reread obsessively, with fanatical attention to detail (Eco 1992); they may attribute texts to genres or even languages other than the ones the author seems to have intended (Waquet 2001 [1998]: 104–105); they may ignore their endings (Ahmed 2010: 88–89), insert new characters (Dobinson and Young 2000), cut them up and stick them in scrapbooks (Garvey 2013).

This chapter begins by introducing the important theoretical distinction between the addressee of a book, or its 'implied reader', and real-life readers. It then provides an overview of theories of reception which centre on the text/reader relationship. These theories are plotted on a spectrum from text-centred, in which the text guides the reader's response, to reader-centred, in which the reader actively intervenes in or even alters the text. Text-centred approaches involve studying addressivity and communication as an aspect of texts, while reader-centred approaches include historical and ethnographic methods for studying real readers. This chapter thus begins by looking at theories of reception and 'the reader' which emphasize the way texts address readers, but do not look at readers themselves. It ends with theories and studies which invert this emphasis, emphasizing the reader's capacity to produce meaning to the point where 'the text . . . becom[es] expendable' (Gray 2006: 37).

'THE' READER: MOCK, IMPLIED OR REAL

There is a significant ambiguity in the word 'reader' as it is used in literary criticism. It sometimes refers to the addressee of a text, as an observable feature of that text, and sometimes to the person in the real world who picks up a text and reads it. It is important to draw a clear distinction between real readers, the people in the real world who engage with the text in specific contexts and for specific purposes, and the 'reader' to whom a text is addressed and who is, in Susan Suleiman's (1980: 8) words, 'created by the work'.

Many different names have been given to the reader created by the text, including the model reader, the mock reader, the intended reader, the virtual reader, the ideal reader, the inscribed reader and the encoded reader (Suleiman 1980; Schmid 2013). The term 'implied reader' is now the most commonly used, and it is the one I will use in this chapter. The concept, although not the term, is elaborated in Wayne Booth's (1961) book *The Rhetoric of Fiction* and the term 'implied reader' itself became popular in the 1970s after it was used to translate the German phrase *impliziter Leser* ('implicit reader') in Wolfgang Iser's books *The Implied Reader* (1974 [1972]) and *The Act of Reading* (1978 [1976]). As commonly used, the phrase 'implied reader' bundles together several slightly different models, levels and theories of the textual reader (Schmid 2013: n.p.).

Despite the complexities involved in the term's origin and usage, it is useful because it allows us to make a clear and fundamental distinction between the textual and the real reader. The 'implied reader' is a reader who is 'created by the work', rather than someone who exists in the real world. We can determine their position, characteristics and functions by looking at the text itself, rather than at any actual readers.

In *The Role of the Reader*, Eco (1979b) shows that every decision an author makes about language, style and technique implicitly presupposes what he calls a 'model reader': an implied reader who is capable of understanding the language, appreciating the style and interpreting the techniques used in the text. Children's literature offers particularly clear examples. We can often make quite detailed inferences about the implied reader or addressee of a children's book, since their 'age, sex, interests and propensities are constantly being defined in the text' (Wall 1991: 5). Indeed, as Barbara Wall argues, drawing on Chambers (1977), it is 'subtleties of address [that] define a children's book' (3); 'it is not what is said, but the way it is said, and to whom it is said, which marks a book for children' (4). The nature of the addressee, then, is a defining characteristic of children's literature. We can analyse texts written for children not simply in terms of their formal features and/or the way in which they represent the characters which appear within them, but also in terms of the way they represent their addressee. Wall shows how the narrator of Roald Dahl's *The Twits* 'puts himself in league with an implied child reader against the inevitable disgust[ingness] of adults' (193) when he writes, for example,

> An ordinary unhairy face like yours or mine simply gets a bit smudgy if it is not washed often enough, and there's nothing so awful about that. But a hairy face is a very different matter. Things *cling* to hair, especially food . . . You and I can wipe our smooth faces with a flannel and we quickly look more or less all right again, but a hairy man cannot do that.
>
> (Dahl 2013 [1980]: 12)

In his work on the reader in *The Rhetoric of Fiction*, Booth draws on a 1950 essay by Walter Gibson on the 'mock reader', the earliest attempt to differentiate between the real and the implied reader. Gibson models the distinction on the New Critical distinction between the author of a poem and its narrator or speaker. New Critics 'distinguish carefully between the *author* of a literary work and the fictitious *speaker* within the work of art', so that 'the attitudes expressed by the "lover" in the love sonnet are not to be crudely confused with whatever attitudes the sonneteer himself may or may not have manifested in real life'. In just the same way, Gibson (1980 [1950]: 2) writes, critics must also distinguish between 'the "real" individual upon whose crossed knee rests the open volume, and whose personality is as complex and ultimately inexpressible as any dead poet's', and the 'mock reader'. The mock reader has 'a set of attitudes and qualities' (1) which can be identified in the language of the text and which may be very different from those of the real reader: the mock reader of *The Twits* is a smooth-faced child, while its real readers include hairy men.

In the 1980s, Annette Kuhn (1984: 23) drew an analogous distinction between the 'social audience' and the 'spectator' in the context of film. The social audience is 'a group of people who buy tickets at the box office, or who switch on their TV sets': the spectator is the addressee of the film, who is characterized by the film's techniques of address in particular ways that may or may not align with the actual characteristics of the social audience. The difference can be illustrated through the first appearance of Sugar Kane, played by Marilyn Monroe, in *Some Like It Hot* (Wilder 1959). In this twenty-second sequence, shot/reverse shot aligns the spectator's gaze with the gaze of the two male protagonists of the film, one of whom, Joe, will go on to have a romance with Sugar. As sultry jazz music plays, a close-up tracking shot follows Sugar/Monroe along the platform. The shot, centred on her buttocks, legs and high-heeled shoes, cuts her body out of the frame at the waist. Editing, music and framing work together to characterize the film's spectator as a straight man, like Joe, who takes pleasure in watching Sugar's/Monroe's sexy walk. However, many different kinds of people have watched the film, so that its social audience includes, for example, people who are not attracted to Sugar/Monroe; people who are attracted to her, but who find the framing of the close-up tracking shot objectifying and alienating; and/or people who enjoy watching Sugar/Monroe not because they are attracted to her but because they appreciate, and perhaps want to imitate, the strength, skill and grace with which she walks in high heels. The characterization of the spectator does not determine the response of the social audience; but equally, the diversity of the social audience's responses does not mean that the film is not actively working to construct a particular position for its spectator.

Like Gibson and Kuhn, Iser also differentiates the two kinds of reader, most clearly in 'The Rudiments of a Theory of Aesthetic Response' in *The Act of Reading*. 'The implied reader as a concept has his roots firmly planted in the structure of the text; he is a construct and in no way to be identified with any real reader' (1978 [1976]: 34). Although the implied reader is not to be identified with the real reader, for Iser, the two are connected: 'No matter who or what he may be, the real reader is always offered a particular role to play, and it is this role that constitutes the concept of the implied reader' (1978: 35).

For Iser, the implied reader functions as a guide or foil to the real reader. We can see how this works in the repeated addresses to the reader in Henry Fielding's 1749 novel *Tom Jones*. For example, in the second chapter of the novel, the narrator explains:

> Reader, I think proper, before we proceed any farther together, to acquaint thee that I intend to digress, through this whole history, as often as I see occasion, of which I am myself a better judge than any pitiful critic whatever.
>
> (1974 [1749]: 37)

Here the narrator addresses an implied reader who will be sympathetic to his digressions, and in this way guides the real reader to adopt the same attitude.

The implied reader is crucial to Iser's model of reading. He writes that 'literary texts take on their reality by being read' and that the 'meaning' of a text is not inherent within it, but must be 'assembled in the responsive mind of the recipient' (1978: 34–35). The process of assembling a meaning, however, takes place under the text's guidance and is ultimately controlled by the text.

> The impressions that arise as a result of [the reading] process will vary from individual to individual, but only within the limits imposed by the written . . . text. In the same way, two people gazing at the night sky may both be looking at the same collection of stars, but one will see the image of a plough, and the other will make out a dipper. The 'stars' in a literary text are fixed; the lines that join them are variable.
>
> (1972: 287)

For Iser (1980: 119), the reader connects dots or 'fills in the blank[s] in the text'. Here he echoes Tzvetan Todorov's (1980) model of 'reading as construction', and Rosenblatt's (1978) theory of 'literature as transaction', which similarly models reading as the production of meaning by a reader under the guidance of the text.

We will return to the notion of reading as assembling meaning in more detail in the next chapter. In the meantime, one problem for these models of readership-as-construction is that they do not account for acts of reading which disobey the guidance of the text. 'On the one hand', Suleiman writes,

> Iser asserts the primacy of a reader's creative role in realizing the text . . . on the other hand, he suggests that it is ultimately the text itself which directs the reader's realization of it. Iser does not treat the question of idiosyncratic readings directly.
> (1980: 23)

The question of idiosyncratic readings is an important one for theorists who understand the meaning of the text as something assembled or produced by a reader, rather than something that is either inherent in the text, determined by the author's intention or irrelevant to the critical enterprise. On the one hand, as Iser (1978: 34) writes, 'literary texts take on their reality by being read'; on the other hand, the responses of real readers to texts are idiosyncratic, unpredictable and/or undisciplined. The idea of a reader inscribed in the text can, therefore, take on a normative edge, potentially suggesting that there is a correct way to read the text: the way set out for the implied reader. Critics who take this view have to carefully circumscribe their references to 'the reader' in order to rule out what they describe as personal, psychological or idiosyncratic responses to texts.

The influential reader-response critic Stanley Fish, for example, reflecting on his practice, defines 'the reader of whose responses I speak' as an 'informed reader, neither an abstraction, nor an actual living reader, but a hybrid – a real reader (me) who does everything within his power to make himself informed'. Reading, for Fish (1980b [1970]: 87) requires 'the conscious attempt to become the informed reader . . . and the attendant suppressing, insofar as that is possible, of what is personal and idiosyncratic and 1970ish in my response'. Similarly, the Russian theorist Boris Korman writes that 'the method of reception is the process of transforming the real reader into the ideal, conceived reader' (1992 [1977], translated and cited in Schmid 2013) and both Gibson and Booth, in their discussions of the mock or implied reader of the text, argue that reading involves moving into the position set out for us in a text. Booth writes:

> As I read ... I become the self whose beliefs must coincide with the author's. Regardless of my real beliefs and practices, I must subordinate my mind and heart to the book if I am to enjoy it to the full.
>
> (1961: 138)

SUBORDINATING ONESELF TO THE TEXT

Critics have elaborated the idea of subordinating oneself to a text in a number of different ways. The first is Derek Attridge's (2004: 79–80) notion of 'readerly hospitality', defined as 'a readiness to have one's purposes reshaped by the book one is reading'. In order to read hospitably, he writes, echoing Booth, one must 'suspend habitual modes of thinking and feeling' (83).

The idea of subordinating mind and emotions to a book is extended to other forms of art, including visual art, and developed into a full-blown theory of aesthetic response by Charles Altieri in his book *The Particularities of Rapture: Towards an Aesthetic of the Affects*. Altieri believes that we should rethink our evaluation of passivity, which has often been seen negatively, and instead value it positively as part of our capacity, as readers, to be *moved* by works of art. The value of works of art for readers and viewers lies in the way they enable us to 'dwell in affective states until their power begins to rival reason's authority' (2003: 130). By subordinating our own minds and hearts to a text, we become able to take on certain types of identification with others. Ultimately, this involves ethical practices of 'extending the self' (139) as submitting to the text allows us to 'experience a subjectivity not fully at home with the roles that [our] culture imposes' (217).

Altieri argues that we cannot account for artworks without thinking about the ways in which they position us as addressees. His reading of Matthew Arnold's poem 'Isolation: To Marguerite' shows how the poem 'puts those who hear his address in the position of feeling that they somehow have to complete the conversational circuit' (96). Altieri's work, like Eco's and Wall's, isolates the addressivity of an artwork as an element of the reading process that we can analyse. It also advocates a practice of aesthetic response as willingness to move into the position set out for us by the text.

The idea of reading as subordination was described much earlier, in 1931, by Virginia Woolf, who writes:

> Our first duty as readers is to try and understand what the writer is making . . . We must not impose our design upon him; we must not try to make him conform his will to ours . . . .
>
> (2010 [1931]: 272)

Woolf adds, however, that we have a second duty as readers:

> reading, as we have suggested, is a complex art. It does not merely consist in sympathising and understanding. It consists, too, in criticising and in judging.
>
> The reader must leave the dock and mount the bench. He must cease to be the friend; he must become the judge.
>
> (272)

Woolf's two-sided model is echoed by Patriciono Schweickart (1986: 54), for whom 'the necessary subjectivity of reading [is] coupled with the equally necessary commitment to reading the text as it was meant to be read'.

Gibson, Booth, Altieri and Woolf all advocate reading practices structured around the *interplay* between the real reader and the implied reader. This reading practice involves aesthetic and ethical judgement but Gibson and Booth argue that the real reader passes judgement not so much on the author, as Woolf would have it, as on the implied reader. Gibson (1980: 5) defines 'a bad book' as 'a book in whose mock reader we discover a person we refuse to become, a mask we refuse to put on, a role we will not play'. Booth (1961: 138) cites this approvingly in *Rhetoric of Fiction* and expands on it in a reading of Peter Benchley's 1974 novel *Jaws* in *The Company We Keep* (1988). In order to read, understand and derive pleasure from *Jaws*, Booth argues, he would have to take up the position of the novel's mock reader, which would entail temporarily becoming someone who is 'enjoying the prospect of bloody death for those who don't matter, hoping for (and fully expecting) final safety for the good guys (who don't matter much more)' (203). Annette Federico (2016: 127) summarizes: 'Because Booth doesn't like who he is or what's expected of him ethically when he's reading *Jaws*, he puts it aside after the first few chapters'.

RESISTANT READERS

The idea of refusing to become the reader that the text wants us to be emerged with a more politicized edge in feminist literary and film criticism from the 1970s onwards. In film criticism, discussions of the gendered nature of spectatorship were sparked by Laura Mulvey's (1975) 'Visual Pleasure and Narrative Cinema', which demonstrated that classical Hollywood film was addressed to a male spectator, or to 'the male gaze', and posed specific problems to female members of the social audience. In literary studies, a few years later, Judith Fetterley's (1978) analysis of canonical male-authored American fiction championed *The Resisting Reader*. Fetterley writes that in the fiction she analyses,

> the female reader is co-opted into participation in an experience from which she is explicitly excluded; she is asked to identify with a selfhood that defines itself in opposition to her; she is required to identify against herself.
>
> (xii)

Fetterley's reading of Washington Irving's short story 'Rip Van Winkle' makes the gender of the reader into an important element of the process of identification. In the story, set at the time of the American Revolution, the protagonist, Rip Van Winkle, is continually nagged by his 'termagant wife' because of his 'insuperable aversion to all kinds of profitable labor' (1996 [1819]: 35). One day, to get away from his wife, he walks up into the mountains, where he meets some supernatural beings, shares a drink with them and falls asleep. On waking, he returns to the village where he gradually discovers that he has slept for twenty years; he is taken in by his daughter and lives a happy, idle life, since he has 'got his neck out of the yoke of matrimony, and [can] go in and out whenever he please[s], without fearing the tyranny of Dame Van Winkle' (47).

'How is a woman to read Rip Van Winkle?', asks Fetterley. 'What is an essentially simple act of identification when the reader of the story is male becomes a tangle of contradictions when the reader is female' (1978: 9). The process of 'being moved', which Altieri sees as central to the reading experience, will be very different for different readers of the same text, because different readers start in different places in relation to the text and to the world it represents. A woman reading 'Rip Van Winkle' can attempt to read it from the position of the implied reader, who is male, a practice that Altieri and Woolf might see as ethically or aesthetically valuable, though Woolf would only recommend it as a first stage. Fetterley, however, sees the initial experience of moving into the position of a male implied reader as part of the workings of a patriarchal system which serves to alienate women from their own subjectivity. She points out that in general, 'as readers . . . women are taught to think as men, to identify with a male point of view' (xx). For the female reader, this produces the experience of being divided against herself, which is not something required of male readers of the same text. Her response is that

> [t]he first act of the feminist critic must be to become a resisting rather than an assenting reader and, by this refusal to assent, to begin the process of exorcising the male mind that has been implanted in us.
>
> (xxii)

Suleiman (1976: 173) argues similarly that 'ideological dissent from works of fiction is a reading experience involving the "perception" of certain formal devices as masks for the novelist in his role as manipulator of values'. The act of perceiving such formal devices involves making available to consciousness aspects of the text which had previously gone unnoticed. The very act of perceiving and naming these devices 'is a quasi-willful *act of non-co-operation with the text* on the part of the reader'.

Fetterley's argument, like many of the others we have been engaging with in this chapter, explicitly advocates a particular practice on the part of the reader. Just as Woolf defines 'the first *duty* of the reader' and Altieri claims that 'audiences *have to* pursue mutual recognition', Fetterley writes that 'the first act of the feminist critic *must be* to become a resisting . . . reader' (my emphases). For Fetterley, as for Altieri, the reader should read in order to extend or transform the self by going beyond the 'roles our culture imposes' (Altieri) or the 'mind that has been implanted in us' (Fetterley). For Altieri, however, we achieve this by submitting to the text, while for Fetterley, we do it by resisting.

The notion of resistant reading is similar to that of 'reading against the grain' proposed a few years after Fetterley by the Marxist critic Terry Eagleton. In *Walter Benjamin or Towards a Revolutionary Criticism* (1981), Eagleton (1981: 113) argues that Marxist criticism should proceed in two ways at once. Firstly, it should 'expose the rhetorical structures by which non-socialist works produce politically undesirable effects'. Rhetorical structures are the communicative aspects of the text, the way in which it addresses us, analogous to what Fetterley calls the text's 'palpable designs'. Secondly, Marxist criticism should 'interpret such works where possible "against the grain", in order to appropriate from them whatever may be valuable for socialism' (113). Appropriation, 'reading against the grain', is a political practice whereby 'literary texts are to be violated, smelted down, read against the grain and so reinscribed in new social practices' (116–117).

For Eagleton, criticism involves active intervention into the text. The task of the critic is not to establish and describe the aesthetic unity of the text as an art object removed from the domain of broader social practice but, on the contrary, to violate the integrity of the text and to reposition the text in social practices of resistance to power. Eagleton's work draws on a model of criticism as 'symptomatic reading' (Belsey 2002: 95–113), developed by the French Marxist theorists Pierre Macherey (1978 [1966]) and Louis Althusser and Etienne Balibar (1970 [1968]), and extended by Frederic Jameson (1981) in *The Political Unconscious: Narrative as a Socially Symbolic Act*.

Symptomatic reading starts from the psychoanalyst Sigmund Freud's crucial distinction between 'latent' and 'manifest' meaning. It proposes that, in addition to their manifest meanings, texts have latent meanings that must be 'unmask[ed]' by the critic (Jameson 1981: 20). The text never 'means just what it says' (61). Instead, its 'surface' meanings must be understood as a series of symptoms, which provide clues through which the critic, working like a psychoanalyst, can uncover the unconscious ideological conflicts which ultimately produce and structure the text through an interplay between what is said and what is not said. 'It seems useful and legitimate', Macherey (1978: 85) states, 'to ask of every production what it tacitly implies, what it does not say'.

The African-American novelist and critic Toni Morrison (1992: 17) drew on the notion of the text's productive silences in her book *Playing in the Dark: Whiteness and the Literary Imagination*, where she argues that although black characters may appear to be marginal or absent in most of US literature, this does not mean that US literary texts are not deeply engaged with, and helping to construct, the ideological problem of race. 'Explicit or implicit', she writes, 'the Africanist presence informs in compelling and inescapable ways the texture of American literature . . . Even, or especially, when American texts are not "about" Africanist presences or characters or narrative or idiom, the shadow hovers in implication, in sign' (46–47).

In the twenty-first century and in contexts other than Morrison's work the notion of 'symptomatic reading' has begun to be criticized, in part because it casts the reader/text relationship as 'adversarial' (Best and Marcus 2009: 16) or even a 'violent intervention' (Crane 2009: 92). Where the 'strong critic' (Jameson 1981: 13) violates the text and heroically brings its hidden meanings into the light, the advocates of various forms of 'surface reading' 'embrace the surface', which 'involves accepting texts, deferring to them instead of mastering them or using them as objects', or 'assumes that texts can produce their own truths because . . . what we think theory brings to texts . . . is already present in them' (Best and Marcus 2009: 10–11). The debate between symptomatic and surface reading, then, returns us to the question of resistance vs subordination to a text.

AUDIENCES, POWER AND FREEDOM

If 'reading' a text can be a form of violent intervention, then how free are readers to decide how to read a text – and how free should they be? The answer we provide, or presuppose, to this question will stem to some extent from to our critical orientation as reception scholars. If we think of texts as manipulating or coercing their audiences into particular positions – having 'designs' on us, in Fetterley's words – we will emphasize resistance to the text. If, on the other hand, we think of texts as having something new, unpredictable and worthwhile to say to us, which we may miss if we do not learn how to listen but instead impose our own concerns upon them, we will value subordination to the text. In practice, most readings will involve a complicated dynamic which combines subordination with resistance, as real readers negotiate a position from which to read, but we can use the spectrum of resistance and subordination, or reader-dominant and text-dominant models of reception, to make useful distinctions between various strands of reception scholarship.

Literary critics have tended to be anxious about the reader's power over the text, and consequently often lean towards text-dominant models of reception. Even reader-response criticism sometimes stresses the importance of suppressing idiosyncratic responses and of subordinating the (real) reader's beliefs and values to those of the text in the reading process, arguing that the more closely we can align ourselves with the mock or implied reader, the more scrupulously we follow the protocols it lays down for reading, the better our reading will be. By contrast, scholars and critics of popular and mass culture have worried more about the power of the text over readers, viewers or audiences, and have often embraced reader-dominant models of reception.

The turn to reader-dominant models is in part a reaction against early-twentieth-century approaches to audiences and media reception theory (Miller 2008). In the first half of the twentieth century, behaviourist theories dominated the field, so that research tended to focus on the effects of media on audiences' beliefs and behaviours. This approach derived from a long history of anxiety about the effects of new cultural forms and media technologies on audiences, especially non-elite audiences: women, working-class people and young people. Thus, for example, in eighteenth-century Europe reading contemporary novels rather than classical texts and the Bible was seen as highly dangerous, particularly to women (Littau 2006: 62–65). In the 1930s, popular fiction was seen as a threat to working-class readers by Q. D. Leavis (2011 [1932]: 14–15), who wrote that 'the reading habit is now often a form of the drug habit'; in the 1950s, Wertham (1954) characterized the effect of comic books on young readers as *The Seduction of the Innocent*. In the 1980s, the rise of VCR (video cassette recorder) technology meant that films could be watched in private, domestic spaces, creating a sustained moral panic about 'video nasties' (Barker 2003 [1997]);

from the 1990s onwards, similar anxieties have clustered around video games, the Internet, smartphones and tablets.

In general, non-elite audiences have historically been seen as less rational than elite males, and hence more vulnerable to manipulation and more in need of protection from the 'bad' messages that they receive from cultural texts. The notion of the vulnerable audience implicitly relies on what has been called the 'injection' model of reception, whereby texts are seen as injecting their messages into audiences as if by hypodermic syringe (Abercrombie and Longhurst 1998: 5).

A different and more sophisticated model of the way in which popular texts can negatively affect audiences was put forward in the 1930s by the Marxist cultural critic Theodor Adorno, in dialogue with his friend and colleague Walter Benjamin. Both Benjamin and Adorno argued that specific media could produce specific 'perceptual modes' (Staiger 2005: 31). Benjamin believed that film, then a relatively new medium, produced a way of seeing the world that was potentially revolutionary. Adorno responded that popular music produced modes of listening that were politically regressive, positioning its listeners in such a way as to produce obedient subjects who 'listen according to formula' and lose 'the capacity to make demands beyond the limits of what [is] supplied' (2001 [1938]: 45).

Since the 1960s, however, theorists have criticized both the 'injection' model and Adorno's more complex understanding of popular texts. Stuart Hall's influential 1973 paper 'Encoding/Decoding' is a particularly effective critique of the 'injection' model in the context of TV news. The 'message' of a TV programme is not injected whole and entire into a viewer, producing a direct and predictable effect on her behaviour or beliefs. Instead, the production, circulation and reception of that 'message' involve a series of encoding and decoding processes. Importantly, the decoded meanings which affect a viewer are not necessarily identical with the meanings that the programme-makers intended: 'we are not speaking about a one-sided process which governs how all events will be signified' (Hall 1980 [1973]: 134–135). However, this also does not mean that decodings are purely 'selective, random, or privatized': 'unless they are wildly aberrant, encoding will have the effect of constructing some of the limits and parameters within which decodings will operate' (135).

Encoding in television does aim to communicate a 'preferred meaning' to the audience, although it does not always succeed. Hall also calls this preferred meaning the 'hegemonic signification of events' (136), borrowing the notion of hegemony from the Marxist theorist Antonio Gramsci. Hegemony, as Davis (2004: 46–47) summarizes, 'rests on an idea of negotiated power whereby members of a class are able to persuade other classes that they share the same class interests'. By encoding news events within a hegemonic viewpoint, the media seeks to convince a mass audience of the legitimacy of its version of events, thus securing assent to the dominant view and playing an important role in the maintenance of hegemony.

Hall identifies three hypothetical positions from which viewers may decode programmes: dominant-hegemonic, negotiated and oppositional. Dominant-hegemonic readings decode a programme according to the codes used to encode it, and take the preferred meaning 'full and straight' (1980: 136). A negotiated reading 'contains a mixture of adaptive and oppositional elements' (137); most often, according to Hall, a viewer will accept the programme-maker's overall framing of a topic, but will 'negotiate' exceptions to the rule in the light of her specific position and interests. An oppositional reading, on the other hand, consciously decodes the message of the TV programme according to a different code from the one used by the programme-makers.

Hall's essay maps the workings of broad social, cultural and technological structures for the production, circulation and reception of meaning. That is, he is looking at reading, rather than readers, so I will return to his essay briefly in the next chapter. His appearance at this point in my argument underscores the way in which thinking about readers requires at least some attention to the reading practices and systems which readers employ. Hall's theoretical model of reading was in fact taken up and tested in empirical work on actual readers, most notably by David Morley in *The 'Nationwide' Audience* (1980), which identified real-life examples of Hall's 'hypothetical' positions in ethnographic interviews with viewers of a popular television news programme in the 1970s. The notion of testing the 'hypotheses' of reception theory was more broadly important for early ethnographic work on real readers, as we will explore in the next two sections of this chapter.

REAL READERS

We need not look any further than the text itself to see how it positions its implied readers and/or how it structures or guides readers' interpretations.

The way a text constructs an implied reader or viewer, or seeks to produce a particular subject position or mode of perception, is an important part of a text, and theories of implied readership help us to analyse this. However, as we have seen, real readers are able to take up a range of different positions with respect to implied readers: subordinate, resistant, negotiated, oppositional, and so on. For this reason, we cannot know how real readers or audiences respond to the protocols and positions set out in a text simply by looking at the text in isolation.

It is important, then, to distinguish between claims about the implied reader of a text, which can be supported or challenged by evidence from the text, and claims about real readers, which can only be supported or challenged by evidence from or about those real readers. As Tony Bennett has pointed out, it is not the case that 'readings, and especially popular readings, can be inferred from the analysis of popular texts' (1983: 6). Jonathan Rose neatly reverses Wimsatt and Beardsley's 'affective fallacy' to call this 'the receptive fallacy': 'critics . . . try to discern the messages a text transmits to an audience by examining the text rather than the audience' (2010: 4). The French sociologist Michel de Certeau similarly insists that it is important to look not just at cultural productions, but at the meanings that real consumers find in them and the uses they make of them. He writes:

> Once the images broadcast by television and the time spent in front of the TV set have been analysed, it remains to be asked what the consumer *makes* of these images and during those hours. The thousands of people who buy a health magazine, the customers in a supermarket, the practitioners of urban space, the consumers of newspaper stories and legends – what do they make of what they 'absorb', receive and pay for? What do they do with it?
>
> (2003 [1980]: 108)

An important strand of reception study, then, involves listening to real readers, and looking at the historical evidence left behind by real readers of the past. In the next two sections of this chapter, we will look at historical and ethnographic/sociological approaches and methodologies for the study of real readers.

READERS IN HISTORY

Attending to real readers in history allows us to avoid Rose's 'receptive fallacy' and to rewrite our understanding of readers and reading on the basis of new forms of evidence, often characterized in terms of 'two poles of approaches' to the history of reading: the micro-historical and the macro-historical (Towheed, Crone and Halsey 2011: 2–3). Macro approaches, which are usually quantitative, track broad trends in the publication and circulation of texts and/or in the diffusion of literacy: what is being published, how many copies are sold, how do books circulate nationally and internationally, what is the demographic makeup of their readership, what proportion of the population is able to read? Micro approaches, which are usually qualitative, focus on individual readers or small groups, and often ask how readers make meanings out of texts or otherwise put them to use.

Moretti (2000; 2005: 1), an advocate of the transformative power of macro-historical approaches, has developed a series of data-driven techniques for what he calls 'distant reading'. He sees this as an important corrective to the dominance of 'close reading', the tendency of literary scholars to focus on detailed interpretation of individual texts. A literary history based on those works which have survived and are canonical for us in the present necessarily misrepresents the past, which should be grasped as a collective system:

> A canon of two hundred novels, for instance, sounds very large for nineteenth-century Britain (and is much larger than the current one), but is still less than one percent of the novels that were actually published: twenty thousand, thirty, more, no one really knows ... A field this large cannot be understood by stitching together separate bits of knowledge about individual cases, because it *isn't* a sum of individual cases: it's a collective system, that should be grasped as such, as a whole.
> (2005: 4)

Moretti has used the phrase 'the slaughterhouse of literature' to designate the mass of short-lived books which may be popular at a given moment, but which are not read for longer than a generation. These books are significant because, as Margaret Cohen (1999: 7) points out, 'the identity of a literary historical moment is defined not by the canonized masterworks but rather by struggles involving a broad range of writers, readers, and texts'. In terms of the theories of inter-textuality discussed in the last chapter, it is the broad range of texts and struggles which forms the 'matrix of possibilities' against which individual texts are received and interpreted.

The methods needed to track these large-scale patterns of produc-tion, circulation and reception are being developed especially in the field of digital humanities. For example, the digital humanities scholar Katherine Bode works with the online database AustLit, which was designed to provide 'a comprehensive record of [Australia's] creative writing and associated critical works' and contains exhaustive biblio-graphic and biographical details about authors, organizations and literary and critical works in a vast range of genres (AustLit, n.d.). 'Mining, modelling and analysing data in a digital archive', instead of focussing on 'the great authors' and 'the canonical texts', allows Bode (2012: 1) to 'write a new history of Australian literature'.

New digital methods for storing and analysing information can provide new data about what was being read, by whom and where. This in turn enables us to identify broader patterns in the production, circulation and reception of texts. Over the nineteenth and twentieth centuries, in English-language literatures, a number of popular genres emerged and a number of others disappeared, as Moretti tracks in the 'Graphs' chapter of his book *Graphs Maps Trees*. It is often assumed that these genres correspond to specific and discrete communities of readers. Moretti himself writes that 'when an entire generic system vanishes at once, the likeliest explanation is that *its readers vanished at once*' (Moretti 2005: 20). However, Julieanne Lamond, who stud-ied the borrowing records of readers in Lambton, NSW between 1902 and 1912, counters: 'We do know that . . . genres of popular fiction . . . took specific and solidified form in this period but I am not sure that we know how discrete the readerships were for these emerging genres' (2014: 90). In fact, the borrowing records of the Lambton readers show 'patterns of common reading clustered around books that do not appear to share generic characteristics' (91). Lamond identifies a shared interest in risk and travel, for example, and we may wonder whether the Lambton readers, mainly immigrants from Wales who had 'taken great (personal and financial) risks to migrate to Australia in search of work' (97), used their library reading to explore these ideas and experiences.

On the basis of library records alone, however, we can only wonder about what the Lambton readers made of the books they read. Robert Darnton, an early scholar of the history of reading, famously wrote: 'to pass from the *what* to the *how* of reading is an extremely difficult step' (1984: 222). Focussing on the *what* of reading can be transformative in itself, as Lamond's work shows. Other examples include Jonathan Rose's (2010) demonstration of the importance of classic and canonical literature to working-class readers in Britain in the nineteenth and early twentieth centuries, arguing against the assumption that working-class readers have a separate 'canon' of popular texts, and Kate Flint's 1993 demonstration that 'middle-class girls in the [Edwardian] period preferred the *Boy's Own Paper* to its putatively gender-appropriate spinoff, the *Girl's Own*' (Price 2004: 305).

However, to move from the 'what' to the 'how' of reading means focussing on qualitative data, rather than on *Reading by Numbers*, the method which gives Bode's book its title. Rose's history of the reading life of the British working classes lists among his sources an enormous volume of autobiographical writing, both published and unpublished, as well as 'oral history, educational records, library records, sociological surveys, and opinion polls, letters to newspaper editors (published or, more revealingly, unpublished), fan mail, and even the proceedings of the Inquisition' (Rose 2010: 1). Other critics have studied annotations, marginalia and glosses in manuscripts and printed books from the medieval period to the present day (Reynolds 1996; Jackson 2001; Griffiths 2014); early modern and eighteenth-century 'commonplace books' (Beal 1993; Darnton 2000); nineteenth-century scrapbooks (Garvey 2013; Marcus 2013); and many other sources, in order to find out *how* readers in the past interpreted texts and used them for their own purposes.

One influential example is Lisa Jardine and Anthony Grafton's essay '"Studied for Action": How Gabriel Harvey Read His Livy', an analysis of the 'purposeful reading' practices of one early modern reader. Their analysis of Harvey's reading leads them to argue that

> if we use our own understanding of the salient features of the
> text of Livy (say) to identify the points of crucial importance to

> an Elizabethan reader we are very likely to miss or to confuse
> the methods and objects at which reading was directed.
>
> (1990: 30)

Jardine and Grafton's work thus challenges the basis of text-dominant approaches to reception. As we saw, Iser (1972: 282) claims that 'the "stars" in a literary text are fixed; the lines that join them are variable' but what counts as a 'star' in a literary text is itself also variable.

Attending to historical readers thus defamiliarizes the interpretative strategies that we take for granted, and even the notion of reading itself. Darnton writes of 'the mystery of reading' that

> both familiar and foreign, it is an activity that we share with
> our ancestors yet that never can be the same as what they
> experienced ... Even if their texts have come down to us
> unchanged ... our relation to those texts cannot be the same
> as that of readers in the past.
>
> (Darnton 1986: 5)

SOCIOLOGICAL AND ETHNOGRAPHIC RESEARCH

Like historical research into past readers, sociological and ethnographic research into present-day readers and reading communities derives from the insight that readers' interpretations are not predictable. The interpretative practices of contemporary real-life readers, their affective responses and the things they do with texts, cannot be inferred from those texts, but must be studied in their own right.

Ethnographic research involves talking to actual readers and/or studying accounts that actual readers have produced of their interpretations of texts and their reading habits. As Radway (1987 [1984]: 5) puts it, ethnographic reception study attempts to 'move beyond the various concepts of the inscribed, ideal or model reader and to work with actual subjects in history'. Radway's own book, *Reading the Romance*, is an early and still influential example of ethnographic work on real readers. The readers she studied were a group of female romance fans, regular customers of a particular bookseller in a town in the Midwest of the United States known in the book by the pseudonym of 'Smithton'. *Reading the Romance* opens with a critique of the way in which 'literary critics tend to move immediately from textual interpretation to sociological explanation' (20), citing the contemporary feminist critic Ann Douglas whose polemic against romance novels proceeded by analysing the texts, finding 'a more overtly misogynist message [than in earlier romances] at the heart of the genre', and then claiming that the rising popularity of romance must mean that readers are actively seeking out 'that new message' (20, summarizing Douglas 1980). Thirty years later, a 2011 paper on Stephenie Meyers' wildly popular vampire romance series *The Twilight Saga* by Lydia Kokkola follows exactly the same argumentative logic as Douglas. (Kokkola 2011: 44) produces her own interpretation of *The Twilight Saga* as 'glorif[ying] female submissiveness in heterosexual relationships, and valoriz[ing] self-abusive behaviour as if it were a sign of "true love"'. Without consulting any readers of the book other than herself, she concludes that the popularity of the books is a sign of the 'evident appeal' of 'these elements' – that is, the ones she identified in her own reading – to 'large numbers of readers'.

Radway argues, however, that without ethnographic enquiry scholars cannot assume that they have correctly identified *which* elements of romances appeal to readers. Like Gabriel Harvey, the Elizabethan reader of Livy discussed above, readers of *Twilight* may single out and enjoy different elements of the text in their reading from those that Kokkola identified. Indeed, research into young Australian readers of teenage romance novels by May Lam in the 1980s suggested that the central heterosexual love plot of these novels was not readers' primary focus. Instead, readers said that they enjoyed the genre because it routinely emphasized and explored feelings and emotions as an important component of daily experience (Lam 1986). Similarly, Radway's work with the Smithton women showed that they had a coherent and shared set of interpretative rules and expectations for romances which derived from their shared investment in and practices of reading romances, rather than from publisher's categories.

PROFESSIONAL AND LAY READERS

One key principle of research into readers, both historical and ethnographic, is that we cannot assume that our own reading patterns are shared by other readers: that 'they' will see what 'we' see in the text, or that they will respond in the ways that we do. This is an important challenge to the convention in literary studies critiqued by Anouk Lang (2009: 125), whereby literary critics 'refe[r] to [their] own . . . interpretation as that of "the reader"'. Lang points out that literary-critical readings are not neutral, but situated within a particular interpretative context and community, just like the Smithton readers. For this reason, she believes that any attempt to refer to a generalized 'reader' simply 'obscure[s] the way interpretive differences flow from differences in the subject position, geographical location and educational training of readers'.

Lang's last factor, educational training, is a key differential for reading practices. Indeed, 'studies of classroom relations have made it clear that what is actually taught in the literature classroom is *not* "the text", but the proper mode of responding to it' (Dale 1997: 4). Thus academic and non-academic reading practices do differ from each other, in ways which are often mapped as a distinction between critical and uncritical, or even 'naïve', reading (Warner 2004). Critical reading, the mode of response taught at university, is intellectual: it proceeds through formal analysis, historical contextualization and political critique. Uncritical reading is emotional: it is oriented around immersion in a fictional world, narrative suspense and identification with characters.

The critical/uncritical distinction, Michael Warner shows, is explicitly or implicitly evaluative. It encodes the assumption that critical or academic reading practices are better than uncritical or popular ones. In particular, critical reading is often asserted to be more intellectual, more politically engaged and/or more ethical. However, those assertions have been challenged in the last fifteen years or so, in two interrelated ways.

Firstly, John Guillory and others have pointed out that even if academic and popular reading practices are different, one is not necessarily better than the other. Guillory (2000) frames the difference between academic and popular reading practices not as a critical practice versus an uncritical one, but in less charged terms, as a professional activity versus a lay one. 'Professional reading and lay reading have become so disconnected that it has become hard to see how they are both reading' (34), he argues, not only because they have differing 'conventions of interpretation' (31), but because they are different *kinds* of activity. Professional reading is work, while lay reading is a leisure activity;

professional reading is communal and vigilant, 'stand[ing] back from the experience of pleasure', while lay reading is solitary and 'motivated by . . . pleasure' (31–32). Rita Felski sums up Guillory's challenge to the notion that professional reading is a superior mode:

> That one person immerses herself in the joys of *Jane Eyre*, while another views it as a symptomatic expression of Victorian imperialism, often has less to do with the political beliefs of those involved than their position in different scenes of reading.
>
> (2008: 12)

In the next chapter, we will return to another aspect of Guillory's work which more explicitly deals with the ways in which educational institutions mediate between texts and readers. In the meantime, Felski's own work goes on to articulate the second challenge to the critical/uncritical divide, by demonstrating that professional and lay reading practices 'share certain cognitive and affective parameters' (14) rather than being sharply differentiated, although their common ground is often disavowed. Something similar has also been demonstrated in the unlikely context of the history of philology, or Classical scholarship. Constanze Güthenke (2014) has shown that the notion of empathic attachment to the past is central to the scholarly and theoretical work of nineteenth-century German philologists. T. P. Wiseman and Edmund Richardson have traced the 'tangled discourses of spiritualism and classical scholarship' (Richardson 2016: 221) in the nineteenth and twentieth centuries, focussing respectively on Jackson Knight, who consulted the spirit of Virgil via a medium in preparation for his translation of the *Aeneid* (Wiseman 1992), and Gilbert Murray, Regius Professor of Greek at Oxford University, President of the Society for Psychical Research and a well-known telepath (Richardson 2016). Sebastian Matzner, meanwhile, demonstrates that the desires 'for recuperation, communion and community' which structure queer engagements with history, as gay people go looking for people 'like us' in the past, 'also motivate and drive' 'straight' scholarly work on the Classics (2016: 191).

In fan studies, scholars have suggested that fan writing can be understood as 'vernacular theory' (McLaughlin 1996), a mode of engagement with texts which is as rigorous and as valid as scholarly writing, but expressed in a different vocabulary. Fan fiction draws on affective and narrative techniques rather than the argumentative techniques of the scholarly essay, but can still explicate a critical reading of a text (Jenkins 2000), or produce particular forms of knowledge of texts and pasts. Non-fictional fan writing on media texts, similarly, is differently oriented from scholarly criticism, but produces and communicates valid insights into the text. As Matt Hills (2013: 5) writes in a book on the long-running BBC science fiction series *Doctor Who*, 'both [academic and fan approaches] are valuable and important ways of thinking through *[Doctor] Who*. To order these hierarchically . . . merely blocks any productive relationship between them'.

In contrast to Hills' and Felski's optimistic belief in the possibility of a 'productive relationship' or a common ground between professional and lay, academic and fannish reading, however, Lynne Pearce (1997: 23; emphasis original) argues that what she calls 'hermeneutic' and 'implicated' models of reading are, ultimately, 'mutually incompatible'. Her work on the practices of feminist readers draws attention to 'the massive *discomfort*' felt by those who 'regularly "commute" between these two discourses/models of reading'.

Whatever conclusion is reached about the relationship between different discourses or models of reading, ethnographic research into real readers is always underpinned by an understanding that different modes of reading coexist. It is characterized, in particular, by a willingness to accept lay modes of reading and response to texts as valid, even or especially when they do not align with the reading practices of professionals.

ACTIVE AUDIENCES 1: INTERVENTION AND INVENTION

Researchers who have asked audiences about what they find in texts and what they do with texts have discovered a range of active interpretative strategies which frequently appear disobedient or, in the term used by de Certeau, 'impertinent', especially in contrast to professional interpretative strategies which tend to emphasize the coherence and unity of texts.

One example is the way in which female and/or gay readers de-emphasize or ignore the endings of texts. John Fiske's work on female viewers of the 1980s female-centred cop show *Charlie's Angels* showed that the narrative closure of each episode is strongly patriarchal, as is the pleasure offered by the visual style of the program, and a textual or ideological analysis would conclude that patriarchy is recuperating signs of feminine liberation. Yet many women have reported reading *Charlie's Angels* selectively, paying attention to the strong women detectives and almost ignoring the signs of the patriarchal closure. Some said that they would typically leave the TV set before the end of the episode and thus avoid altogether one of the main moments of patriarchal narrative power.

(Fiske 1989a: 143)

Similarly, in 1952, when Vin Packer wrote *Spring Fire,* which would become the first bestselling lesbian pulp novel, she was told that it could only be published if it did not have a happy ending. 'My heroine has to decide she's not really queer . . . and the one she's involved with is sick or crazy' (2004: vi). In her introduction to a new edition of the book in 2004, Packer reflected that the unhappy ending she provided 'may have satisfied the post office inspections, [but] the homosexual audience wouldn't have believed it for a minute. But they also wouldn't care that much, because much more important was that there was a new book about us' (vii; cf. Ahmed 2010: 88–89).

Cheryl Dobinson and Kevin Young's (2000: 109) work on lesbian cinema spectators found that 'lesbians can take the seemingly unrelated experiences of characters in films and apply them to their own personal circumstances', as when one respondent empathized with Jodie Foster's character in the film *Nell* because 'she could never have what she really wanted which was her sister back . . . I identified with that . . . because . . . I felt that I could never have what I wanted which was a relationship with another woman' (108). Lesbian viewers may also 'superimpose a lesbian theme on women's friendships' (112) or even 'kind of change the story', as another respondent reports:

I did that with *The Piano*, I changed the whole movie around in my head. I actually made up a new character that was a woman that [Holly Hunter] fell in love with and of course lives a much better life.

(116)

Readers from other marginalized groups similarly use a range of actively interventionist and creative interpretative strategies to open texts onto readers' own lived experiences, concerns and desires. The black feminist theorist bell hooks, in an essay on 'The Oppositional Gaze', makes the case that

> Manthia Diawara's 'resisting spectatorship' (Diawara 1988) is a term that does not adequately describe the terrain of black female spectatorship. We do more than resist. We create alternative texts . . . As critical spectators, black women participate in a broad range of looking relations, contest, resist, revision, interrogate and invent on multiple levels.
>
> (1992: 128)

Alternative texts may be created imaginatively as a reader reads a book or a viewer watches a film. For example, the group of black women interviewed by Jacqueline Bobo about their viewing of the film of Alice Walker's novel *The Color Purple* turned out to have 'edit[ed]' it 'mentally' (1995: 106). They deleted or de-emphasized whole sequences as they watched, selecting out aspects of the film and realigning it around their own concerns and priorities.

Ethnographic work in fan studies has similarly shown that fans of colour use a range of viewing and reading strategies to 'contest, resist, revision, interrogate and invent' aspects of media texts. They may write fiction that centres on characters of colour who are mis- or under-represented in mainstream media texts, so that 'forgotten characters reappear, not quite undoing but remembering their marginal status' (Carrington 2016: 212), or create alternative versions of texts which alter the ethnicity of characters stated or assumed to be white. One well-known example is the fictional character Hermione Granger, who was played in the *Harry Potter* films by the white actor Emma Watson, but who has been read as black by many fans (Bennett 2015). Fans created a range of alternative texts featuring a black Hermione, including fan fiction and fan art. In 2015, a black actor, Noma Dumezweni, was cast to play the adult Hermione in J. K. Rowling's play *Harry Potter and the Cursed Child*. This decision was understood by most observers as a conscious response to, and acceptance of, a minority reading of the character. In this instance, the reception of a mainstream text by a group of marginalized viewers has had an observable impact on the earlier text, confirming Mieke Bal's claim, discussed in Chapter One, that later artworks can alter the meaning or significance of earlier artworks, in an inversion of our usual model of influence as flowing from past to future. Rowling (2015) wrote on Twitter that 'white skin was never specified' for Hermione in the books, retroactively insisting that the character's race is an open question within the 'original' text, not just in the alternative texts created by resisting spectators.

IDENTIFICATION AND DISIDENTIFICATION

Readers of black Hermione can be understood as practising a form of 'disidentification', a term used by José Esteban Muñoz (1996: 152–153) to describe the ways in which minority audiences can 'transfigur[e] an identificatory site that was not meant to accommodate' their identities. 'To disidentify', Muñoz writes,

> is to read oneself and one's own life narrative in a moment, object, or subject that is not culturally coded to "connect" with the disidentifying subject . . . It is a mode of *recycling* or reforming an object that has already been invested with powerful energy.
>
> (149)

Identification is often assumed to be a naïve or even politically regressive relation to texts, especially for minority subjects who are often asked to identify against their own interests, as we saw in Fetterley's analysis of women readers. The idea of disidentification, however, suggests that readers and spectators are able to use the energies and pleasures of identification for resistive and subversive ends.

Disidentification also works against the assumption that real readers identify in straightforward ways with characters who are 'like them'. This assumption, which partly underpins the injection model of audience research, has been critiqued from both theoretical and empirical viewpoints. Elizabeth Cowie's groundbreaking essay 'Fantasia', first published in 1984, uses Freud's theory of conscious and unconscious fantasy. The 'unconscious' at work here is the viewer's, rather than the text's, as in Macherey's and Jameson's symptomatic reading. In Cowie's model of spectatorship, viewing practices are not organized by a straightforward relationship of identification between a viewer and a character. Instead, they are underpinned by complex patterns of unconscious desire and fantasy which position the reader in a shifting and unstable set of relations to multiple characters on-screen. Films set out 'a scenario of desire . . . where the subject positions are not fixed or completed' (1997 [1984]: 149). Instead of fixed positions of 'identification', there is a 'continual circulation of exchange and substitution' (161). Thirty years later, Martin Barker's (2005) global-scale empirical audience research on the *Lord of the Rings* films showed that viewers relate to characters in a range of different and unpredictable ways which are interwoven with broader aspects of their viewing and interpretative practices.

ACTIVE AUDIENCES 2: INGENUITY AND PLEASURE

All these theoretical and empirical enquiries into readers and their practices challenge the devaluation of lay or 'uncritical' reading, and forcefully oppose the injection model of mass-media audiencing. Reading, especially for disempowered readers, becomes a highly active, productive and skilled process of interpretation and invention. Fiske (1989b: 73) writes of Australian Aboriginal film audiences that they are 'ingenious almost to the point of deviousness in finding black pleasures and meanings in white texts'. A good example is the 1985 film *Rambo: First Blood Part II*, which, as reported by the anthropologist Eric Michaels, was avidly consumed by the Warlpiri people among whom he was living in the 1980s. They 'could find neither sense nor pleasure in [John Rambo's] "patriotic", nationalistic motivation. Instead they constructed for him a tribal or family motivation by inserting him into an elaborate kinship network with those he was rescuing'. John Fiske explains:

> The fact that the film was a favorite with both Ronald Reagan and Australian Aboriginals must not lead us to assume any affinity between the two, nor between the meanings and pleasure that each produced from the same cultural commodity.

(61)

Fiske's emphasis on, and association of, 'meanings and pleasure', is symptomatic of his model of readership or 'audiencing'. This model draws on Michel de Certeau's understanding of reading as poaching and sees audiences as constructing meanings in such a way as to produce subversive pleasures for themselves. Because different groups are positioned differently by their society and culture, they will take different kinds of pleasure and thus produce different meanings.

Fiske's approach focusses on the agency, creativity and resistant power of audiences. It serves to counter models of mass-media audiencing which see the audience as vulnerable and/or as fundamentally passive recipients of unsound messages, and hence risk underestimating the agency of audiences and their power to resist manipulation by texts. However, the celebration of the active power of audiences epitomized by Fiske but shared by many media and cultural studies scholars is itself open to criticism from a number of directions.

Firstly, like all reader-dominant models, it can be seen to deny any agency, otherness or specificity to the text. As the Italian theorist Emilio Betti asked, 'If the object is not other than its observer and if it does not, of itself, speak, why listen?' (cited in Palmer 1969: 56). Secondly, Fiske's focus on positive affect, especially pleasure, has more recently given way to an interest in a wider range of readers' and viewers' affective responses. In fan studies, following Jonathan Gray's (2003) work on 'anti-fans and non-fans', there has been increasing interest in negative fan affects and experiences of unpleasure, like those collected by Lise Dilling-Hansen (2015) in her ethnographic work with Lady Gaga fans: '"so nervous my stomach is in knots. Feel like I'm gonna hurl"; "Uhg [*sic*] I feel so shitty. Just need to sleep"'. In literary studies, too, Poletti et al. (2014) have written on the negative affects experienced by student readers including 'being bored, hating characters, feeling stupid', and demonstrated that these affects also work to generate and structure reading experiences.

Finally, Fiske's model of reading or viewing as 'semiotic warfare' assumes that reading is ultimately and necessarily a political and antagonistic/resistive act, and that readers produce meanings out of their politically determined subject positions. As we saw in the last chapter, fans have often been seen as the ultimate resistant readers or 'textual poachers'. More recently, however, work in reception study has begun to focus on aspects of popular reading practices that are *not* disobedient, unruly, resistive or impertinent, to the point where Rhiannon Bury has described certain fannish interpretative practices as 'textual gamekeeping' (2008: 63, redeploying a term from Hills 2002: 36). Bury analyses the reception of the HBO television series *Six Feet Under* by looking at posts on the official HBO forum. Her analysis shows that viewers are 'firmly steeped in the reading practices of bourgeois aesthetics' (Lang 2012: 8), including heteronormative assumptions. Where Alexis Lothian sees some fans' 'reconfigurations of dominant media' as 'hav[ing] a powerful capacity' to 'push away from media's racism and sexism' (2017: 248), Bury (2008: 61) found, by contrast, that in this community, at least, 'the majority of forum participants were . . . collectively *straightening out* the gay storyline'. Similarly, Janet Staiger's (2008) analysis of online fan discussions of David Lynch films finds that, far from being creative, impertinent or disobedient, they tend to 'model interpretive behaviours that can be traced to the US film education movement which began in the 1920s' – for example, looking for symbolism, identifying directorial style, analysing the parts of the film in relation to its aesthetic and formal unity, and valorizing ambiguity (Lang 2012: 8).

READING AS SOCIAL ACTIVITY

Whether resistant or obedient, feeling pleasure or unpleasure, all these readers are engaged in acts of interpretation. Janice Radway, however, questioned the way in which reading is made synonymous with interpretation. In her introduction to the British edition of *Reading the Romance*, she reflects on the process of researching and writing the book. At the beginning of her work, she writes, she 'conceived of reading in a limited fashion as *interpretation* and saw the project largely as one focussing on the differential interpretation of texts' (1987: 7). However, she found that 'the Smithton women repeatedly answered my questions about the meaning of romances by talking about the meaning of romance *reading* as a social event in a familial context' (7). In order to account for the responses of her interview subjects, Radway had to differentiate between 'the significance of the *event* of reading and the meaning of the *text* constructed as its consequence', with the result that the book gradually became ... less an account of the way romances as texts were interpreted than of the way romance reading as a form of behaviour operated as a complex intervention in the ongoing social lives of actual social subjects, women who saw themselves first as wives and mothers.

(7)

Radway's work points to the non-interpretative dimensions of reading: the importance of reading as a social act. In the case of the Smithton women, romance reading was seen as a 'declaration of independence' (7), a withdrawal from the space of the family. Similarly, bell hooks' work on the oppositional gaze opens from the observation that the act of looking, especially looking at white people, was/is itself a dangerous and forbidden act for black people under slavery and in its wake. Reading and looking are, then, social acts as well as interpretative ones.

Long (1993: 181) points out in an influential essay on 'Textual Interpretation as Collective Action' that 'our understanding of reading is . . . governed by a . . . powerful and . . . partial picture of the solitary reader', which locates 'reading in the private sphere or, most extremely, in the heads of isolated individuals' (190). This, she argues, 'neglects two important aspects of [the] collective nature' of reading (190): firstly, the 'social infrastructure of reading', the institutions which enable reading, including education, publishing, bookselling and piracy; and, secondly, 'the ways in which reading is *socially framed*' (192). 'The habit of reading', she concludes, 'is profoundly social. As mid-century American empirical studies of adult reading show, social isolation depresses readership, and social involvement encourages it. Most readers need the support of talk with other readers' (191).

As readers, we produce a kind of evaluative knowledge of a text through our interactions with other readers. We do this both by comparing texts to other texts, and by comparing our interpretations and responses to other people's. Booth (1988: 76) calls this interpretative process 'coduction', neither induction nor deduction, emphasizing its collaborative nature. For him, reading and interpreting is an ongoing process in which 'we do not first come to know our judgment and then offer our proofs; we change our knowledge as we encounter, in the responses of other readers to our claims, further evidence'. He gives as an example a (fictional) conversation with his wife. They have just watched *The Color Purple* together:

> I weep at several points . . . Then, when leaving the cinema, I notice that my wife, Phyllis, is absolutely dry-eyed. She looks at me and says 'How corny can you get?'
>
> 'What do you mean, corny? It really got to me.'
>
> 'You mean you weren't troubled by the obviousness of all those contrivances, those romps in the daisies, that loading of the dice against Mister Mister, by . . .'
>
> 'Well, ah . . .' – and I may very well embark on an immediate reconsideration of my tears. Or she may begin to wonder whether her resistance was unduly cynical. Thus the 'work itself' is being re-performed and transformed by us as we hold our conversations about it.
>
> (74)

The usefulness of Booth's model is confirmed by ethnomethodological research, for example in Daniel Allington's and Bethan Benwell's analysis of a discussion of Jackie Kay's long poem *The Adoption Papers* by an Edinburgh book group. Allington and Benwell (2012: 224) use a method called close discourse analysis to show in detail how one reader 'adopts a series of different responses to [one] part of the poem before alighting on a strategy that elicits a take-up from another member'. 'Book group opinions', they conclude, 'are partly constructed in response to evidence of approval or support from the other members' (226). Further, 'the social dimension of reading does more than intrude on readers' accounts of their private responses; it provides the occasion for those accounts, and is the medium in which they are constructed' (230). Accordingly, Allington and Benwell caution us to be aware that the stories about reading that readers produce 'may appear to be literal *reports* of events taking place in a pre-existing reality, but . . . must be seen as *accounts* constructing reality' (218). Accounts of reading are produced within particular social and cultural contexts, for particular purposes, and will be shaped by 'the social interactional contingencies of whatever setting it is produced in', whether that is a Goodreads review, a reading group or an interview with an academic ethnographer of reading (Edwards and Stokoe 2004: 505).

Allington and Benwell emphasize the normative power of the group social interaction, and the ways in which interpretation and its articulation is constrained by group behaviours. Elizabeth McHenry's work on the literary societies set up by free blacks in the United States between 1828 and 1860, however, sees social practices around collective reading as a crucial part of liberatory and transformative black politics:

> Never had there been greater need for free blacks to assert in strong public voices their commitment to liberty and equality. These voices developed and found maturity through collective reading and literary activities such as those sponsored and sustained by . . . early African American libraries and reading rooms.
>
> (2011 [2007]: 320)

Whether the experience of collective reading is liberatory or constraining, it is, as Lynne Pearce writes, to some extent inevitable.

> No reading experience is ever an exclusive, private, bilateral exchange between text and reader . . . Any dialogical relationship (and this includes the text–reader one) always involves some sort of third party – who . . . may be seen to direct (or, more menacingly to 'police') our reading. Reading . . . is thus always a 'reading to': an act of engagement and/or interpretation somehow, and somewhere, determined by another (silent) witness who sits in active judgment, whether critical or benign, on our response.
>
> (1997: 195)

The experience of collective interpretation is not just a question of reflecting in company *after* a solitary reading experience. The interpretations we produce in our most private moments are produced with other people in mind. This is not a new phenomenon: Suzanne Reynolds' (1996: 32) work on annotations, or 'glosses', in medieval manuscripts reveals that glossators were teachers and the interpretations they suggested were specifically shaped by the needs of their students. Similarly, Allington and Benwell analyse the face-to-face interactions of a reading group, and Booth's parable of coduction is a conversation with his wife. In other contexts, as we saw in Chapter One, readers may read in company with past interpreters of texts, creating a 'community of mind' (Johnston 2012: 634) across great historical distances. In his essay 'Homer's Deep', Shane Butler traces just such a transhistorical community, made up of those readers who interpret Homer's characters Achilles and Patroclus as lovers. Such readers, as Butler sees them, are neither right nor wrong. Their interpretation cannot be either supported or disproved by appealing to the authority of any text, whether Homer's or a later version, because this reading does not itself frame the text as authoritative. Rather, the love of Achilles and Patroclus, as textual object, crystallizes out of a network of readings and readers across time and space, which Butler (2016: 39) calls 'tradition'. Here, reader-to-text relationships fade into reader-to-reader ones, and the object of reading becomes an effect of the chain or network of receptions that make it visible or bring it into being.

TALKING ABOUT BOOKS – AND OTHER THINGS

The emphasis placed on interactions and conversations between readers by the theorists we have just discussed suggests that it is possible to see reception, in some cases, not as a text-to-reader process, but as a reader-to-reader process. Indeed, the conversations that we have about books (or other texts) are not always *about* the books themselves. Talking about books, films, TV programmes or other texts can be a way of opening conversation about topics covered in the texts. In his bibliomemoir *My Reading Life*, the US author Pat Conroy writes about reading *Look Homeward Angel* with his mother:

> The book made areas accessible to us that had carried the impediment of taboo before. We began to talk more freely about my father's violence . . . It was Thomas Wolfe's father who opened that door of conversation in my hurt, traumatized family.

(2010: 254–255)

Similarly, Marie Gillespie's (2003 [1995]) work on the way British Asian teenagers talked about the Australian soap opera *Neighbours* in Southall, West London, in the 1990s, shows how they tacked back and forth between 'soap talk' and talk about 'real life'; the two were used to make sense of one another and to negotiate and solve problems. In particular, the close-knit, gossipy community of *Neighbours'* Ramsay Street, and the way in which the adult characters exercised surveillance and control over the teenagers, were seen as homologous to the workings of the British Asian community in Southall.

Gillespie's case study raises two important points. The first is that, as with the Aboriginal readings of *First Blood*, we have an example of a 'white' text being used by members of a minority ethnic group, countering the idea that readers will necessarily identify with or seek out texts about people from their own identity categories. Indeed, *Neighbours* has been criticized since its inception for its unrealistic representation of suburban Australia as an Anglo monoculture, and for its racist representations of non-Anglo people, including an Indian character, Vickram, introduced a few years after Gillespie carried out her field research. This underscores the importance of distinguishing between critiques of representation and claims about reception. Vickram is undoubtedly, as Susan Howard writes, 'a caricature' (Howard 1994), but an analysis of *Neighbours'* representational strategies does not enable us to predict the meanings and uses that Indian viewers will find in the text in which he appears – in de Certeau's terms, what they will *do* with *Neighbours*.

Secondly, we see how readers can use texts as pre-texts for talking about other things. Gillespie (2003: 320) shows that the 'meanings' of *Neighbours* are constructed collaboratively through talking about the show but she also writes that 'the local importance of *Neighbours* . . . lies in the various functions served by talking about it', rather than in its meanings as such. Is there, then, a distinction between the meanings of *Neighbours* and the functions it serves in a local context? And at what point do acts of engagement with texts stop being acts of 'reading' those texts?

I have argued that the term 'reception' embeds a communications metaphor in our thinking about reading, viewing and listening. But as James Carey (1989 [1975]: 15) points out, drawing on John Dewey's (1916) *Democracy and Education*, we can think about 'communication' in two different ways: as the transmission of information, 'a process whereby messages are transmitted and distributed in space for the control of distances and people', or as 'a ritual', where 'communication is directed not toward the extension of messages in space but toward the maintenance of society in time; not the act of imparting information but the representation of shared beliefs' (18). In its ritual form, communication is that which 'produces the social bonds . . . that tie men together and make associated life possible' (22). Thus, instead of thinking about the messages, information or meanings that *Neighbours* transmits to its audience, we think about the social bonds that are produced by collective watching and talking.

This model of communication has been taken up particularly by scholars of television, for whom, as Abercrombie and Longhurst (1998: 68–69) write, 'being a member of an audience . . . is constitutive of everyday life'. Its impact has been slower to be felt in literary studies, for two reasons. The first is a long and historically sedimented investment in the idea of reading as a solitary act of self-making, which, as we saw in the Introduction, dates back to the Protestant Reformation in the sixteenth century and was reinforced by the notion of 'self-culture' in the nineteenth and twentieth centuries. The second reason is, as Leah Price (2004: 305) writes, 'that literary critics tend to act as if reading were the only legitimate use of books. They forget that the book can take on a ritual function . . . it can serve as a gift . . . an investment . . . even an engineering challenge'. In her book *How to Do Things with Books in Victorian Britain*, Price attends to ways in which people use or engage with books other than reading. She aims to

> excavate the often contentious relation among three operations: reading (doing something with the words), handling (doing something with the object) and circulating (doing something to, or with, other persons by means of the book – whether cementing or severing relationships, whether by giving or receiving books or by withholding and rejecting them). Often pictured as competing, in practice these three modes almost always overlapped.
>
> (2012: 5–6)

As Price shows, it is possible to engage with a book in all kinds of meaningful ways other than, or as well as, reading. Not reading can be an act of fairly straightforward refusal of or resistance to a text, as when Amy Hungerford defends 'Not Reading DFW' in a 2016 essay, arguing that she has gleaned enough from other sources to make an informed decision that her time would not be well spent in reading the critically acclaimed US novelist David Foster Wallace, author of *Infinite Jest*, one of *Time* magazine's 100 Best Books of 1923–2005 (Grossman 2010: n.p.).

Not reading a text is, however, not the same as not knowing about it or not engaging with it. In fact, 'not reading' is a complicated phenomenon which encompasses several modes of engagement with texts. As Benwell, Procter and Robinson put it,

> not reading might be best understood as part of a continuum of reading, rather than reading's opposite: partial reading, selective reading, sectional reading, readings based on extracts, reviews, and second-hand information – these activities have all been labelled 'not reading' in book controversies.
>
> (2011: 95)

Indeed, in controversies such as the one over Salman Rushdie's 1988 novel *The Satanic Verses,* which contained three dream sequences retelling stories related to the life of the prophet Mohammed that caused profound offence to some Muslims, 'vocal "non-readers"' . . . constitute a significant interpretative community' (Ranasinha 2007: 46).

There are other contexts in which readers have a clear sense of, and even a strong opinion on, particular texts without reading them. Well before the rise of Internet sites like Sparknotes, the Translation Studies scholar André Lefevere writes that

> when . . . the majority of readers . . . say they have 'read' a book, what they mean is that they have a certain image, a certain construct of that book in their heads. That construct is often loosely based on some selected passages of the actual text of the book in question (the passages included in anthologies used in secondary or university education, for instance), supplemented by other texts that rewrite the actual text in one way or another, such as plot summaries in literary histories or reference works, reviews in newspapers, magazines,

or journals, some critical articles, performances on stage or screen, and, last but not least, translations.

(Lefevere 1992: 6–7)

In other words, as Gray (2006: 37) wrote twenty-five years later, 'we actually consume some texts through paratexts and supportive inter-texts, the text itself becoming expendable'. It is, then, possible to pro-duce a reading of a text which one has never, in fact, read, if a 'reading' of a text is understood to be a coherent interpretation of it, produced collectively in relation to specific social and historical norms and artic-ulated to another person. For example, I have never read Laurence Sterne's *Tristram Shandy* (1759–1766) but as someone working in the field of English literature, I have picked up a knowledge of its com-plex narrative structure, its metafictional elements, its play with tem-porality and some details of its material production like its famous all-black page; I could produce a fairly plausible reading of it. That is, in Lefevere's terms, I could describe the 'image' of it that I have in my head, and that image will be roughly consistent with the one in the head of a colleague who *has* read the novel.

In *How to Talk About Books You Haven't Read*, Pierre Bayard claims that *all* readings, not just those mediated through rewritings and other paratexts, can be characterized in this way. 'Reading is first and foremost non-reading' (2008 [2007]: 6), in part because reading is always mediated in one way or another, and in practice can only consist of the construction of an image of a book through partial appropriations of that book. Reading, for Bayard, is a fuzzy phenom-enon, always partial and provisional, which 'does not obey the hard logic of true and false' (129), and which is determined far more by other readers and cultural norms, which mediate our relationship to texts, than by texts themselves.

Non-readers, resistant readers and active audiences shape their responses collaboratively, read partially and selectively, mentally edit and otherwise intervene in texts. They use texts as jumping-off points for social interactions and conversations to the point where, in some cases, the 'meaning' of the text, or even the text itself, barely figures at all. The readers revealed by ethnographic, sociological and his-torical methods could not be further from 'the reader' envisaged by Iser and Fish, who suppresses her idiosyncratic responses and obeys the text's directions. Yet the implied reader remains an important element in the dynamic of reading and receiving texts. The acts of refusal to read with which we end this chapter hark back to Gibson's, Booth's and Fetterley's refusal to become the person a text wants us to be. All these models of reading, whether text-dominant or reader-dominant, ultimately involve a two-way dynamic between reader and text.

In the next chapter, we will look at some of the factors which enable and structure that encounter even before it takes place. Some of the more celebratory accounts of resistant reading we have seen in this chapter might suggest that readers are absolutely free to make meaning, but in fact meaning exists only within languages and sign systems, which are social and collective, not the property of any individual. Here we have looked at approaches to reception which focus on readers: in the next chapter, we move on to approaches which take as their object the sociocultural and technological system that is *reading*.

3

READING

In the last chapter, we saw how individual readers receive and respond to texts in historically and culturally grounded but ultimately unpredictable ways. Readers generate meanings and interpretations which may be guided by the text, but are certainly not entirely determined by it. Reading, we saw, is a social act as well as a process of individual interpretation.

In this chapter, we extend the notion of reading as a social act and shift the focus from readers to reading itself. In order to become a reader in the first place, one has to learn to read a particular language and script, or, more broadly, a particular sign system. Learning to read, which takes place in both formal and informal settings, also involves learning the interpretative techniques and conventions which structure both the cognitive and the affective dimensions of reading. These conventions vary socially, culturally and historically. Encounters between readers and texts are enabled, mediated and structured by these specific historical and sociocultural factors, which are also inseparable from the material technologies by means of which texts are received through the learned bodily practices of readers, viewers and listeners. Reading is thus best understood as a complex 'sociocultural system' (Johnson 2010: 11) in which cognitive processes, interpretative and affective norms, bodily practices, and writing and reading technologies are bound up together in practices of reception.

In 1996, Alberto Manguel wrote that 'we, today's readers, have yet to learn what reading is' (23); fifteen years later, Piper (2012: x) reiterated that 'we really have no idea what it is people do when they read'. Rethinking reading in terms of reception helps us to clarify and expand our understanding of this 'fundamentally opaque practice' (Piper 2012: x), by reframing the reader/text encounter to take account of the complex and interdependent array of social, cultural, institutional, material, physiological and technological factors which open up and mediate that encounter.

This chapter, accordingly, looks at theories and methodologies for reception which map the sociocultural and technological factors that construct the frameworks within which individual readers receive and respond to texts. Beginning from the interpretative codes, conventions, frames, filters and cultural competences which readers bring to bear on texts, the chapter then shifts from the cognitive/interpretative dimensions of reception to its affective, bodily and technological aspects. It concludes by interrogating and expanding the notion of literacy itself, before we move on to examine theories of language and meaning in the last chapter.

CODES, CONVENTIONS AND RULES

As we have seen in the last two chapters, texts are interpreted differently by different readers. The coexistence of multiple interpretations raises an important question, articulated clearly by Steven Mailloux (1984: 149) in his book *Interpretive Conventions*: 'What exactly constrains the production and acceptance of interpretations?' If we agree with the idea that reading is a productive act, where a reader constructs or assembles meaning, how does the reader know, or choose, *how* to construct or assemble meaning from a particular text?

Iser (1978 [1976]: 25; cf. Allen 1991) believes that texts contain 'instructions for meaning-production'. Readers produce meanings as they read by following the instructions that the text provides. One example of such 'instructions' might be what Peter Rabinowitz (1987: 53) calls 'rules of notice'. These rules 'tell us where to concentrate our attention', stressing certain features of the text which then 'serve as a basic structure on which to build an interpretation'. As readers navigate through the richly signifying field of a novel or a film, full of extraneous detail, rules of notice direct their attention to particular features, on which they will base their overall interpretation of the text. For example, in the sequence from *Some Like It Hot* discussed in the last chapter, we are instructed by the soundtrack, the framing of the close-up tracking shot and the use of shot/reverse shot, to notice Sugar Kane's hourglass figure and sexy walk, and to understand Sugar Kane as an object of sexual desire and a potential romantic lead for the film's male protagonist.

Rules of notice structure the reception of texts in important ways, and different readers obey different rules of notice, depending on cultural, social and also neurological factors. In 2000, researchers at Yale University used eye-tracking technology to compare the ways in which autistic and non-autistic adults viewed the 1966 film *Who's Afraid of Virginia Woolf*, and found significant differences at the level of notice, which corresponded to differences in interpretation (Klin et al. 2002). For example, in one scene, the protagonist, Martha, is flirting with a young man, Nick: her husband George watches in the background, but does not speak. The visual composition of the scene is triangular, with George at the apex, directing the spectator's attention to George as well as Martha and Nick.

Tracking the eye movements of neurotypical (non-autistic) viewers showed a triangular movement back and forth across Martha, Nick and George, focussing on the characters' eyes. Neurotypical viewers concentrated their attention on the details of the mise-en-scène which reflected the triangulated nature of the characters' emotional interaction. Autistic viewers, however, focussed on the mouths of the speaking characters and never on George; following different 'rules of notice', they ultimately ascribed a different significance to the scene.

What this empirical research also seems to show, however, is that the rules being followed by viewers and readers in the production of meaning are not inherent in the text, since the same text can be interpreted according to different rules of notice. In fact, as Rabinowitz points out, there are actually two sets of procedures or rules which enable readers to construct meaning. The first are 'the text's directions': framing, soundtrack, focalization and other techniques for positioning or guiding the reader's response. The second are 'the readerly presuppositions that allow those directions to work' (Rabinowitz 1987: 38). For example, neurotypical viewers presuppose that the eyes of characters will always be among the significant details in a scene, so they are able to follow the 'directions' embedded in the triangular visual composition of the scene in *Who's Afraid of Virginia Woolf?* where autistic viewers cannot.

Iser's (1978 [1976]: 61, my emphasis) claim that the literary text 'relates to conventions *which it carries with it*', then, as Rabinowitz claims, 'smudges the line between' two separate sets of procedures or rules. Developing Iser's metaphor of the text's 'instructions for meaning-production' and differentiating between two sets of instructions, Rabinowitz (1987: 38) writes that one can think of a text as an 'unassembled swing set'. It 'comes with rudimentary directions, but you have to know what directions *are*, as well as how to perform basic tasks. It comes with its own materials, but you must have certain tools of your own at hand'. In other words, the text can only instruct us how to read it if we already know how to follow its instructions. For this reason, Mailloux answers his own question about the constraints on interpretation in this way:

> The most important . . . constraints are what I call 'interpretive conventions': shared ways of making sense of reality. They are communal procedures for making sense of the world, behavior, communication, and literary texts . . . [They] are group-licensed strategies for constructing meaning.
>
> (1984: 149)

Jonathan Culler (1975: 104) places particular emphasis on the importance of interpretative conventions for acts of reception, arguing that a poem, for example, 'has meaning only with respect to a system of conventions which the reader has assimilated. If other conventions were operative, its range of potential meanings would be different'. Culler elaborates on this point by saying that 'the easiest way to grasp the importance of these conventions is to take a piece of journalistic prose . . . and set it down on the page as a poem'. At the beginning of his 1997 book *Literary Theory: A Very Short Introduction*, Culler does just this with the opening sentence of the book *From a Logical Point of View* by the analytic philosopher W. O. Quine:

> The curious thing about the
> ontological problem
> is its
> simplicity

(Culler 1997: 25, citing
Quine 1980: 1)

In the new layout, 'the properties assigned to the sentence by a grammar of English remain unchanged': however, the line breaks prompt us, as readers, to read the sentence as a poem, and thus to interpret it according to a different set of expectations and conventions. 'The different meanings which the text acquires', Culler states,

> cannot therefore be attributed to one's knowledge of the language but must be ascribed to the special conventions for reading poetry which lead one to look at the language in new ways, to make relevant properties of the language which were previously unexploited, to subject the text to a different series of interpretive operations.

(1975: 101–102)

Similarly, Yvonne Sherwood's (2000: 50) account of the reception history of the book of Jonah shows how 'between the early Christian period and critical biblical studies, [it] manages to rotate in meaning *through one-hundred-and-eighty-degrees*', as Jonah moves from being interpreted as a Christ figure to standing for 'the Jew as the antithesis of a benevolent Christianity'. 'If all these readings are somehow *in* the text, in essence', writes Sherwood, 'then the 48-verse book of Jonah must be an immensely rich concentrate' (49).

It is not the text alone, then, that directs the reader's interpretation, but the set of interpretative conventions which we bring to the text. The text does not carry these conventions with it, as Iser claims; they change over time and with cultural and social context, so that the 'same' text may be read according to different conventions, and thus mean different things.

This insight produces a new way of thinking about the question of resistant and subordinate reading, discussed in Chapter Two. Instead of resisting the text, as Judith Fetterley suggests, or resisting the implied reader, as does Wayne Booth, we might understand resistant readings as readings which resist dominant interpretative conventions. The queer theorist Eve Kosofsky Sedgwick (1994 [1993]: 3) makes this point when she writes that the reading strategies she developed as a young queer person, 'founded on [her] basic demands and intuitions', 'had necessarily to run against the grain of the most patent available formulae for young people's reading and life'.

'The most patent available formulae', or dominant reading conventions, determine which interpretations of a given text are legitimated and which are positioned as marginal or 'dissident' (Sinfield 2005). For example, currently, dominant reading conventions instruct readers to interpret interactions between male and female characters as sexually charged, but *not* interactions between characters of the same sex. In reality many readers do not obey these conventions, and do interpret the intense emotional and physical interactions between, say, Sam Gamgee and Frodo Baggins in *The Lord of the Rings* as indications of a sexual or romantic relationship (Smol 2004). However, as Alexander Doty (1993: xii) points out, these readings are regarded as '*sub*-textual, *sub*-cultural, *alternative* readings' according to 'conventional heterosexist paradigms' of interpretation.

This is not because of the directions given by the text: the hugs, touches, lingering looks and expressions of affection exchanged between Sam and Frodo are no different from those exchanged between, say, Fox Mulder and Dana Scully in an early season of *The X-Files*. But according to the dominant rules of notice and significance operating in our historical and cultural context, we attend to these interactions in a different way, and attribute different significance to them, depending on whether the characters are of different sexes or the same sex. Queer reading thus involves a resistance not to the text, but to the 'heterosexist paradigms' or 'most available formulae of reading' which direct us to interpret the details of the text in a particular way. Queer readings transform texts, finding new meanings in them, by applying different rules to them (Willis 2006).

In the context of race, rather than sexuality, the feminist critic Joanna Russ gives a detailed account of the way a text can be transformed when different operations of reading are applied to it, in the Afterword to her book *How to Suppress Women's Writing*. She writes about being accused by her colleague Elly Bulkin of overlooking black women writers. In response, Russ tells us,

> I went to the library, got Black novelist Zora Neale Hurston's classic *Their Eyes Were Watching God*, and read it.
>
> It was episodic.
>
> It was thin.
>
> It was uninteresting.
>
> The characters talked funny.
>
> It was clearly inferior to the great central tradition of Western literature (if you added these authors' wives', daughters', mothers', sisters' and colleagues' books). I'd been vindicated. Why go on?
>
> But Elly must have put a virus in my tea or otherwise affected me, as shortly thereafter I returned from the library with an armful of books and from the bookstore with another, all these about women of color. There were novels, short story collections, books containing literary criticism, literary journals and a few slender pamphlets from small presses. Then I read John Langston Gwaltney's *Drylongso*, Gerda Lerner's *Black Women in White America*, Barbara Christian's pioneering study *Black Women Novelists*, *Conditions: Five, the Black Women's Issue*, Toni Cade Bambera's *Black Women: An Anthology* . . .
>
> Then I went back and read *Their Eyes Were Watching God*.
>
> It was astonishing how much it had improved in the meantime.
>   (1983: 136)

Russ's punchline makes the same point as Culler and Sherwood. Saying '*it* had improved' attributes the change to Hurston's novel, when in fact what has changed is the reading practices that Russ brings to the book. Read according to the conventions of the white literary tradition, *Their Eyes Were Watching God* appears to be 'thin', 'episodic' and 'uninteresting'. Reading more literature by black women, as well as critical explications of the conventions and traditions of black literature, gives Russ a new set of rules. The book becomes less 'thin' when she is able to see its relation to a different set of intertexts, of which she was previously unaware; its episodic structure is no longer seen as a flaw when read in relation to the conventions of African-American narrative, rather than a white tradition which valorizes linearity and unity of plot; and it is not 'uninteresting' once she has learned a new set of rules of notice and significance within which to plot the details of the text.

In this instance, 'what appears to be a dispute about aesthetic merit is, in reality, a dispute about the *contexts of judgement*', as Annette Kolodny puts it. What is at stake in disagreements like Russ's with Bulkin is not the objective properties of the text but rather 'the adequacy of the prior assumptions and reading habits brought to bear on the text' (Kolodny 1985 [1980]: 158). In other words, as Rabinowitz explains in *Before Reading*:

> When a text fails to respond to the rules applied to it, it is not always clear whether the text or the reader is at fault. To put it in other terms, there are two ways of rethinking your reading experiences when a text fails to respond to the strategies with which it is approached: You can keep the text and change the strategy, or you can keep the strategy and toss out the text on the assumption that it is thin or incoherent.
>
> (1987: 211)

Russ resists the temptation to 'keep the strategy and toss out the text' and instead changes the strategy with which she approaches *Their Eyes Were Watching God*, by learning a new set of rules for assembling the meaning of the text. Her experience suggests that if we bring the wrong rules to bear on a text, we may fail to appreciate or even understand it. In Eagleton's (1983: 125) words, 'the competent reader is the one who can apply to the text certain rules; but what are the rules for applying rules?'.

GENRE

One of a number of answers to Eagleton's question might be genre. Rabinowitz defines genres as 'preformed bundles of operations performed by readers in order to recover the meanings of texts' (Rabinowitz 1987: 177); in other words, more or less, rules for applying rules. We understand texts by assigning them to genres. In E. D. Hirsch's

(1967: 76) words, 'all understanding of verbal meaning is necessarily genre-bound'.

John Frow writes, in terms which hark back to Mailloux's question about the constraints on interpretation:

> Genre guides interpretation because it is a constraint on ... the production of meaning; it specifies which types of meaning are relevant and appropriate in a particular context, and so makes certain senses of an utterance more probable, in the circumstances, than others.
>
> (2015: 110)

He goes on to summarize: 'genre is not a *property* of a text but is a function of reading' (11). Reading, not readers:

> Genre is neither a property of (and located 'in') texts, nor a projection of (and located 'in') readers; it exists as part of the relationship between texts and readers, and it has a systemic existence. It is a shared convention with a social force.
>
> (112)

Genres can and do change over time and they vary between cultures and even subcultures. Some groups of readers will recognize, define or even invent genres and classifications which are not meaningful to other groups, but which do affect the way in which those readers read. For example, we might wonder whether Julieanne Lamond's Lambton readers, analysed in the last chapter, could be said to have produced a 'genre' of 'books about risk' through their collective reading habits. Long's (2003: 132) analysis of the Leisure Learning Group, a book club in Houston in 1986–1988, shows how their collective discussions led to their formulation of a new 'literary category', 'women-in-pain books', which 'became a routine part of the group's generic mapping of modern literature'. 'Women-in-pain books' are not recognized as constituting a literary genre beyond the Leisure Learning Group, but even this local and/or temporary genre is a collective and social form, produced through ongoing group negotiation and discussion and providing bundles of rules which direct and limit interpretation.

The importance of genre to interpretation can be clearly seen in a paragraph constructed by the genre theorist Heather Dubrow, which will be interpreted differently depending on the generic conventions we use to read it. The difference depends on whether it opens a murder mystery entitled *Murder at Marplethorpe*, or a novel of individual growth and development (*Bildungsroman*) entitled *The Personal History of David Marplethorpe*:

> The clock on the mantelpiece said ten thirty, but someone had suggested recently that the clock was wrong. As the figure of the dead woman lay on the bed in the front room, a no less silent figure glided rapidly from the house. The only sounds to be heard were the ticking of that clock and the loud wailing of an infant.
>
> (1982: 1)

Categorizing the text as a murder mystery, 'we mentally file the allusion to the clock as a clue that might later help us to identify the murderer', and 'become alert for any further clues about the peculiarities of this unreliable machine' (1). Reading it as a *Bildungsroman*, 'we read that allusion [to the clock] symbolically, as a hint that time is disordered in the world that our novelist is evoking', and 'become alert not for additional details about the mechanics of the clock but rather for further images of and ideas about time' (2). Other details, too, are read differently: has the dead woman been murdered, or died in childbirth?

Dubrow's paragraph is an invented example of the real-life phenomenon that Gary Saul Morson calls 'boundary works', works which could belong to two different genres. In such cases 'it is uncertain which of two mutually exclusive sets of conventions govern a work', so that, 'doubly decodable, the same text becomes, in effect, two different works' (Morson 1989: 48). The attribution of a text to a different genre changes the reading strategies or conventions we will bring to it as readers, and thus changes the meanings that we will be able to find within it. And if the same text can be decoded either as a murder mystery or as a *Bildungsroman*, then, in Morson's terms, two people may have read the same *text* as another person, but not the same *work*. This recalls the arguments in the last chapter that 'not reading' and 'reading' 'might be best understood as . . . a continuum' (Benwell, Procter and Robinson 2011: 95). If I read *Marplethorpe* as a murder mystery, and you read it as a *Bildungsroman*, then have I read the book that you are talking about? Defying the 'hard logic of true and false' (Bayard 2008 [2007]: 129), the answer must be both yes and no.

Genre thus at least partly determines the way we read texts, our affective response to them, the significance we attribute to their details and the kinds of pattern or coherence we discover, or construct, in them. In his essay 'The Art Cinema as a Mode of Film Practice', David Bordwell shows that the genre of art cinema is defined ultimately not by any formal properties in a given film, but by the reading procedure it solicits. The art film 'foregrounds deviations from the classical norm – there are certain gaps and problems' within its structure (Bordwell 1979: 60). But when a film is viewed as an art film, these gaps and problems are understood as problems for the viewer to solve, rather than as flaws in the composition of the film. For example, in the final section of David Lynch's 2001 film *Mulholland Drive*, Lynch commits what appears to be an error of film 'grammar'. In a shot/reverse shot sequence, the position occupied by one character, Camilla, in the first reverse shot, is occupied by another, Diane, in the second (McGowan 2004: 68). This is what Bordwell calls a 'prohibited camera movement', amounting to a 'breakdown of the motivation of cinematic space and time by cause-effect logic' (59). In a low-budget film or one by a student director, this would be interpreted as a compositional flaw. However, in the case of an art film, Bordwell argues, viewers solve such problems and produce coherence by appealing either to realism ('in life things happen this way'), or to the director's intention ('the ambiguity is symbolic') (60). In the case of *Mulholland Drive*, Todd McGowan (2004: 68) does indeed incorporate the 'disruption of a shot/reverse shot sequence' into his interpretation of the film, invoking Lynch's intention to represent the incoherence of desire through this lapse in grammar.

The same logic applies to literary texts and other forms of 'elite' or 'high' art. Mary Louise Pratt (1977: 170) writes that 'in literary works . . . the range of deviations which will be construed as intentional [and hence significant] is much larger' than in popular forms, while Rabinowitz points out that

> in elite art we demand – and seek out – greater and more elaborate forms of coherence. We are, for instance, more apt to look at apparent inconsistencies as examples of irony or undercutting, whereas in popular novels, we are apt to ignore them or treat them as flaws.
>
> (1987: 188)

Thus, for example, when we read in Arthur Conan Doyle's short story 'A Study in Scarlet' (1887) that the character Dr Watson has a war wound in his shoulder, and in 'The Sign of Four' (1890) that his injury is in his leg, we assume that Conan Doyle made a careless mistake in the composition of his popular *Sherlock Holmes* stories. But when Geoffrey Chaucer seems to make a similarly straightforward error in his poem *The House of Fame*, scholars work harder to recuperate it, incorporating the apparently mistaken detail either into the poem's complex aesthetic design, or into the broader context of Chaucer's tradition. In *The House of Fame*, Chaucer gives the Trojan hero Aeneas two sons when Virgil's *Aeneid* makes it clear that he only had one, albeit with two names: Iulus and Ascanius. Some scholars argue that Chaucer is in fact referring to a different, non-Virgilian version of the myth, in which Aeneas did have two sons. In this case, his reference to 'Iulo/ and *eke* Askanius *also*' (1.177–1.178, my emphasis) 'is possibly no error at all', or if it is, 'the mistake . . . is not due to ignorance, but to too much information' (Rand 1926: 222, 224). More recently, Ralph Hexter has interpreted the 'error' as intentional, part of the poem's design: Chaucer is 'sending up a simple-minded reader', and it is this reader, not Chaucer, who has made the error about the number of Aeneas's sons (Hexter 1996).

What we see in a text, then, depends on where we are looking from: the same words could be either an error of ignorance or a learned joke. As Tompkins (1985: 8–9) puts it, 'it is never the case that a work stands or falls "on its own merits", since the merits – or demerits – that the reader perceives will always be a function of the situation in which he or she reads'. The 'rules for applying rules' that Eagleton asks about thus derive from the situation in which the reader finds herself. Genre, as 'a shared convention with a social force' (Frow 2015: 112), is part of the situation, but numerous other factors also mediate, guide and shape readers' encounters with texts. A key example, as we saw in the last chapter, is education.

In an influential book from 1993, *Cultural Capital: The Problem of Literary Canon Formation*, John Guillory analysed the history of the formation of the 'literary canon', an imaginary list of great or serious works of literature, clearly differentiated from popular forms. Canonical texts tend to be the ones set for study at schools and universities. The principles on which texts are designated canonical are, of course, culturally and historically variable. Guillory (1993: ix) argues, however, that the function of the list as such is always the same: it produces, regulates and distributes 'cultural capital'. Educational institutions, in complex relation to their broader social and cultural contexts, function to legitimate certain texts as worthy of serious attention, by including them on syllabi and teaching the 'correct' way of responding to them (Dale 1997: 3). Students who master these texts and responses obtain the symbolic currency of cultural capital: 'a kind of knowledge-capital whose possession can be displayed upon request and which thereby entitles its possessor to the cultural and material rewards of the well-educated person' (Guillory 1993: ix). Thus 'reading is "framed" not only by genre', Dale (1997: 3) argues, 'but by institutions like schools and universities that "teach English"'.

FRAMES AND READING FORMATIONS

Dale's phrasing indicates her debt to frame theory, a broad theoretical paradigm which encompasses all the generic, institutional and conventional 'rules' which we bring to texts. The sociologist Erving Goffman (1974) developed the idea in *Frame Analysis*, and it has since been used to theorize reading. Jonathan Rose asks:

> How do we interpret not only books, but all the raw sensory data that is constantly showering on us? Goffman developed the useful concept of the 'frame', meaning 'the organization of experience', our ground rules for processing information, 'the basic frameworks of understanding available in our society for making sense out of events'. The frame . . . determines how we read a given text or situation: whether we treat *Alice's Adventures in Wonderland* as a bedtime story or a Freudian fable, *Finnegans Wake* as densely meaningful or gobbledygook, the morning newspaper as biased to the left or the right, Bible stories as truth, lies, or parables.
>
> (2010: 6)

'Readers can adopt any frame they choose', he continues, 'provided it produces some kind of meaningful reading, and provided the readers have learned the rules laid down by the frame' (7).

The importance of the idea of a frame is that, in Frow's (1982: 28; cf. 2015: 116–117) words, it 'does not simply separate an inside from an outside but mediates between the two'. As Frow elaborates the notion, a frame provides a way of thinking about reading as the complex inter-action between text and reader. In the last chapter, we saw how Iser ultimately saw reading as guided by the text, while reader-centred para-digms like Fetterley's tended to see differences between readings as produced, albeit in complex ways, by differences between readers. For Rose and Frow as they take up Goffman, differences between readings are produced by differences in *framing*: Frow (1982: 29) calls the frame 'the culturally determined . . . conventions determining the reception of the work'.

Gérard Genette suggests that we might be able to discover what those conventions are, not from the text itself, as Iser claimed, but by studying the 'paratexts' which surround and accompany the work like a series of frames:

> [A] text is rarely presented in an unadorned state, unre-inforced and unaccompanied by a certain number of verbal or other productions, such as an author's name, a title, a preface, illustrations. And although we do not know whether these productions are to be regarded as belonging to the text, in any case they surround it and extend it, precisely in order to *present* it, in the usual sense of this verb but also in the stron-gest sense: to *make present*, to ensure the text's presence in the world, its 'reception' and consumption in the form (now-adays, at least) of a book.
>
> (1997b [1987]: 1)

Some paratexts are included in the text as physical object. Genette calls these peritexts. In visual media, DVD 'extras', such as directors' commentaries and 'making-of' features, are increasingly an import-ant form of peritext, influencing the way viewers interpret and reinter-pret films (Egan and Barker 2008). In a book, peritexts include things like the author's name; the front and back cover, which may include a publisher's blurb and quotations from reviews; in school or scholarly editions, an introduction, footnotes and/or marginal annotations; and in popular editions, especially of women's fiction, suggested reading-group questions, an author's note and other material, for example a collection of recipes. All of these frame our reading of the book, directly or indirectly: a scholarly introduction will make explicit statements about which aspects of the text are significant, while the inclusion of recipes implicitly underscores the significance of descriptions of food and cooking in a novel. Recipes also cross the boundary between the fictional and the real world as we engage in the same activities as the fictional characters we have been reading about, but produce real food that we can really eat. Peritexts may also provide information about the implied reader of a text, as when the novelist Jenny Colgan writes, in a recipe at the end of *Christmas at Rosie Hopkins' Sweet Shop*, 'These snowballs are delicious . . . And they have booze in them. And even *more* important than that, they are so easy you could let the children make them (but perhaps do the booze yourself)' (2013: 393). Colgan's implied reader ('you') is not a committed or expert baker; she has no religious objections to drinking alcohol, nor is she a member of the teetotal straight-edge punk subculture; and she has caring responsibilities for children.

In addition to peritexts, which physically frame the 'text itself', Genette also defines epitexts: information and conventions which direct our reading of a text but which are not physically present alongside the text. These might include newspaper reviews, biographical information about an author, interviews, publisher's reputation and almost anything else: 'in principle, every context serves as a paratext', writes Genette (1997b [1987]: 8). Russ's reading of other texts by and about black women provided her with a number of epitexts, allowing her to reframe *Their Eyes Were Watching God*.

Paratexts are relatively concrete frames, or perhaps concrete evidence for the more abstract cultural framing practices that Tony Bennett calls 'reading formations'. In an essay on the function of Marxist criticism which explicitly builds on Frow's notion of framing, Bennett writes:

> By a reading formation, I mean a set of discursive and intertextual formations that organize and animate the practice of reading, connecting texts and readers in specific relations to one another by constituting readers as reading subjects of particular types and texts as objects-to-be-read in particular ways.
>
> (1985: 7)

To take reading formations as the object of study, Bennett continues,

> is to question conventional conceptions of texts, readers, and contexts as separable elements, fixed in their relations to one another, by suggesting that they are variable functions within a discursively ordered set of relations. Different reading formations, that is to say, produce their own texts, their own readers, and their own contexts.
>
> (10)

FILTERS

How, though, can we recover and study the reading formations which produce and structure acts of reading? The first problem is that acts of reading themselves do not necessarily leave behind any evidence or physical trace, as James Machor elaborates:

> The dead do not speak very openly or extensively about their reading acts. When they do, the traces of their voices are frequently buried in musty, obscure volumes and far-away archives. It is difficult for us to hear and understand those voices not only because they are hard to find but also because the dead do not give up their traces of responses without mediation – in the form of further reading acts.
>
> (2011: ix)

The problem is intensified when we are trying to discover reading formations or the presuppositions which underlie acts of reading, because these are almost always, by definition, left unspoken in any account of reading: they are what is taken for granted, what goes without saying, in interpretative acts. Nonetheless, as Machor again argues, 'a historical hermeneutics needs to reconstruct the shared patterns of interpretation for a specific historical era to define the reading formation of particular interpretive communities' (7).

Carlo Ginzburg's (1980 [1976]) book *The Cheese and the Worms* tackled these problems directly and demonstrated the possibility of reconstructing, from written evidence, the unspoken and unformulated strategies for reading available for use by one exceptional and long-dead reader. *The Cheese and the Worms* focusses on a sixteenth-century miller, Domenico Scandella, known as Menocchio, who was tried for heresy in 1583 and 1599, and finally executed. The title of the book refers to one of Menocchio's most striking heresies, his belief that God did not create the universe. 'In my opinion', Menocchio explained in his interrogation on 7 February 1584,

> all was chaos, that is, earth, air, water, and fire were mixed together; and out of that bulk a mass formed – just as cheese is made out of milk – and worms appeared in it, and these were the angels.
>
> (1980 [1976]: 5–6)

Ginzburg reconstructs Menocchio's reading from records of his interrogations and trials. Comparing Menocchio's ideas to the texts he recalls, Ginzburg finds that

> more than the text . . . what is important is the key to his reading, a screen that he unconsciously placed between himself and the printed page: a filter that emphasized certain words while obscuring others, that stretched the meaning of a word, taking it out of its context, that acted on Menocchio's memory and distorted the very words of the text. And this screen, this key to his reading, continually leads us back to a culture that is very different from the one expressed on the printed page – one based on an oral tradition.
>
> (33)

Menocchio applies the conventions, knowledges and discursive strategies of oral culture to print texts, producing what appear to be idiosyncratic readings but which derive, in fact, from the historically and culturally specific reading formation in which he was positioned.

CULTURAL COMPETENCES

The way we read a text is, then, determined not so much by the text itself, nor by our unique individual subjectivity, as by the set of interpretative conventions we bring to bear. These conventions are culturally determined and learned; different readers, with their different experiences and interests, will have assimilated different conventions to different degrees, although readers from the same culture and historical period will probably have broad similarities in their reading practice. For example, historical norms about whether to read aloud or silently (Saenger 1997), to keep a 'commonplace book' filled with quotations from one's reading under various headings (Darnton 2000), or to think of literature as something that one might love (Lynch 2014) all inflect individual processes of reception and response.

'Every reading', then, in the words of the semiotician and cultural critic Roland Barthes (1989a [1970]: 31), 'derives from trans-individual forms . . . The most subjective reading imaginable is never anything but a game played according to certain rules'. These rules are not determined by the author, the reader or the text itself, but 'come from . . . a symbolic form which constitutes us even before we are born – in a word, from that vast cultural space through which our person (whether author or reader) is only one passage'. In other words, both authors and readers are working to produce meanings from within sign systems and their associated conventions of meaning and interpretation.

One implication is that what we experience subjectively as the expression of our personal taste may in reality be the operation of learned rules, which we have internalized and apply unconsciously. We learn those rules in part intuitively, informally and through experiences of what Wayne Booth calls 'coduction': reading a lot of texts, talking to a lot of readers, and comparing texts and interpretations. We also learn them through formal education.

This foundational argument was advanced by the influential French sociologist Pierre Bourdieu (1984 [1980]: 3), in his book *Distinction*. Bourdieu makes the claim that our 'aesthetic disposition', or the way in which we respond aesthetically to a work of art, 'is inseparable from a specific cultural competence'. In other words,

> the encounter with a work of art is not 'love at first sight' as is generally supposed, and . . . the art-lover's pleasure presupposes an act of cognition, a decoding operation, which implies the implementation of a cognitive acquirement, a cultural code.

(1984 [1980]: 3)

'The capacity to *see* (*voir*) is a function of . . . knowledge (*savoir*)', so that

> a work of art has meaning and interest only for someone who possesses the cultural competence, that is, the code, into which it is encoded. The conscious or unconscious implementation of explicit or implicit schemes of perception and appreciation which constitutes pictorial or musical culture is the hidden condition for . . . the familiarity with the internal logic of works that aesthetic enjoyment presupposes. A beholder who lacks the specific code feels lost in a chaos of sounds and rhythms, colours and lines, without rhyme or reason.
>
> (2)

We are trained to think about aesthetic appreciation not as a cognitive act, the implementation of a learned code, but as a personal and spontaneous response. By contrast, however, Bourdieu argues in *Distinction* that tastes in fact 'function as markers of "class"' (2):

> cultural needs are the product of upbringing and education: surveys establish that all cultural practices (museum visits, concertgoing, reading etc.) and preferences in literature, painting or music are closely linked to educational level (measured by qualifications or length of schooling) and secondarily to social origin.
>
> (1)

Working-class, or popular, and bourgeois, or intellectual, cultures have different aesthetic dispositions and tastes. Popular taste is 'based on the affirmation of the continuity between art and life, which implies the subordination of form to function', so that popular audiences tend to reject artworks whose appeal is based in formal experimentation. Bourgeois taste, by contrast, suspends '"naïve" involvement' with artworks, taking up a critically detached position and insisting on the *dis*continuity between art and life. It is oriented towards the formal and/or representational qualities of a work. We tend to see this as a higher or more critical form of response to artwork, but for Bourdieu, such a response is in reality tied to the class position and class interests of the bourgeois subject: 'Intellectuals could be said to believe in the representation – literature, theatre, painting – more than in the things represented . . . an aestheticism which . . . takes the bourgeois denial of the social world to its limit' (5). The inclusion of recipes in a 'chick lit' novel thus marks it as popular fiction, by suggesting a continuity between the fictional world of the novel and the real world of the reader and reducing the aesthetic distance between the reader and the thing – in this case, a cake – that is represented.

Jacqueline Rose's (1994 [1984]) book *The Case of Peter Pan, or the Impossibility of Children's Fiction* traces the ways in which sharply class-differentiated aesthetic orientations were embedded in schooling in Edwardian England as a matter of government policy. Rose reads government documents produced by the Board of Education and elucidates the principles behind the teaching of English in elementary schools (mainly attended by working-class children, aged 10–14) and in secondary schools (middle-class children, 12–16). In elementary schools, 'the child should read literature for its story, poetry for its matter rather than its form' (1994 [1984]: 120); Rose cites a Board of Education circular from 1912 recommending that when reading and discussing *Robinson Crusoe*, the elementary student should be asked: 'What were the difficulties which Crusoe found in building his boat, and how did he overcome them?' (Board of Education 1912: 26, cited in Rose 1994: 123). In the secondary school, by contrast, the student's attention was to be directed to 'specially fine passages' of literary texts (Board of Education 1910: 6, cited in Rose 1994: 120), 'the aim being to produce an attention to language itself rather than to by-pass it in the name of the concrete event which it records' (123).

The cultural competences a person possesses are determined in part by her formal education, but also, more broadly, by her social and cultural position, history and knowledge. Once again, it becomes difficult to separate out reading practices from readers. If social position partly determines reading practice, then who a reader is and how she reads are entangled from the beginning.

In her 1995 book *Black Women as Cultural Readers*, Jacqueline Bobo (2003 [1995]: 309–310) significantly expands Bourdieu's concept of 'cultural competence', using it to track the 'complex process of negotiation whereby specific members of a culture construct meaning from a mainstream text that is different from the meanings others would produce'. For Bobo as for Bourdieu, what the viewer *sees* (*voir*) in a film is the effect of the *knowledge* (*savoir*) she brings to it. Bobo writes that in

> the specific moment when subjects bring their histories to bear on meaning production in a text cultural competencies come into play. A cultural competency is the repertoire of discursive strategies, the range of knowledge, that a reader brings to the act of watching a film and creating meaning from a work.
>
> (2003 [1995]: 312)

Importantly, Bobo pluralizes Bourdieu's 'competence': different readers and different groups will have different, and multiple, competences. She also includes other axes of difference beyond class, including race and gender.

BEYOND MEANING

The insight that aesthetic pleasure is at least to some extent dependent on cultural competence is an important one. Among other things, it reminds us to be wary of our subjective responses to works of art from unfamiliar cultural contexts, as with Russ's first reading of *Their Eyes Were Watching God*. However, a problem with Bourdieu's account of reading is that it reduces the encounter with a text or an artwork to its purely cognitive and interpretative dimensions. Bourdieu claims that aesthetic experience feels, subjectively, like 'love at first sight', but is actually produced by a cognitive process based in specific knowledge which is acquired through formal and informal training. We believe we are taking pleasure in a text, when really the pleasure comes from our own 'mastery of [particular] interpretative strategies' (Kolodny 1985 [1980]: 154). In this context, it is striking that in the passage of Bobo's book quoted above, 'the act of watching a film' seems to be coextensive with 'creating meaning'.

However, meaning is not the only thing that is created or produced by reading. For example, reading a book produces visual images in the mind, but images of a very particular kind. Peter Mendelsund (2014: 11–15) writes in *What We See When We Read* that 'when we remember the experience of reading a book, we imagine a continuous unfolding of images . . . We imagine that the experience of reading is like that of watching a film. But this is not what actually happens'. Mendelsund (2014: 24) reports conversations with readers who claim to be able to picture the fictional character Anna Karenina 'as if she were standing here in front of me', but cannot answer the question 'What does her nose look like?'. Such readers clearly did not picture a woman without a nose. Mendelsund's point is that the visual images generated by verbal texts are different in quality from those that we experience when looking at visual art or watching a film.

As well as visual images, texts also produce affective and bodily responses: tears, nausea, arousal, the feeling of the hair rising on the back of the neck. Indeed, Robyn Warhol (2002: 7) argues in *Having a Good Cry* that popular narrative forms like soap opera function as 'cultural technologies' for producing affective and bodily responses (gasping, laughing, crying) which in turn have long-term effects on readers' bodies and subjectivities, 'providing structures of feeling in the daily lives of their devotees' and functioning as 'a technology for writing gender on and through our bodies'. Reading and viewing do not just produce interpretations in the minds of readers: they are part of the way we produce and reproduce our gendered bodily experience from day to day.

Helen Slaney (2016: 87) provides a very different theoretical perspective on the bodily dimension of reception, looking at experiences of ancient sculptures and ruins and analysing 'the contribution made by the haptic imagination to the perception of antiquity'. Drawing on an argument by the eighteenth-century theorist Gottfried Herder that the appropriate sense for the appreciation of sculpture is not sight, but touch, she shows how our visual, haptic and motor senses work together in our imaginative perceptions and receptions of three-dimensional spaces. As we look at sculptures, moving around them and imagining how they would feel to the touch, or how our own bodies would feel in the position held by the sculpted body, we 'translate flat visual data into three-dimensional affordance, defining objects in terms of their potential interface with [our] moving, sensing body'. Extending the exercise of the 'haptic imagination' from the third into the fourth dimension, we can also imagine ourselves back in time and 'contact the past intimately, bodily' (102).

As noted in the Introduction, the visual, haptic, imaginative, affective and bodily dimensions of reading have tended to be sidelined in twentieth-century academic and theoretical models of reading in favour of attention to cognitive processes of interpretation and meaning-making. Karin Littau (2006: 10) calls this tendency 'the cognitive fallacy', forty years after Susan Sontag (1966: 7) had decried the scholarly emphasis on interpretation as a form of hostility to aesthetic and affective responses, calling interpretation 'the revenge of the intellect upon art'. As both Littau and Sontag remind us, privileging the cognitive over the affective is a fairly recent development in terms of the long history of reading. 'For the ancients', Littau (2006: 2) writes, 'poetry's capacity for generating affect was a testament to the greatness of the poet'. Contemporary literary criticism, however, still struggles to 'find a language for talking about the reader's body' (Warhol 2002: ix).

Because of the recent critical emphasis on meaning and interpretation, the distinction between cognitive and affective dimensions of reading has tended to be mapped onto the distinction between critical and uncritical, or professional and lay, reading. To take a typical example, in her bibliomemoir *How to be a Heroine: Or, What I've Learned from Reading Too Much*, Samantha Ellis writes:

> After three years of English at Cambridge, being force-fed literary theory, I was almost convinced that literature was all coded messages about Marxism and the death of the self. I crawled out of the post-structuralist desert thirsty for heroines I could laugh and cry with.
>
> (2014: 163)

Ellis represents her desire for a physicalized reading experience – laughter and tears – as itself a physical 'thirst', which arises from the dryness of reading for 'coded messages'. Ellis's imagery draws on a long history of the scholar as dry and passionless, but also contributes to a more recent phenomenon: an increasingly sharp and antagonistic divide between academic approaches to literature, seen as dry and loveless, and lay approaches, consistently associated with love. Leigh Dale writes: 'It could be suggested that in attempting to stand outside (or above) readers' love of literary works . . . literary scholars dismantled . . . the emotional architecture of lay support for the discipline' (Dale 2013: 5; cf. Cottom 2005: 49–52).

In response, some professional critics and teachers of literature have launched what Daniel Cottom calls an 'Erotic Rearmament

Campaign' (51), striving against the cognitive fallacy and seeking to reintroduce affect into scholarly approaches to reading. Rita Felski (2015: 13), for example, asks 'Why is the affective range of criticism so limited? Why are we so hyperarticulate about our adversaries and so excruciatingly tongue-tied about our loves?'

However, while it is important to remember that reading has affective and bodily dimensions as well as cognitive ones, this does not mean that affective and bodily responses are necessarily more authentic or 'real' than cognitive ones. Our embodied and emotional responses to texts do not come naturally. They are learned, and are just as historically and culturally variable as the interpretative and social dimensions of reading.

For this reason, the opposition that Ellis sets up in the passage quoted above is a false one. Ellis frames her ability to 'laugh and cry with' heroines, and her expectation that this is something a text can and should offer, as authentic responses and opposes them to Marxist criticism and post-structuralist theory, which she represents as a set of artificial strategies imposed by a specific educational institution. However, as Deirdre Lynch has shown in her book *Loving Literature*, the discourse of love on which Ellis draws is itself historically constructed. Love of literature is not a natural tendency in the human organism, but was produced out of specific discursive and cultural institutions first developed in the eighteenth century, a period which saw 'the emergence . . . of new etiquettes of literary appreciation' (Lynch 2014: 1).

These 'new etiquettes', or conventional practices of affective relation to literature, emerged as part of broader cultural, social and economic changes in the aftermath of the European Enlightenment, which redrew the boundaries between public and private, feeling and knowing, and recreation and labour (Lynch 2014: 4). As part of this profound alteration in the organization of European societies and their theories of knowledge, 'literature bec[a]me available to readers first and foremost as private, passional persons rather than as members of a rational, civic-minded public' (6–7). Lynch's study of reading practices in this period shows that 'individuals needed to *learn* to develop and to legitimate their own private, individuated relationships with . . . "literature"' (12, emphasis original). Even when we experience reading as a deeply private, personal and affective activity, that experience is itself enabled and structured by a broader cultural and historical construction of reading which produces particular modes of reception and response.

TECHNOLOGIES OF READING

Reading is not a purely individual or purely cognitive act. Acts of reading take place along multiple dimensions and depend on large-scale social and cultural institutions and norms. These institutions and norms structure not only the cognitive and interpretative strategies of readers but also our affective and bodily responses. They do so in large part through technologies of reading and writing, especially when 'technology' is understood in the expanded sense it has in the social sciences, where the term covers not only 'physical objects or artifacts' like print books or e-readers, but also the 'activities or processes' and '"know-how"' involved in the production and use of those physical objects (Bijker, Hughes and Pinch 2012: xlii).

For example, in the High Roman Empire, written texts were produced in *scriptio continua*: all in capital letters with no spaces between the words. Cognitive scientists have demonstrated that, in terms of the physiological features and capacities of the human brain, which have not varied significantly in the last two thousand years, *scriptio continua* is objectively more difficult to read (Johnson 2010: 20). To twenty-first-century readers, with our interest in producing ever-more efficient ways of processing information, this is puzzling: why develop and retain a system of writing that is so inefficient? William Johnson shows, however, that this technical mode is highly congruent with the values associated with reading in the culture of the High Roman Empire. At every level, the Romans prized difficulty, complexity and the display of hard-won skills over simplicity and ease of processing. In this context 'it becomes . . . an insult . . . to mark the phrases of a sentence or the basic units of compositional structure in a speech' (31). The technical aspects of writing and reading thus reflect the cultural value associated with reading: as Johnson writes, 'we can infer a profound symbiosis between this exaggerated idea of reading competency and the idea of a literature that was itself challenging, in many prominent cases necessitating years of advanced study to fully apprehend' (31).

This technological and interpretative system also has consequences for the affective disposition of readers: what they find pleasurable and unpleasurable in reading experiences. Today, difficulty in reading is frequently associated with negative affects. Australian researchers from the Reading Resilience Project have found that, when reading set texts experienced as difficult, university students of English Literature have a range of negative affective responses including 'hating characters, being bored, feeling stupid' (Poletti et al. 2014), or feeling 'embarrassed or ashamed' (Salvatori and Donahue 2005: xi).

In the High Roman Empire, by contrast, intellectual labour on literary texts was seen as an indispensable part of 'a balanced, perfected life', along with exercise, aesthetic contemplation and social interaction (Johnson 2010: 108). For particularly committed readers, literary labour was integrated into leisure time: 'the sort of quiet, concentrated comparing of texts that we associate with scholarly work . . . happen[ed] over dinner' (128).

As well as being cognitively, culturally and affectively dissimilar to the acts we think of as 'reading', Roman reading was also a very different physical activity. The reading of literary texts, especially, took place standing up and aloud: scrolls needed to be held with two hands and would usually have been supported on a lectern. Reading was so physically demanding that some ancient medical works 'include[d] reading among healthful forms of physical exercise' (Price 2004: 309, citing Cavallo 1999: 75). Although we call both of them 'reading', interacting with a scroll written in *scriptio continua* draws on a very different repertoire of bodily and cognitive functions, a very different set of affective dispositions and a very different set of social and cultural competences and norms from, say, reading on a Kindle.

Early marketing materials and reviews of Amazon's Kindle, as Yung-Hsing Wu demonstrates in her paper 'Kindling, Disappearing, Reading', stressed the invisibility of the technical interface. Compared to the sleek aesthetic of Apple products, the first Kindle was perceived as plain and unattractive in design. Its quality of plainness, however, reinforced its capacity to disappear as physical object. In an early video endorsement by the 'geek-chic' superstar Neil Gaiman, he says that while reading the Kindle 'I'd done the thing that you do with books where you're actually on the other side of the text . . . there's nothing between you and the story . . . you're in book-reading land' (cited in Wu 2013: 11). The specific technology of the Kindle thus reflects an important aspect of the twenty-first-century construction of reading as an immersive experience or 'virtual reality'. The contemporary emphasis on the transparency of the medium is very different from the embodied, physical experience of reading in the High Roman Empire.

We will return to some of the broader implications of the emergence of digital reading technologies below. In the meantime, what the contrast between the Roman scroll and the contemporary Kindle makes clear is that reading technologies are not simply neutral carriers of information. Rather, the technical, material, physical and physiological aspects of reading form part of a broad sociocultural system, together with the cognitive, interpretative and affective norms that we have looked at in this chapter so far.

The system as a whole involves both technological forms and what Lisa Gitelman calls 'their associated protocols':

> a vast clutter of normative rules and default conditions, which gather and adhere like a nebulous array around a technological nucleus. Protocols express a huge variety of social, economic and material relationships. So telephony includes the salutation 'Hello?' (for English speakers, at least), the monthly billing cycle, and the wires and cables that materially connect our phones. E-mail includes all of the elaborately layered technical protocols and interconnected service providers that constitute the Internet, but it also includes both the QWERTY keyboards on which e-mail gets 'typed' and the shared sense people have of what the e-mail genre is . . . And protocols are far from static.
>
> (2008: 7–8)

Gitelman's model of media as 'socially realized structures of communication, where structures include both technological forms and their associated protocols' (7) helps us to understand the complexity of processes of reception. Far from being synonymous with 'the cognitive processing by the individual of the technology of writing' (Johnson 2010: 12), for Gitelman, the reception of and response to texts involves a 'nebulous array' of 'normative rules' and 'default conditions', bound up with 'a huge range of social, economic, and material relationships'.

The film theorist and historian Richard Dyer (1997: 83) similarly argues that 'all technologies are at once technical in the most limited sense (to do with their material properties and functioning) and also always social (economic, cultural, ideological)'. In a chapter of his book *White*, he shows how the technology of photographic and cinematic film, especially colour film, cannot be separated out from an ideology which privileges whiteness. On a material level, photography works with light, and different skin colours reflect light differently. On an ideological and cultural level, faces are seen as the most important elements in a photograph, and white faces are positioned as the norm. Consequently, since the 1840s, 'experiment with, for instance, the chemistry of photographic stock, aperture size, length of development and artificial light all proceeded on the assumption that what had to be got right was the look of the white face' (90); the technology of photographic media and film lighting thus evolved in such a way that 'photographing non-white people is typically construed as a problem' (89). Technology and ideology are inseparable elements in the history of the photographic and cinematic construction of whiteness and blackness.

Another clear example of the way that technological forms are bound up with much broader social, cultural and economic forces and structures is the change in the dominant form of writing technology in late antiquity and the medieval period, analysed by Paul Saenger. As Saenger shows, in the first few centuries CE, the Roman-style scroll was replaced as the dominant form of physical text by the codex. The scroll is a continuous strip of papyrus which is held in both hands and unrolled, while the codex is a small, bound volume with rectangular pages that are turned – the same basic form as today's printed books. Gradually, from the seventh century CE to the thirteenth century CE, *scriptio continua* fell into disuse in Europe and spaces between words were introduced, facilitating silent reading. The rise in silent reading, as mentioned in the Introduction, is associated with a change in the conception of reading from a communal and social activity to a solitary, private and individual one. This change in reading technologies, practices and systems led to significant alterations in the physical layout of texts and libraries. It also enabled readers to have more intense private affective and physical experiences while reading, including sexual and religious ones. 'The practice of private reading encouraged the production of salacious writing', writes Saenger; it also 'gave laymen the means of pursuing the individual relationship to God which had been the aspiration of erudite Christians since Saint Augustine' (Saenger 2011 [1982]: 122–123). Again, the technological dimension of reading is inseparable from broader social, ideological and religious factors.

Another significant transformation in writing and reading technologies is taking place now: the transition from print to digital culture. Changes in reading practices accompany technological change, encouraging a tension between social relations and the forces of technology that produce forms of behaviour that outstrip those relations and challenge their efficacy. Drawing on cognitive and neurological research into reading, Maryanne Wolf (2016) suggests that online reading tends to be shallow or extensive rather than deep or intensive; empirical research suggests that readers are less likely to remember what they have read on-screen than what they read on paper (Noyes and Garland 2003). On the other hand, some scholars believe that digital technologies and 'new media literacies' enable new forms of 'deep reading' to evolve in the context of networked 'participatory culture' (Clinton, Jenkins and McWilliams 2013: 11). Once again, changes in reading technology are linked to changes in the organization of social networks and subjectivity, this time shifting us away from the privatization of reading experience traced by Saenger and towards new forms of networked, collective interpretation, where the distinction between creative and critical responses to texts begins to break down (Clinton, Jenkins and McWilliams 2013: 3–23).

Like the shift from oral to silent reading traced by Saenger, the shift from print to digital culture promises to have far-reaching consequences for human subjectivity and social relations. Saenger's book, however, was written with the benefit of centuries of hindsight, while digital technologies are still emerging, and we can only speculate about the impact they will ultimately have (Lang 2012: 4–6). However, we can develop a framework for thinking about digital culture and its possible consequences by theorizing and historicizing the relationship between reading technologies and broader cultural and social forms.

Littau (2006: 58) writes: 'It is technology and not human agency which ultimately has effects on, or even determines, cultural practices such as reading, writing and thinking'. Indeed, some media historians and historians of literacy attribute large and profound consequences to changes in media technologies. One very influential thinker who argues that the move from orality to literacy produced a fundamental shift in human thought, subjectivity and social organization is Walter Ong. 'More than any other single invention', Ong (1982: 77) writes in a much-quoted line, 'writing has transformed human consciousness'.

For Ong (1982: 94), literate thought has 'different contours from those of orally sustained thought'. Specifically, alphabetic script transforms our relationship to the word, memory, the past and knowledge. In oral cultures, information about the past is not recorded and then retrieved, but kept alive through continuous retellings. Retellings are always embedded in a specific, face-to-face communicative context, and thus are conditioned by the social relationships which structure that context. Ong (1982: 53) provides the example of an illiterate Uzbekistani worker asked by the ethnographer Alexander Luria in the 1930s to explain what a tree is, who responded 'Why should I? Everybody knows what a tree is. They don't need me telling them'. The respondent is quite right that the researcher knows what a tree is: his response is oriented towards the interpersonal situation, rather than towards an abstract realm of correct knowledge about trees. For Ong (1982: 45), this realm of abstract knowledge is opened up when writing 'separates the knower from the known'. Without writing, and especially print, the forms of abstract knowledge developed in the European Enlightenment could never have come into being.

Ong's large-scale comparison of orality to literacy, by which he really means the culture of alphabetic print, is valuable because it makes visible some broad contrasts between oral and print culture. Other scholars have attributed similarly large-scale effects to other changes in writing and information technology: the development of printing (Eisenstein 1979; Anderson 1983); the invention of film and phonography (Kittler 1990 [1985]); and the invention of radio and television (McLuhan 1964). All these versions frame media history as a sequence of 'revolutions', with new technologies ushering in successive new modes of reading, new social and economic structures, and new forms of consciousness. As such, they help us to see the broad differences between historical regimes of reading and the possibilities and constraints afforded by particular technologies and protocols.

Such historical accounts are, however, examples of what Raymond Williams (1977: 121) calls '"epochal" analysis', in which 'a cultural process is seized as a cultural system, with determinate dominant features: feudal culture or bourgeois culture [here, perhaps, 'print culture or digital culture'] or a transition from one to the other'. Epochal analyses overemphasize change rather than continuity, and do not account for the dynamic nature of cultures, including reading cultures, in which dominant forms and practices coexist with residual and emergent ones (121–127). As Simon Gaunt and Sarah Kay point out, although Saenger is right that the Middle Ages did see the rise of silent, individual reading, oral and sociable forms of reading also continued to flourish alongside the new practices:

> Most Old and Middle French texts were composed to be recited to an audience . . . or indeed to be sung . . . or to be performed or mimed by a group . . . 'reading' medieval literature was thus a social, public activity, sometimes committed to professional performers, either travelling troupes of *jongleurs* or else minstrels attached to a particular court.
>
> (2008: 5)

In our own period of print/digital transition or interplay, Lang (2012: 4) characterizes reading as a set of 'hybrid practices' which 'rarely present an entirely new formation but rather create a meshing of old and new technologies and established and emergent modes of interaction', with 'many points of continuity . . . between [contemporary] modes of reading . . . and those of previous eras'.

Hybrid practices are thus born out of moments of historical transition from one reading culture to another. They also come about at particular historical moments when different reading cultures encounter each other, something which often takes place in the fraught and violent circumstances of colonialism, invasion and settlement.

ORALITY AND LITERACY REVISITED

Once again, the theoretical picture is complicated by historical and empirical enquiry into real readers and reading practices in moments of interaction between oral and literate cultures. Ong 'believ[es] writing to be an autonomous engine of cultural development'; that is, he 'assumes that writing's impact is inherent in the nature of alphabetic script and "literacy itself"' (Van Toorn 2006: 9). However, work on the interaction between print culture and oral culture in the context of European colonization of Australia and New Zealand shows that the impact of literacy is not determined by the qualities of alphabetic script. Instead, it depends on 'constructions or ideologies of literacy, and on the specific purposes, means and institutions through which those conceptions [are] introduced and enforced' (9).

In an influential article from 1984, 'The Sociology of a Text: Oral Culture, Literacy, and Print in Early New Zealand', D. F. McKenzie analyses the literacy practices and protocols at work in the signing of the Treaty of Waitangi, New Zealand's 'founding document'. The Treaty was drawn up by the British Lieutenant-Governor William Hobson, translated into Maori by the missionary Henry Williams and his son Edward and signed by Hobson on behalf of the British Crown, and by about 540 Maori chiefs (*rangatira*). On the basis of this treaty British sovereignty over New Zealand was declared in May 1840. One of the issues at stake involves translation; for example, 'sovereignty' was translated as 'kawanatanga' in the Maori version of the Treaty, which the majority of the chiefs signed. McKenzie writes:

> The question here is what the English meant and the Maori understood by the word 'Sovereignty'. Did it mean that the chiefs gave up to the Crown their personal power and supreme status within their own tribes, or was it only something more mundanely administrative, like 'governorship'? In fact the word used by Henry Williams to translate 'Sovereignty' was precisely that: *kawanatanga,* a transliteration of 'Governor' *(kawana)* with a suffix to make it abstract ... What he significantly omitted in translating the 'Sovereignty' which the Maori were being asked to surrender was the genuine Maori word *mana,* meaning personal prestige and the power that flowed from it, or even the word *rangatiratanga,* meaning chieftainship.
>
> (1984: 360–361)

Layered onto the literal meaning of the words and the problematics of translation, however, is the question of what Gitelman would call the protocols surrounding the signing of a legal document, and what

McKenzie calls 'the subtler, much more elusive and indeterminate technology' of 'literacy' (338). He enumerates some of the components of print literacy, as a protocol for interacting with written texts, as follows:

> the reduction of speech to alphabetic forms, an ability to read and write them, a readiness to shift from memory to written record, to accept a signature as a sign of full comprehension and legal commitment, to surrender the relativities of time, place and person in an oral culture to the presumed fixities of the written or printed word.
>
> (336–338)

'What the English meant' and 'what the Maori understood' by the Treaty, both in terms of the words on the page and in terms of the process and consequences of signing, were very different things. In the terms of Stuart Hall's essay, discussed in the last chapter, the English 'encoded' and the Maori 'decoded' the Treaty in very different ways.

In *Writing Never Arrives Naked*, Penny Van Toorn (2006: 75) gives an account of 'early Aboriginal cultures of writing', analysing the ways in which Aboriginal people adopted and appropriated aspects of the European system of alphabetic literacy, including the material forms in which they encountered texts. She points out that when Aboriginal people encountered them, 'alphabetic characters . . . were always on tangible objects that formed part of the alien material culture of the settle society', so that 'these objects and the distinctive lettering styles used on them would have [partially] shaped Aboriginal people's understandings of the nature and function of alphabetic script'. Aboriginal appropriations of European alphabetic writing were also shaped by interaction with existing Aboriginal signifying practices, as when a Wiradjuri club from the 1860s is decorated both with traditional cross-hatched and zig-zag markings and with specific European letters whose diagonal lines harmonize with the traditional patterns: V, M, W, X, N. The decorative or ideographic use of alphabetic writing reveals, as van Toorn argues, that 'the defining characteristic of any script – its capacity to "be" phonographic, ideographic or pictographic – is not intrinsic to it, but held in place by culturally and historically conventions of reading' (73). Even the properties of alphabetic script, then, are artefacts of the reading conventions and traditions brought to bear on that script, not intrinsic within a script or writing technology.

What this work shows, then, is that there is no 'level zero' of reading which is pure literacy in a given script. In this chapter, we have been thinking about what enables readers to make sense of texts, and to connect with them emotionally: what social and cultural systems generate and structure the multidimensional experiences that happen when we read. But in order to be able to read, a reader must, at the very least, recognize written signifiers as such, and be able to translate them into signifieds according to the rules of a particular script and language. We might think, then, that literacy, the sheer capacity to decode letters and words in written language, is the sustaining or neutral ground on which higher-level cultural competences are founded. However, work like McKenzie's and Van Toorn's shows us that we cannot securely separate out the technical capacity to read a given script from higher-level cultural competences. Thinking about reading always means thinking about the complex technological/sociocultural systems which produce and structure communication between texts and readers.

Van Toorn's work helps us to account for the complexity of individual reading events and practices, by reminding us to attend in detail to the materialities, technologies and literacies involved in any single reading event. In the next chapter we will extend her interrogation of literacy and alphabetic script to look at the notion of meaning itself, and the features of language and other sign systems which make acts of communication and reception possible in the first place.

4

MEANING

Over the last three chapters we have explored a range of theoretical, historical and empirical approaches to reception: different models for understanding how readers, viewers and audiences receive, interpret and respond to texts. All the approaches we have mapped, despite their differences, have a fundamental insight in common: the insight that intertextual relations, readers and reading are necessarily part of what we study when we study literary texts.

Some scholars and critics understand the everyday business of literary studies to be the formal or contextual analysis of texts, and regard the study of the reception of texts as a separate matter. On this view, a literary critic and a reception scholar carry out different activities on different objects. The first would perform a textual analysis of, say, Harriet Beecher Stowe's *Uncle Tom's Cabin*, looking at the text itself, and perhaps at the context of its original publication. The second, by contrast, would not read the novel, but would instead map changing or diverse interpretations of the book by investigating a different set of documents, ones which recorded readers' responses to the text (Hochman 2011). There is some truth to this: as we have seen throughout the previous chapters, different approaches to reception do require the use of different forms of evidence and different methodologies.

However, the theories and methods that we have surveyed so far have also problematized the idea that it is possible for any critic to look only at the text itself.

Thinking about reception means that we can no longer understand the text, as the New Critics did, as 'an object, like a machine, whose parts can be analyzed without reference . . . to the observer (or reader)' (Rosenblatt 1995: 267). The insights of reception indicate that the object of literary study is more complex than this. 'The status, shape and meaning of texts are functions of reading activities' (Machor 2011: 4), so that texts cannot be studied without reference to readers and/or reading.

Texts are only texts if they *mean* something to a reader, as Sheldon Pollock (2009: 957) argues, asking: 'What mode of existence does a text have for us when it has no meaning, when it means nothing to us?'. We can turn to the semiotician Charles Sanders Peirce (1931–1958 [1894]: 2.172) for an answer to that rhetorical question: 'Nothing is a sign unless it is interpreted as a sign'. Signs which are not interpreted are not signs; texts which do not mean anything are not texts, but inert physical objects. The implications of this idea are explored in 'The Author of the Acacia Seeds', a 1974 short story by the science fiction author Ursula K. Le Guin. The setting of the story in the near future is indicated not through an extraterrestrial setting or allusions to advances in technology or science, but rather through improved techniques in 'therolinguistics', the capacity to read texts written in various animal languages, including the 'group kinetic texts' created by penguins (1983 [1974]: 7) and the 'Acacia Seeds' of the title. The first 'text' read in Le Guin's short story is a manifesto 'written in touch-gland exudation on degerminated acacia seeds'; its author is a revolutionary ant (3). The last, as yet unreadable text, is the 'passive, wholly atemporal, cold, volcanic poetry of the rocks', to be deciphered one day by the 'geolinguist' (7). What makes an object – an acacia seed, a rock – into a text is an act of reception; a text is something, anything, that is read. And to read something, as Le Guin's short story also makes clear, requires hard-won knowledge of a language, a script and a set of interpretative conventions (Willis 2014).

Texts thus come to be texts only within systems and relations of signification and meaning. Studying texts in the light of reception requires us to articulate, and to address, broad conceptual and theoretical questions about the nature of meaning, language, sign systems and interpretation, questions which underpin all literary study and textual analysis. In this chapter, I explore four reasons why attention to readers, reading and interpretation is inevitably part of the process of textual analysis, whether or not this is explicitly acknowledged. Four reasons, in other words, why we cannot study texts without thinking about reception. The first reason is the constructed nature of the text, as something which is co-produced by an interpreter, or, really, a number of interpreters. The second is the non-existence of a fixed meaning for any statement or sign prior to an act of interpretation. The third is the dialogic nature of interpretation and the inextricability of the interpreter from the text. The fourth is the irreducibly polysemic nature of linguistic meaning, which can only be fixed or determined by appealing to extratextual authority.

STABLE TEXTS

As we have seen throughout this book, what is 'in' a text depends in part on the frames, conventions and competences that a reader brings to it. Even when we accept the existence of multiple and variable interpretations, however, we still tend to attribute some kind of stability to the text itself, locating variability and multiplicity in the responses of readers or the framing techniques that they bring to the text. Stanley Fish (1978: 627) puts it this way: '[we] assume that on some (perhaps molecular) level what is in the text is independent of and prior to whatever people have said about it, and that therefore the text is stable, even though interpretations of it may vary'. Fish counters this assumption, however, by saying that 'there is always a text', but 'what is in it can change, and therefore at no level is it independent of and prior to interpretation'.

As we saw in the discussion of genre in Chapter Three, the significance that we attribute to aspects of texts does indeed change according to the interpretative conventions used by readers. We might still attribute some sort of independence and stability to the 'text itself', however, if we think of the text as consisting of particular words in a particular order: the words on the page, prior to their reception by a reader. But even these words and their ordering are, in practice, the result of interpretative acts.

Biblical studies brings this issue into sharp focus. Recent archaeological discoveries have cast into doubt the very existence of an 'original text' for the books of the Bible. Brennan Breed summarizes the situation and its implications:

> We now know that several biblical books existed in multiple, irreducible versions in antiquity, and that some textual differences presumed to be later corruptions or recensions are in fact alternative ancient versions, often composed in the 'original' Hebrew ... Upon inspection, it appears that the history of a biblical text is a long process that often has indistinct beginnings, discontinuities and irreducibly different versions of the same text ... It is 'reception all the way down'.
>
> (2015: 97)

Even for texts with less long and complex histories of composition, circulation and reception than the books of the Bible, the existence of a 'stable text' is itself the result, not simply the basis, of interpretative acts. In *The Textual Condition*, Jerome McGann points out that this is unavoidably true on the level of the words on the page for literary texts. At the point where they reach readers, literary texts have always been co-produced by multiple individuals and institutions: texts are the result of 'a collaboration between the author and all those (amanuenses, proof-correctors, editors, publishers) who had an opportunity to alter that text' (Howard-Hill 2009: 15, summarizing McGann 1983). Far from there being 'words on the page' which are simply given as the basis for the interpretative work of readers, those words are already the outcome of the interpretative judgements of editors and others, who decide on the 'best' version of the text. As McGann puts it, 'All editing is an act of interpretation' (McGann 1991: 22). Thus

> it is a mischaracterization to regard the textual operations on a text (no matter how seemingly 'minute') as somehow 'prehermeneutic' (i.e., 'prior to ... meaning'); for all such operations, from a decision to use old or modern spelling to the selection and evaluation of variants to the question of when

and how to annotate (and for what sort of reader) are already
deeply hermeneutic.

(Greetham 2009: 23)

Furthermore, the very perception of something *as* meaningful, the
decision or capacity to treat something as a text or a sign, is itself the
outcome of an act of interpretation. What counts as a meaning-bearing
aspect of a text, script or material object is historically and culturally variable. For example, Van Toorn (2006: 77) points out that 'when
Aboriginal people initially encountered alphabetic characters, they
would have had no way of knowing which features of the characters
"carried" meaning (in the eyes of literate Europeans) and which did
not'. Aboriginal people had to evaluate, for example, whether the
presence of serifs altered the significance of a letter; whether letters like
M and W had to have a specific number of zigs and zags; and whether
the spatial orientation of a letter altered its meaning, as when letters
appear 'upside-down' in inscriptions around the edge of a coin.

Similarly, for some readers and in some reading acts, the material
properties of a text are framed as meaningless or as obstacles to
meaning. A student reading a second-hand copy of a set text will be
frustrated if a page is torn out or scribbled over, and will not draw
attention to such gaps, or to stains and dog-ears on the pages, in the
'readings' she produces for her tutor in class discussion or an essay.
But such gaps and marks may be profoundly significant to reception
historians as evidence of the ways in which books were handled and
interacted with by users, as with Kathryn Rudy's work on the marks
left by lips and fingers on medieval prayer books (Rudy 2010), or
Emma Smith's 'biography' of Shakespeare's First Folio, which tells
the book's history through the ink blots, cat footprints, wine-glass
rings and marginalia left on individual copies (Smith 2016).

LITERAL MEANING

As Fish says, then, what is 'in' a text can change according to our
perceptions of what is meaningful; there can be no stable text which
precedes interpretation. In the same way, he argues, we cannot appeal
to the notion of a determinate literal meaning which remains constant
at a level below or beneath the creative operations of interpreters.

This is because the meaning of any sequence of words is not an inherent property of those words or that sequence; instead, meaning is determined by the communicative situation in which the sequence of words is uttered and received.

Fish demonstrates that a context can always be found, imagined or invented, within which a sentence can 'mean' whatever you like. He uses an example from the philosopher of language John Searle, who imagines a conversation between two students: student X says 'Let's go to the movies tonight', and student Y replies 'I have to study for an exam'. Searle argues that the statement 'I have to study for an exam' *functions* as a rejection of the proposal, even though there is nothing in the *meaning* of the sentence itself – the dictionary definitions of the words and their syntactical and grammatical relations to one another – which says anything about going to the movies. Searle (1975: 60–62) goes on to say that 'statements of this form do not, in general, constitute rejections of proposals', and that if the second student 'had said *I have to eat popcorn tonight* . . . in a normal context', this would not have functioned in the same way as 'I have to study for an exam'.

Fish, however, asks:

> Normal for whom? Or, to put it another way, is it possible to imagine a set of circumstances in which 'I have to eat popcorn tonight' would immediately and without any chain of inference be heard as a rejection of X's proposal?

He answers:

> It is not only possible, it is easy . . . Let us suppose that student Y is by profession a popcorn taster: that is, he works in a popcorn manufacturing plant and is responsible for quality control . . . If Student X knows this, he will hear 'I have to eat popcorn tonight' as a rejection of his proposal because it will mean 'Sorry, I have to work'.

> (1978: 639)

The 'literal' meaning of a sequence of words, therefore, does not pre-exist interpretation, but is produced by the context: the total communicative situation in which the sequence of words was uttered. Fish concludes that 'there are no inherent constraints on the meanings a sentence may have' (644). What constrains or determines the interpretation we place on a sequence of words is not the inherent properties of those words or that sequence, but the properties of the contextual and communicative situation within which those words are uttered and received.

This, however, seems to miss a more fundamental dimension of meaning: the properties of language as a system of signs with assigned meanings. Fish's and Searle's example assumes that their speakers are both fluent in the same language. In order for 'I have to eat popcorn tonight' to succeed in meaning 'I can't come to the movies', both parties to the dialogue have to have a certain degree of linguistic knowledge: they have to know what the word 'popcorn' means.

Many theorists have tried to deal with this problem by drawing a distinction between different levels of meaning, so that the words 'meaning' and 'means' in the last sentence of the last paragraph refer to slightly different processes or relationships. Tzetvan Todorov, for example, distinguishes a basic level of signification and a higher, interpretative level of symbolization. He explains with reference to Benjamin Constant's 1816 novel *Adolphe*:

> Ellenore's trip to Paris is *signified* by the words in the text. Adolphe's ultimate weakness is *symbolized* by other factors in the imaginary universe, which are themselves signified by words. For example, Adolphe's inability to defend Ellenore in social situations is signified; this in turn symbolizes his inability to love. Signified facts are *understood*: all we need is knowledge of the language in which the text is written. Symbolized facts are *interpreted*; and interpretations vary from one subject to another.
>
> (1980: 73)

The media theorist John Corner distinguishes three levels of 'meaning', and the responses they elicit, arguing that they are often conflated:

> The first is the literal recognition of what is said or shown (words, objects, actions, events). The second is the 'connotative' level, grasping that any of these is operating metaphorically or symbolically, and what those connotative additions might be.

The third level is wider: 'What does it all mean, and mean to me?', the finding of coherent patterns in which we can anchor ourselves.

(Barker 1997: 21–22, summarizing
Corner 1991: 267–284)

These models posit a level of 'understanding' or 'recognition' below or prior to the level of interpretation. In the light of these distinctions, Fish's argument that 'literal' meaning is dependent on context seems to refer only to the level of what Todorov calls symbolization and Corner calls connotation or pattern-finding. It has no bearing on Todorov's signification or Corner's 'basic recognition of words'.

These differentiated levels of meaning also correspond to a distinction drawn by some linguists and philosophers of language between 'semantics' and 'pragmatics'. 'Semantics' derives from a Greek word meaning 'sign', and refers to the meaning of a word within a language; 'pragmatics' derives from a Greek word meaning 'action' or 'practice', and refers to the way a word is used in practice, to communicate in a given situation. Within a given language, then, words have a particular range of meaning, or semantic range. 'Popcorn', for example, means 'a variety of maize, the dried kernels of which swell up and burst open with a small explosive sound when heated' and 'the heated kernels of the popcorn served as a food snack' (*Oxford English Dictionary*, definition A1a). Pragmatically, the word can be *used* in a given context, as we have seen, to signify something about going to work, but this does not mean that its semantic range has expanded.

However, as Mark Gaipa and Robert Scholes point out, 'a glance at any dictionary will expose the problems' with the distinction between semantic and pragmatic meaning, 'for most of the words listed come not with a single literal meaning, but with a range of probable or potential meanings'. Indeed, even the relatively narrow-ranging word 'popcorn', according to the *Oxford English Dictionary*, might also mean 'Something that is vacuous or merely entertaining; *spec.* an undemanding film' (definition A2) or 'made of or having raised stitches resembling popcorn' (definition B1). Gaipa and Scholes continue:

In any given situation, a reader or listener must sift through those possibilities, using the appropriate codes and contextual

> information to select the 'literal' meaning for that particular
> case . . . Because different codes and contexts generate differ-
> ent significations out of the same signifiers, understanding
> always depends on these factors . . . Meaning is always a prod-
> uct of both semantics and pragmatics.
>
> (Gaipa and Scholes 1993: 168)

On this model, then, a literal meaning is something selected by a reader in a given contextual and communicative situation, out of a range of possible options and according to a variety of possible principles of selection.

Just as there is no invariant text which grounds and stabilizes all interpretations, so the semantic dimension of language does not ground and stabilize the pragmatic dimension. In other words, the semantic level does not provide an invariant meaning or ground which remains the same across the various pragmatic uses to which words are put in practice. Pragmatics determine semantics just as much as semantics determine pragmatics. Again, attending to particular instances of reception can illustrate this chiastic formulation, and can help us to challenge, nuance or re-evaluate theories of meaning. Interpretation can and does occur in practice even when a receiver or interpreter is unaware of the semantic principles of a given language or script. One example comes from Pierre Jakez Hélias's account of his childhood experience of hearing the Greek and Latin words used in Catholic mass as if they were in his own language, Breton. Thus 'Kyrie eleison' (Lord, have mercy) became 'there were heaps of carts' (Hélias 1995 [1975]: 133; cf. Willis 2014: 487–488). Hélias's practice might be understood as a simple error, but Françoise Waquet (2001: 104) theorizes it differently. According to her, Hélias has succeeded in 'translating into intelligible words a reality whose literal meaning the linguistic barrier has . . . transformed into mere sounds'.

The same principle underlies homophonic translation, in which a translator deliberately renders the sound, rather than the sense, of a poem's words in the words of a different language. A well-known example is the 1969 translation of the works of the Latin poet Catullus (c. 84–54 BCE) by Celia and Louis Zukofsky. The first two lines of Catullus's poem 70 are *Nulli se dicit mulier mea nubere malle/quam mihi, non si se Iuppiter ipse petat*. A 'literal' translation, rendering the sense of the words, would run: 'My woman says that she would prefer to marry no-one other than me, not even if Jupiter himself asked her'. The Zukofskys translate:

> Newly say dickered my love air my own would marry me all whom but me, none see say Jupiter if she petted.
>
> (1969: 70)

Their homophonic translation, as Horáček (2014) argues, directs our attention to the material and sonorous properties of Catullus's Latin words, locating their 'meaning' or significance there, rather than on the semantic level.

Meaning, therefore, is always bound up with particular contexts and practices of communication, or what the philosopher Foucault (2001 [1969]: 99–118) has called the 'enunciative function' of language; that is, the property of being uttered, communicated or 'enunciated' which characterizes all linguistic statements. Foucault argues that meaning cannot be assigned to a statement on the basis of purely linguistic or semantic rules. He gives the example of a famously 'meaningless' sentence, proposed by the linguist Noam Chomsky: 'Colourless green ideas sleep furiously'. For Chomsky, the sentence is grammatically correct but meaningless because it is semantically self-contradictory and cannot correspond to any 'visible reality'. Foucault shows, however, that to call this sentence meaningless is already to 'exclud[e] a number of possibilities – that it describes a dream, that it is part of a poetic text, that it is a coded message, that it is spoken by a drug addict' (101–102). It is at this level, the level of enunciation or being-uttered, that the meaning of a sentence or statement can be specified. In Foucault's words, 'the relation of a sentence with its meaning resides within a specific, well-stabilized enunciative relation' (102) and not within the relationships between words and meanings that we might find in a dictionary.

Enunciative relations can be complex and nested. When Claudius, the King of Denmark in Shakespeare's *Hamlet* who has murdered his brother, married his widow and taken his throne, refers to himself as having 'an auspicious and a dropping [weeping] eye' (I.2.11), within the play's fictional universe he means to convey that he is divided between joy at his marriage and grief at his brother's death. However, the enunciative status of this sentence as Claudius's utterance influences the audience's response to it. Claudius is framed as a suspicious character, and our emotional reaction to his utterance is accordingly combined with a critical one. We are not sure he is telling the truth. It could be said that the relation of enunciation between Claudius and the characters to whom he speaks is nested within another enunciative relation, between the text and its audience: in this context Claudius's utterance 'means' his untrustworthiness. The two enunciative framings inflect one another, producing complex effects of meaning and response.

Meanings are assigned, then, not at the level of language but at the level of enunciation and ultimately the level of discourse, the broad cultural system which organizes and regulates the way that statements are produced and related to one another (Mills 1997: 7).

INTERFACE, DIALOGUE AND RESONANCE

Meaning is thus not to be found 'in' texts or utterances, but this does not necessarily mean that it is to be exclusively found 'in' readers, viewers or listeners either. In *Interpreting Film*, the media reception theorist Janet Staiger (1992: 35–36) groups theories of reception into three categories: text-activated, reader-activated and context-activated. Text-activated theories, like those I called 'text-centred' theories in Chapter Two, 'suggest. . . that meaning or significance is "in" the text for the reader to interpret'. Reader-activated theories locate meaning '"in" the reader's interpretation', and context-activated theories proceed on the basis that 'the text and the reader are equally significant in creating meaning, that historical context is very significant for the interaction, and that meaning or significance is "in" that contextual intersection'. In the example from *Hamlet* given above, we see text and reader working together to create the 'meaning' of Claudius's line, through the words of the sentence, its enunciative function and the complex response of the audience.

For Staiger, context-activated theories offer the most convincing account of the way that meaning is produced in the 'contextual intersection', or the *encounter* between texts and readers, viewers or listeners. The classical scholar William Batstone, similarly, argues that if 'meaning is realized at the point of reception' (Martindale 1993: 3), then that 'point' must be understood not as a point where meaning can be 'isolated or stopped' but as 'the ephemeral interface of the text; it occurs where the text and the reader meet and is simultaneously constitutive of both' (Batstone 2006: 17).

One particularly persistent image for the intersection or interface between text and reader is the dialogue. The notion of reception as dialogic has been theorized most thoroughly by the hermeneutic philosopher Hans-Georg Gadamer, who taught both Wolfgang Iser and Hans Robert Jauss at the University of Heidelberg.

For Gadamer (1989: 57), the key factor in reading is not so much 'meaning' as 'understanding'. Human beings necessarily 'speak and write in order to be understood'; reciprocally, the aim of reading is to understand a text. The model of understanding that Gadamer (2004 [1960]: 155) develops is based on dialogue or conversation. 'Literary art . . . speaks to us', he claims, and 'our understanding is not specifically concerned with its formal achievement as a work of art but with what it says to us'. Understanding a text is not a question of decoding its 'correct' meaning once and for all; instead, understanding is fundamentally relational, and 'only the person who allows himself to be addressed – whether he believes or doubts – understands' (328). In other words, as Robert Evans (2014: 248) explains, 'understanding the text *presupposes a relationship to what it says*'. We do not, and cannot, understand a text from a neutral or detached position, but only when we know what it has to say to us. Gadamer (2004: 296) writes that 'every age has to understand a transmitted text in its own way . . . The real meaning of a text . . . is always co-determined . . . by the historical situation of the interpreter'.

The metaphor that Gadamer uses for this dialogic process of understanding is the 'fusion of horizons'. A text is written within a particular context, or 'horizon of expectations': a reader comes to it from within a different horizon. Both horizons, the writer's/text's and the reader's, must enter into the process of understanding: 'the horizon of understanding cannot be limited by what the writer originally had in mind' (396). If we attempt to 'see the past on its own terms' by 'just disregarding ourselves' and entering fully into the horizon of the past text, then we '*think* we understand', but 'in fact . . . we have given up the claim to find in the past any truth that is valid and intelligible for ourselves' (302–303, my emphasis). We only know what the writer meant, not what the text says to us, and this is not true understanding.

Gadamer emphasizes, however, that the converse is also true: historical understanding does not entail 'subordinating another person to our own standards', and 'it is constantly necessary to guard against over-hastily assimilating the past to our own expectations of meaning' (304). This would be monologic rather than dialogic. Thus, for Gadamer, understanding involves the 'fusion of horizons'. The reader does not seek to dismiss or downplay her own historical and cultural situation, since she wants to know what the text has to say to her where she is; but she also takes into account the position from which the text 'speaks'.

Gadamer's student Jauss developed his teacher's dialogic theory of understanding, writing that

> a dialogue consists not only of two interlocutors, but also of the willingness of one to recognize and accept the other in his otherness . . . Literary understanding becomes dialogical only when the otherness of the text is sought and recognized from the horizon of our own expectations . . . and when one's own expectations are corrected and extended by the experience of others.
>
> (2001 [1985]: 9)

For Jauss, the 'fusion of horizons' was neither possible nor desirable; instead, he used the term 'conjunction' of horizons.

> It is the task of historical understanding to take both horizons into account through conscious effort. To believe that it is possible to gain access to the alien horizon of the past simply by leaving out one's own horizon of the present is to fail to recognize that subjective criteria, such as choice, perspective, and evaluation, have been introduced into a supposedly objective reconstruction of the past.
>
> (7–8)

In both Jauss's and Gadamer's terms, we can only access the past by taking into account our own situation in the present. For Gadamer and Jauss, because we are historically constituted in our very being, any attempt to reach an ahistorical or objective 'meaning' for a text could only be an act of bad faith. As a reader, one should not try to 'leav[e] out one's own horizon', writes Jauss. Gadamer argues, further, that the expectations and pre-judgements, or 'prejudices', that we bring to the text do not necessarily hinder our understanding. They may, on the contrary, enable it. Indeed, part of the reader's task is to 'distinguish the true prejudices, by which we *understand*, from the *false* ones, by which we *misunderstand*' (2004: 298, emphasis original). We make this distinction only in our encounter with the text. The important point here, however, is that Gadamer seeks to do away with the negative connotations of 'prejudice': prejudices or 'fore-understandings' are 'conditions of understanding' (277). We cannot do without them, because they are part of our historical being, which is an irreducible part of our subjectivity and existence.

In her paper 'A Theory of Resonance', Wai Chee Dimock puts forward a rather different model of interpretation and reading which, nonetheless, like Gadamer's and Jauss's, is opened up and enabled, rather than threatened, by what the reader brings to the text. Dimock (1997: 1063) elaborates a metaphor of texts as 'resonating' through time, using noise 'as an apt analogy for . . . interpretive context'. Noise, she demonstrates, does not simply interfere with the 'correct' reception of a text: instead it can be 'beneficial . . . it enriches the dynamics for interpretation'. 'This argument is counterintuitive', she continues, 'yet it echoes a recent scientific hypothesis about the beneficial effects of random noise on the detectability of sounds'. In a phenomenon known as stochastic resonance, 'a weak signal is boosted by background noise and becomes newly and complexly audible'. Dimock argues that as texts travel through time, encountering 'new ways of imputing meaning' (1061), they are made to resonate in different ways against different patterns of background noise:

> An effect of historical change, noise is a necessary feature of a reader's meaning-making processes. And even as it impinges on texts, even as it reverberates through them, it thickens their tonality, multiplies their hearable echoes, makes them significant in unexpected ways.
>
> (1063)

Thus, for Dimock as for Gadamer, the meaning of a text should not be 'assumed to be the property of the historical period in which it originated' (1060–1061). Rather, the historical change that the text undergoes as it travels through time into the future is a dynamic process which 'release[s]' 'interpretive energies' (1062), and renders the text as 'the "object" of literary studies . . . an object with an unstable ontology, since a text can resonate only insofar as it is touched by the effects of its travels' (1061).

The idea that a text is affected by its journey through history is extended by the Sanskrit scholar Sheldon Pollock (2014: 399) in his model of reading 'in three dimensions'. He defines this as 'a philological practice that orients itself simultaneously along three planes of a text's existence: its moment of genesis; its reception over time; and its presence to my own subjectivity'. In Pollock's model, the dialogue is expanded to a three-way interaction. 'There are . . . three, potentially radically different, dimensions of meaning (the author's, the tradition's and my own)' (401), and '"making sense" of a text resides in the sum total of the varied senses generated on these three planes, their lively copresence to our mind' (400).

In his discussion of the plane of tradition, Pollock invokes Jauss (1982: 20), who argues that understanding is 'sustained and enriched by a chain of receptions'. Pollock, however, points out that Jauss, like Gadamer, believes that 'earlier interpretations can be "falsified"' (2014: 405). In strong contrast, Pollock argues that 'in relation to the meanings and truths of Plane 2 [the plane of tradition], there can be no such thing as an incorrect interpretation' (406). He expands on this provocative claim, stating that 'Since all interpretations are embodiments of human consciousness, which have been called into being by certain properties in the text, such forms of consciousness cannot be correct or incorrect *in their historical existence*' (406). Pollock's point is, primarily, that an interpretation could only be 'incorrect' if the 'correct' meaning of the text could be determined and made available for comparison. More broadly, Pollock is here staking out a position similar to Tony Bennett's, discussed in Chapter One: 'marginalized, subordinate, quirky, fantastic, or quixotic [meanings] are just as real, just as ontologically secure, just as much wrapped up in the living social destinies of texts as are dominant ones' (1983: 8). Every interpretation that survives is a piece of historically extant evidence that a text was able to be read in a particular way, by a particular reader, at a particular time. As we saw with Hélias's reading of Latin Mass via the Breton language, even receptions of texts by readers who do not understand the language in which the text is written are 'interpretations . . . which have been called into being by certain properties in the text' (Pollock 2014: 406) – in this example, by the sonorous properties of Latin words.

For Staiger, Batstone, Gadamer, Jauss, Dimock and Pollock, in different ways, meaning is produced by or at the interface between texts and reader/s. Time, historical change and tradition are important parts of this interface, as two- or three-way interactions between text, reader and tradition are opened up. Meaning and response are co-produced by text and interpreter, and are matters of historically bound human consciousness.

LINGUISTICS, SEMIOTICS AND DECONSTRUCTION: BEYOND COMMUNICATION

All of these theorists foreground the communicative dimension of language and, in some cases, model the interpretation of literary texts on the relationship between two human subjects who seek to understand each other.

On this view, meaning is ultimately the product of human minds. However, a different model of meaning, as the product of language itself, has been enormously influential in literary and cultural studies since at least the 1960s. This model was developed out of the analysis of language presented by Ferdinand de Saussure in *A Course on General Linguistics* in 1916.

As we saw in the Introduction, Saussure defined the basic unit of meaning as the linguistic sign. The sign combines a particular signifier (the sound of the spoken word or the shape of the written word) with a particular signified or concept (the meaning of the word within a given language). He argued that signs have meaning only within a given sign system:

> It is a great mistake to consider a sign as nothing more than the combination of a certain sound and a certain concept. To think of a sign as nothing more would be to isolate it from the system to which it belongs. It would be to suppose that a start could be made with individual signs, and a system constructed

by putting them together. On the contrary, the system as a united whole is the starting point.

(2013 [1916]: 133)

Saussure's argument that 'the system as a united whole is the starting point' prompts a shift in thinking about meaning. Meaning is no longer seen as something which is generated in a person's mind and expressed through language, but as a property of language itself. That is, instead of accepting language as a neutral tool for the expression of meanings which are produced inside a speaker's mind, Saussurian semiotics regards language as determining the range of possible meanings and concepts that a person has at their disposal. In a gesture that reverses the notion that language is merely instrumental, Saussure claims that it is language that speaks through us, rather than we who speak a language.

Saussure's model has another important implication. This is that meanings derive not from the relationship between a signifier (the letters that comprise the word 'tree') and a signified (the concept of 'tree'), or between a sign (the word 'tree') and a thing (an actual tree), but from the differences between signs within a system. Saussure writes:

In . . . language itself, there are only differences. Even more important than that is the fact that, although in general a difference presupposes positive terms between which the difference holds, in a language there are only differences, *and no positive terms*. Whether we take the [signified] or the [signifier], the language includes neither ideas nor sounds existing prior to the linguistic system, but only conceptual and phonetic differences arising out of that system. In a sign, what matters more than any idea or sound associated with it is what other signs surround it.

(140–141, emphasis original)

Linguistic meaning, then, is a more complex and dynamic process than a dictionary model that presupposes a direct referential connection between word and object might imply. For Saussure, linguistic signs *mean* neither because they straightforwardly express the thought of a speaker or writer nor because they have a positive, one-to-one relationship with the object they refer to. Instead, meaning is produced by the relationships between terms within a system ('langue') which pre-exists and contains the utterances of individual speakers ('parole').

The implications of this model of linguistic meaning for literary studies in particular were followed up by a group of French critics, philosophers and theorists known as the *Tel Quel* group, including Julia Kristeva, Roland Barthes and Jacques Derrida (Mowitt 1992). For them, Saussure's model radically alters the way in which we read texts, both because the writer cannot be seen as fully in control of the meaning that the text holds or produces, and because signs mean only with reference to other signs, rather than pointing to an extratextual 'meaning' beyond, behind or outside the text. These writers ground their work in Saussure's model, but go much further than Saussure in decentring the speaker or writer as the origin of meaning. Jonathan Culler, an American critic strongly influenced by the *Tel Quel* group, explains:

> A whole tradition of thought treats man as essentially a thinking being, a conscious subject who endows objects around him with meaning. Indeed, we often think of the meaning of an expression as what the subject or speaker 'has in mind'. But as meaning is explained in terms of systems of signs – systems which the subject does not control – the subject is deprived of his role as a source of meaning.
>
> (1981 [1977]: 32–33)

This notion underpins the work of the philosopher and deconstructionist critic Jacques Derrida. In one of his most explicit discussions of his theory of meaning and reading, Derrida writes that, because meaning is a property of systems of signs which are not under the control of any individual speaker or writer,

> the presumed subject of [a] sentence might always say . . . more, less, or something other than what he *would mean* . . . The writer writes *in* a language and *in* a logic whose proper system, laws and life his discourse by definition cannot dominate absolutely. He uses them only by letting himself, after a

fashion and up to a point, be governed by the system. And the reading must always aim at a certain relationship, unperceived by the writer, between what he commands and what he does not command of the patterns of the language that he uses.

(1976 [1967]: 157–158)

'Understanding' a text is thus not a matter of understanding or reconstructing what a writer means, or what she has to say to us as readers, as it is for Gadamer.

Derrida's thinking about language as a system extends and critiques Saussure's to tease out the radical implications of the insight that the meanings of signs are not fixed, but dynamically produced through their interrelationships within a linguistic system or structure. In an important essay from 1966, 'Structure, Sign and Play in the Human Sciences', Derrida shows that most post-Saussurean thinkers accept some degree of relativity in meaning and interpretation, but ultimately believe that 'the organizing principle of the [linguistic] structure . . . limit[s] what we might call the *play* of the structure . . . by orienting and organizing the coherence of the system'. They assign a stable centre to the linguistic system, thus allowing the system itself to limit and fix the play of meaning.

The concept of centered structure is in fact the concept of a play based on a fundamental ground, a play constituted on the basis of a fundamental immobility and a reassuring certitude, which itself is beyond the reach of play.

(2001 [1966]: 352).

By contrast, Derrida argues that there is no centre or fundamental ground which could structure or limit the free play of signification. If meaning is produced by difference, and signs mean only in relation to other signs, then meaning plays across and between signs in unstable signifying chains which are not ultimately grounded or fixed, any more than the system of language has an immobile centre of meaning.

Derrida gives a demonstration of the reading practice opened up by this model of signification in a 1968 essay on *Phaedrus*, a discussion by the Greek philosopher Plato (c. 429–347 BCE) of alphabetic writing as a technology. Derrida analyses the *Phaedrus* by tracing the ways in which it deploys the word *pharmakon,* which recurs through-out the text. Rather like the English 'drug', *pharmakon* means both 'remedy' and 'poison'; furthermore, it is related to a number of other words in Greek including *pharmakos*, scapegoat. By attending scru-pulously to the way in which the multiple possible meanings of the word *pharmakon* and its cognates interact with one another, Derrida teases out the complex logic of Plato's text. He shows that the text both opposes the ideas of 'remedy' and 'poison' to one another and, at the same time, identifies them with one another. Attending to the play of language and its polysemic workings in Plato's text brings to light a complex and self-contradictory picture of writing, one which under-mines the very conceptual categories and distinctions which we might usually seek to use to understand Plato's text. Derrida argues that

> the word *pharmakon* is caught in a chain of significations. The play of that chain seems systematic. But the system here is not, simply, that of the intentions of an author who goes by the name of Plato. The system is not primarily that of what some-one *meant-to-say*. Finely regulated communications are estab-lished, through the play of language, among diverse functions of the word and, within it, among diverse strata or regions of culture . . . These links go on working of themselves. In spite of him? thanks to him? in *his* text? outside his text? but then where? between his text and the language? for what reader? at what moment?

> (2004 [1968]: 98)

For Derrida, if meaning is produced in and by the play of signification rather than by the intentions of an author, then reading cannot be a matter of understanding what an author 'meant to say'. Instead, it involves tracing a systematic chain of significations, a set of connec-tions and links which 'go on working of themselves'. He argues that 'reading . . . cannot legitimately transgress the text toward something other than it, toward . . . a signified outside the text whose content could take place, could have taken place outside of language' (1976: 158), and that the mode of deconstructive reading which he elaborates must not 'leap over the text toward its presumed content, in the direc-tion of the pure signified' (159).

Barthes, similarly, argues for a mode of reading which does not attempt to 'leap over the text' in order to find a meaning which would exist before or behind the text. Again like Derrida, he bases this argument partly on the fact that meaning, as a property of language, cannot be confined to what the author meant to say, since words can always mean more or other than what we intend to express by them. 'To assign an Author to a text', he writes, 'is to impose a brake on it, to furnish it with a final signified, to close writing . . . once the Author is found, the text is "explained"' (1989c [1968]: 53). By contrast, in the mode of reading that Barthes advocates,

> everything is to be *disentangled* but nothing *deciphered*, structure can be followed, 'threaded' (as we say of a run in a stocking) in all its reprises, all its stages, but there is no end to it, no bottom; the space of writing is to be traversed, not pierced; writing constantly posits meaning, but always in order to evaporate it.
>
> (53–54)

For both Barthes and Derrida, 'classical reading' tries to find a 'meaning' which is, ultimately, beyond, beneath or before the text itself. It tries to explain the text, to close the text upon a 'final signified', or to 'leap over the text' towards its content. Yet if signs have meanings neither because they express the intention of a speaker or author nor because they point towards an extratextual reality, then these procedures are ultimately illegitimate. Language is inherently and essentially polysemic, and any attempt to determine the meaning of a text therefore involves closing down certain possibilities of meaning in favour of others. There is nothing in language itself that tells us *which* possibilities for meaning we should prioritize over others.

As we have seen, Fish and many other critics argue that context effectively determines or constrains meaning: Derrida (1982 [1971]: 317), however, shows in 'Signature – Event – Context' that 'a written sign carries with it a force of breaking with its context . . . No context can enclose it'. 'It belongs to the sign to be legible', he writes, 'even if the moment of its production is irremediably lost'. In other words, signs, by definition, have the capacity to continue to mean, to continue to be legible, even when they are out of their original context.

If they do not have this capacity, they cannot mean anything at all. Decontextualization, the possibility of being interpreted outside of an original context, is not a danger or risk that may befall a particular utterance; it is what makes language language. For this reason, context alone cannot tell us which possibilities for meaning we should prioritize over others, any more than language alone can. Our responses to texts, then, must take into account the complex dynamic of decontextualization and recontextualization that is involved in the readerly production of meaning, rather than appealing to 'context' as the ultimate determinant of the meaning of a sequence of words. Here we return, perhaps, to the discussion of rewriting and interpretation in Chapter One, where we saw that the redeployment of an old text in a new context can release new possibilities of meaning and interpretation, and that this process is never finished. As Derrida specifies, 'This does not suppose that the mark is valid outside its context, but on the contrary that there are only contexts without any centre of absolute anchoring' (1982: 321). In other words, 'no meaning can be determined out of context, but no context permits saturation' (1979: 81).

The basis on which we determine a singular or coherent meaning for a text, then, is not given to us by the properties of the text or by context. Instead, for both Barthes and Derrida, power and authority are always at work in acts of reception which seek to close down, fix or limit the meaning of a text. Derrida consistently asks 'what authorizes us' as readers to overlook the multiple possibilities for meaning in the language of a text, including where those possibilities appear contradictory or incoherent, suggesting that all attempts to determine a singular meaning for a text involve an appeal to authority: an appeal to interpretative conventions, which are always bound up with cultural and social norms. Similarly, in 'The Theory of the Text', Barthes (1981 [1973]: 33) argues that textual meaning is 'arrested' by the insistence on a set of 'authoritarian . . . rules' for reading, which are designed to produce a single meaning; by contrast, his semiological 'theory of the text extend[s] to infinity the freedoms of reading' (42).

As James Machor and Philip Goldstein (2001: 320) point out, most reception theory 'assumes that the conventions of interpretive practice limit the play of the signifier', as when Steven Mailloux (1984: 149) argues that 'the most important . . . constraints [on interpretation] are what I call "interpretive conventions": shared ways of making sense of reality'. Derrida and Barthes also see interpretative conventions precisely as constraints on interpretation imposed by cultural and social norms. As a result, they advocate a mode of reading which is ceaselessly attending to, and trying to subvert, the interpretative conventions which frame, limit and arrest meaning. For Derrida in particular, these are not just the local or institutional conventions discussed in Chapter Three, such as genres (Frow 2015), heteronomativity (Sedgwick 1994), or the norms of bourgeois taste (Bourdieu 1984), but the whole system of Western metaphysics, including our notions of truth and reality.

Both Derrida and Barthes regard reading as a productive practice: readers *make* meanings by playing (with) the possibilities of the text. In the discussion of his reading practice cited above, Derrida writes that 'the reading must always aim at a certain relationship, unperceived by the writer, between what he commands and what he does not command of the patterns of the language that he uses'. He goes on to say that 'this relationship is . . . a signifying structure that critical reading should *produce*' (1976: 158, emphasis original). For Derrida, then, critical reading entails taking responsibility for the ways in which one produces meaning out of a text. It also entails attending to the polysemic nature of linguistic meaning in an attempt to subvert or circumvent as far as possible the norms of classical reading which would make a reading practice complicit with Western metaphysics. As John Mowitt explains,

> by foregrounding the production of what he calls a 'signifying structure' . . . [Derrida's] reading makes available. . . a methodological space wherein the process of generating a text's meanings . . . can be examined – an examination that does not avoid the text, but which treats the text as a construct for which the [reader] is to some extent responsible.
>
> (1992: 95)

Once again, in Derrida and Barthes' model, meaning is not something inherent in the text, or waiting to be discovered behind or beneath the text. However, their understanding of 'meaning' differs from the other models we have looked at in this chapter because, following and extending Saussure, they shift the locus of the production of meaning from the communicative situation, or the dialogue between text and reader, to the dynamic play of language and signification itself. Because of the very nature of linguistic meaning, a writer 'might always say . . . more, less, or something other than what he *would mean*', and 'nothing initially authorizes us to overlook . . . [or] to impoverish' this excess of meaning (1976: 309). This model inverts the idea of the singular, stable text with multiple interpretations. Instead, we have an irreducibly multiple, polysemic text, which interpretations can only close down, fix and render singular. The question, as Gadamer put it in an exchange with Derrida, is 'where the multiplicity of meaning is really located' (1989: 115).

Like many of the critics we have looked at, especially in Chapter Two, Derrida and Barthes can be seen as advocating a particular theory and practice of reception, one which foregrounds polysemy and creative play, as part of a larger political project to democratize the reader. They can also be seen, however, as working to expose the mechanisms which underpin all acts of reception and response: the complex and dynamic functions of language and sign systems which produce, structure and enable all the different ways of reading we have explored in this book.

THE TEXT ITSELF

The four versions of language and meaning that we have surveyed in this chapter overlap to some extent, but ultimately draw on different conceptions of meaning and interpretation. What they all have in common, however, is the transformative insight that we cannot appeal to 'the text itself' to determine its meaning: that there is no final or stable distinction between a text and its interpretation. In the Conclusion, we will examine some of the implications of this insight for the ways in which we think about literary and textual analysis.

5

CONCLUSION

The emphasis upon the reception of texts as a product of reading practices has opened up a huge area for research beyond what was traditionally seen as the domain of literary studies. Drawing on historical and ethnographic methods, including book history and media history, reception scholars use a wide range of documents and methodologies to examine the ways in which texts survive and circulate, and the ways in which they are received, read, interpreted, rewritten, remixed and put to use by a variety of audiences. The basic insight that texts are a form of communication vastly extends the kinds of things that we do as literary scholars.

Throughout I have argued against a model of reception as a postscript or ancillary activity, separable from textual analysis proper. The theoretical insights and empirical findings of reception theory/studies transform the whole field of literary and textual analysis, by transforming the way in which we conceive of the text as object.

Reception, as I have conceived it in this book, has an ambiguous relationship to the field of literary and textual analysis. On the one hand, reception is simply coextensive with textual analysis: to analyse a text is to interpret it, and therefore requires us to take account, implicitly or explicitly, of the norms of interpretation which determine our own and others' reception of the text. On the other hand, the theoretical insights and empirical findings of reception challenge, undermine and transform many of the assumptions, definitions and practices of 'straight' literary criticism, including the very notion of the text.

All the theorists discussed in Chapter Four radically undermine, though in different ways, the possibility of drawing a clear distinction between a text's original meaning and the meanings it acquires in its reception. The Biblical scholar William John Lyons spells out the implications of this: 'The rejection of the distinction between "original" and "reception" means that we should openly acknowledge, without prejudice, that what we are all working on is reception history in some form' (Lyons 2015b: 6). Twenty years earlier, Charles Martindale (1997: 12) made the same point in relation to the discipline of Classical studies: 'reception and interpretation are closely intertwined', he wrote, making the case that present-day scholarly readings of Classical texts must be understood as just another part of the reception history of those texts, whose 'meaning and interpretation [are] inseparable from what readers and reading communities . . . have made of them' (8).

We cannot, then, analyse texts without reference to the acts of reception and systems of interpretation and signification within which those texts mean, and without an awareness that they may mean, and almost certainly have meant, something different to a different reader. The text is a particular kind of object, one which indeed has an 'unstable ontology', in Wai Chee Dimock's (1997: 1061) words, because it is co-produced by its receiver. To put it another way, reception permanently puts in question the boundaries of the text, since what is 'in' a text varies from reader to reader, context to context, protocol to protocol. Gayatri Spivak (2012 [1987]: 138) argues that only 'ethico-political strategic exclusions define a certain set of characteristics as an "inside" at a certain time', and that '"the text itself" [and] "the poem as such" . . . are such strategic definitions'.

Reflecting in 2008 on her own 1984 book *Reading the Romance*, Janice Radway (2008: 336) critiques the way her earlier analysis had relied on the categories of 'genre . . . reader, writer, text, author, and book'. All these categories, she finds, are in fact 'a function of the very idea of the book': 'the modern notion of "the book" as a discrete entity is an effect of particular printing, binding and circulation technologies, as well as of an entire juridical regime that coagulates social process and communication into intellectual property'.

Radway points out that practices of reading, structured by technologies, juridical regimes and norms of interpretation, produce 'the book' as what appears to us to be a self-contained and self-evident object of analysis. Reception, as I have conceived of it, involves thinking about all the factors which mediate and produce text–reader encounters, rather than relying on the self-evidence of the categories 'text' and 'reader'.

In 1971, Barthes compared the text–reader encounter to the experience of taking a walk:

> The reader of the Text might be compared to an idle subject . . . [who] strolls (this has happened to the author of these lines, and it is for this reason that he has come to an intense awareness of the Text) along a hillside at the bottom of which flows a *wadi* (I use the word to attest to a certain alienation); what he perceives is multiple, irreducible, issuing from heterogeneous, detached substances and levels: lights, colors, vegetation, heat, air, tenuous explosions of sound, tiny cries of birds, children's voices from the other side of the valley, paths, gestures, garments of inhabitants close by or very far away; all these incidents are half identifiable: they issue from known codes, but their combinative operation is unique, it grounds the stroll in a difference which cannot be repeated except *as difference*. This is what happens in the Text: . . . its reading is semelfactive [a linguistic term referring to verbs which 'express action as single in its occurrence without repetition or continuation' (Merriam-Webster)] . . . and yet entirely woven of quotations, reference, echoes . . . which traverse it through and through, in a vast stereophony.
>
> (1989b [1971]: 60)

The encounter with the text does not take place between a unitary text and a unitary reader. It is made up of multiple 'heterogeneous, detached substances and levels'. The 'book' is made up of many different languages, codes and references, each one decodable in different ways; it is also made of specific materials and technologies. The 'reader', too, is not single but multiple: she has various cultural competences, affective orientations, technical skills, bodily habits, imaginative dispositions, all of which may vary from day to day, from reading to reading. Also at play in the text–reader encounter are the multiple mediating factors we have looked at in this book: other readers, genres, intertexts and interpretative norms which frame and filter the relation between reader and text. All these factors combine in the 'semelfactive', unrepeatable experience of reading, which is unrepeatable because it consists of a unique *combination* of multiple factors.

Fifty years after Barthes, Rita Felski's work on attunement draws on actor–network theory to suggest a way of analysing and organizing the multiple and heterogeneous factors, or actors, that structure and enable encounters with artworks. Attunement, or the 'experience [of] an affinity [with a text or artwork] that is not fully conscious or deliberate', is the multidimensional experience of 'getting' a work in a way that is at once cognitive, sensory, affective, bodily and imaginative. However, the term 'attunement' also alludes to the way in which we become attuned to artworks via networks made up of 'countless things, experiences, events, spaces [which] come together . . . to bring [the artwork] into view'. 'Attunement', Felski writes, 'is a matter of personal receptiveness, but also of catalysts, sparks, triggers – all those human and non-human others that orient us toward certain works, in both predictable and unpredictable ways' (forthcoming).

As I indicated in the Introduction, acts of reception presuppose the existence of a system of communication which structures and enables the text–reader encounter. Barthes' valley provides a striking image of the complexity and multiplicity of that system of communication, while Felski's actor–network-inflected account of attunement shows in more detail how each act of reception is produced and structured by a unique, unrepeatable combination of multiple human and non-human actors whose interactions produce temporary networks of attunement and response. Each act of reception is unique and ultimately unpredictable, but it also depends on broader structures, networks and systems of response which precede and outlast the act of reception itself, and which can be traced and analysed.

In practice, we may never be able to account for all the factors which produce any given act of reading in their complexity and heterogeneity. But our critical approach can be structured by an awareness that all these factors exist, and that our own reading is historically situated, selective and *productive* or co-productive of the very object it purports to analyse. John Mowitt writes:

> By virtue of its ambivalent structure, the text insists that artifacts mean both what we make them mean and what others might make them mean if we stopped trying to represent their interests for them ... Thus, the 'plural' character of the text ... has less to do with some bland notion of multiple meanings, than with an empowerment that enables our constructions to be ceaselessly challenged – not merely contested at the level of conclusions, but subverted at the level of disciplinary legitimation.
>
> (1992: 45–46)

An approach to texts informed by reception, by an awareness of the multiplicity of possible interpretations and our own agency as co-producers of meanings, does not entail dissolving rigorous engagements with texts into individual, solipsistic, subjective opinions, or giving up on the possibility of intersubjective dialogue, disagreement and agreement about books: quite the reverse. As we have seen throughout this book, interpretation can never be solipsistic or purely individual: there is always a public and/or collective dimension to it.

Reception transforms literary studies by challenging us to produce readings with an awareness of the structures of legitimation which underpin our own reading and interpretative practices, and the ways in which these structures are bound up with broader institutional, cultural and discursive power structures. A reception-informed literary criticism finally means an approach to texts which does not seek to establish a single correct interpretation, but proceeds on the basis of an engagement with other possible readings and readers. It involves not just producing and defending interpretations of texts, but accounting for the interpretative strategies we have used, as well as a willingness to bring those strategies into dialogue with others', without necessarily seeking consensus. It entails both a generosity and an openness towards other positions, and a sharpening of our own interpretations in response to those of others.

BIBLIOGRAPHY

Abercrombie, Nicholas, and Longhurst, Brian (1998) *Audiences*, London, Thousand Oaks and New Delhi: Sage.

Abraham, Ibrahim (2015) 'High, Low and In-between: Reception History and the Sociology of Religion and Popular Music', in Emma England and William John Lyons, eds, *Reception History and Biblical Studies: Theory and Practice*, London: Bloomsbury, 241–253.

Adorno, Theodor (2001 [1938]) 'On the Fetish Character in Music and the Regression of Listening', in *The Culture Industry: Selected Essays on Mass Culture*, ed. J. M. Bernstein, London and New York: Routledge, 29–60.

Agger, Ben (1992) *Cultural Studies as Critical Theory*, London and Washington: The Falmer Press.

Ahmed, Sara (2010) *The Promise of Happiness*, Durham, NC: Duke University Press.

Allen, Graham (2000) *Intertextuality*, London: Routledge.

Allen, James Smith (1991) 'Reading the Novel', in *The Public Eye: A History of Reading in Modern France, 1800–1940*, Princeton: Princeton University Press, 275–302.

Allington, Daniel, and Benwell, Bethan (2012) 'Reading the Reading Experience', in Anouk Lang, ed., *From Codex to Hypertext: Reading at the Turn of the Twenty-First Century*, Amherst and Boston: University of Massachusetts Press, 217–234.

Althusser, Louis, and Balibar, Etienne (1970 [1968]) *Reading Capital*, trans. Ben Brewster, London: New Left Books.

Altieri, Charles (2003) *The Particulars of Rapture: An Aesthetics of the Affects*, Ithaca, NY, and London: Cornell University Press.

Anderson, Benedict (1983) *Imagined Communities: Reflections on the Origin and Spread of Nationalism*, London: Verso.

Armstrong, Paul B. (2013) *How Literature Plays with the Brain: The Neuroscience of Reading and Art*, Baltimore: Johns Hopkins University Press.

Arnold, Matthew (2006 [1869]) *Culture and Anarchy*, Oxford and New York: Oxford University Press.

Ashcroft, Bill, Griffiths, Gareth, and Tiffin, Helen (1989) *The Empire Writes Back: Theory and Practice in Post-Colonial Literatures*, London: Routledge.

Attridge, Derek (2004) *The Singularity of Literature*, London: Routledge.

AustLit (n.d) 'About', n.p. www.austlit.edu.au/austlit/page/5961893.

Bal, Mieke (1999) *Quoting Caravaggio: Contemporary Art, Preposterous History*, Chicago: University of Chicago Press.

Bal, Mieke (2006 [1991]) *Reading 'Rembrandt': Beyond the Word-Image Opposition*, Amsterdam: Amsterdam University Press.

Baldick, Chris (1983) *The Social Mission of English Criticism, 1848–1932*, Oxford: Clarendon Press.

Barker, Martin (1997) 'Taking the Extreme Case: Understanding a Fascist Fan of Judge Dredd', in Deborah Cartmell, I.Q. Hunter, Heidi Kaye and Imelda Whelehan, eds, *Trash Aesthetics: Popular Culture and Its Audience*, London and Chicago: Pluto Press, 14–30.

Barker, Martin (2003 [1997]) 'The Newson Report: A Case Study in "Common Sense"', in Will Brooker and Deborah Jermyn, eds, *The Audience Studies Reader*, London and New York: Routledge, 74–91.

Barker, Martin (2005) 'The Lord of the Rings and "Identification"', *European Journal of Communication*, 20(3): 353–378.

Barthes, Roland (1981 [1973]) 'Theory of the Text', trans. Ian McLeod, in Robert Young, ed., *Untying the Text: A Post-Structuralist Reader*, London: Routledge and Kegan Paul, 31–47.

Barthes, Roland (1989a [1970]) 'Writing Reading', in *The Rustle of Language*, trans. Richard Howard, Berkeley and Los Angeles, CA: University of California Press, 29–32.

Barthes, Roland (1989b [1971]) 'From Work to Text', in *The Rustle of Language*, trans. Richard Howard, Berkeley and Los Angeles, CA: University of California Press, 56–64.

Barthes, Roland (1989c [1968]) 'The Death of the Author', in *The Rustle of Language*, trans. Richard Howard, Berkeley and Los Angeles, CA: University of California Press, 49–55.

Barthes, Roland (1990 [1973]) *The Fashion System*, trans. Matthew Ward and Richard Howard, Berkeley, CA: University of California Press.

Bassnett, Susan (2014) *Translation*, London: Routledge.

Batstone, William W. (2006) 'Provocation: The Point of Reception Theory', in Charles Martindale and Richard F. Thomas, eds, *Classics and the Uses of Reception*, Oxford: Blackwell, 14–21.

Bauschatz, Cathleen (1980) 'Montaigne's Conception of Reading in the Context of Renaissance Poetics and Modern Criticism', in Susan Suleiman and Inge Crosman, eds, *The Reader in the Text: Essays on Audience and Interpretation*, Princeton, NJ: Princeton University Press, 264–292.

Bayard, Pierre (2008 [2007]) *How to Talk about Books You Haven't Read*, trans. Jeffrey Mehlman, London: Granta.

Beal, Peter (1993) 'Notions in Garrison: Seventeenth-Century Commonplace Books', in W. Speed Hill, ed., *New Ways of Looking at Old Texts: Papers of the Renaissance English Text Society, 1985–1996*, Binghamton, NY: Renaissance English Text Society, 131–149.

Belsey, Catherine (2002) *Critical Practice*, second edition, London: Routledge.

Bennett, Alanna (2015) 'What A "Racebent" Hermione Really Represents: The Beauty of the *Harry Potter* Character as a Woman of Color', *Buzzfeed*, n.p. www.buzzfeed.com/alannabennett/what-a-racebent-hermione-granger-really-represen-d2yp?utm_term=.yrqKm5NL8#.kf9pxrzVR.

Bennett, Tony (1983) 'Texts, Readers, Reading Formations', *Bulletin of the Midwest Modern Language Association*, 16(1): 3–17.

Bennett, Tony (1985) 'Texts in History: The Determination of Readings and their Texts', *Journal of the Midwest Modern Language Association*, 18(1): 1–16.

Benwell, Bethan, Procter, James, and Robinson, Gemma (2011) 'Not Reading *Brick Lane*', *New Formations*, 73: 90–116.

Best, Stephen, and Marcus, Sharon (2009) 'Surface Reading: An Introduction', *Representations*, 108(1): 1–21.

Bijker, Wiebe E., Hughes, Thomas P., and Pinch, Trevor (2012) *The Social Construction of Technological Systems*, anniversary edition, Cambridge, MA: MIT Press.

Bloom, Harold (1973) *The Anxiety of Influence: A Theory of Poetry*, Oxford and New York: Oxford University Press.

Bloom, Harold (1975) *A Map of Misreading*, Oxford and New York: Oxford University Press.

Boal, Augusto (1985 [1974]) *Theatre of the Oppressed*, trans. Charles A. and Maria-Odilia Leal McBride, New York: Theatre Communications Group.

Bobo, Jacqueline (1995) *Black Women as Cultural Readers*, New York: Columbia University Press.

Bobo, Jacqueline (2003) '*The Color Purple*: Black Women as Cultural Readers', in Will Brooker and Deborah Jermyn, eds, *The Audience Studies Reader*, London and New York: Routledge, 305–314.

Bode, Katherine (2012) *Reading by Numbers: Recalibrating the Literary Field*, London and New York: Anthem Press.

Bohannon, John (2014) 'Dance Your PhD Winner Announced', *Science*. www.sciencemag.org/news/2014/11/dance-your-phd-winner-announced.

Booth, Wayne (1961) *The Rhetoric of Fiction*, Chicago: University of Chicago Press.

Booth, Wayne (1988) *The Company We Keep: An Ethics of Fiction*, Berkeley, CA: University of California Press.

Bordwell, David (1979) 'The Art Cinema as a Mode of Film Practice', *Film Criticism*, 4(1): 56–63.

Breed, Brennan (2015) 'What Can a Text Do?: Reception History as an Ethology of the Bible Text', in Emma England and William John Lyons, eds, *Reception History and Biblical Studies: Theory and Practice*, London: Bloomsbury, 95–111.

Brewer, John (1996) 'Reconstructing the Reader: Prescriptions, Texts and Strategies in Anna Larpent's Reading', in James Raven, Helen Small and Naomi Tadmor, eds, *The Practice and Representation of Reading in England*, Cambridge, UK, and New York: Cambridge University Press, 226–245.

Brodhead, Richard H. (1986) *The School of Hawthorne*, New York: Oxford University Press.

Brooker, Will, and Jermyn, Deborah (2003), eds, *The Audience Studies Reader*, London and New York: Routledge.

Bourdieu, Pierre (1984 [1980]) *Distinction: A Social Critique of the Judgment of Taste*, trans. Richard Nice, London: Routledge.

Bury, Rhiannon (2008) 'Setting David Fisher straight: homophobia and heterosexism in "Six Feet Under" online fan culture', *Critical Studies in Television*, 3(2): 59–79.

Butler, Shane (2016) 'Homer's Deep', in Shane Butler, ed., *Deep Classics: Rethinking Classical Reception*, London and New York: Bloomsbury, 21–48.

Carey, James W. (1989) 'A Cultural Approach to Communication', in *Communication as Culture: Essays on Media and Society*, Winchester, MA, and London: Unwin Hyman, 13–36.

Carrington, André (2016) *Speculative Blackness: The Future of Race in Science Fiction*, Minneapolis, MN and London: University of Minnesota Press.

Carruthers, Jo, Knight, Mark, and Tate, Andrew (2014), eds, *Literature and the Bible: A Reader*, London: Routledge.

Cavallo, Guglielmo (1999) 'Between Volumen and Codex: Reading in the Roman World', in Guglielmo Cavallo and Roger Chartier, eds, *A History of Reading in the West*, trans. Lydia G. Cochrane, Amherst, MA: University of Massachusetts Press, 64–89.

Chakrabarty, Dipesh (2000) *Provincializing Europe: Postcolonial Thought and Historical Difference*, Princeton, NJ: Princeton University Press.

Chambers, Aidan (1977) 'The Reader in the Book: Notes from Work in Progress', *Signal Approaches to Children's Books*, 23: 64–87.

Chew, Dalglish (2015) 'We Have Never Been Critical', *Stanford Arcade*. http://arcade.stanford.edu/content/we-have-never-been-critical.

Christie, Ian (2012), ed., *Audiences: Defining and Researching Screen Entertainment Reception,* Amsterdam: Amsterdam University Press.

Clinton, Katie, Jenkins, Henry, and McWilliams, Jenna (2013) 'New Literacies in an Age of Participatory Culture', in Henry Jenkins and Wyn Kelley, eds, *Reading in a Participatory Culture: Remixing Moby-Dick in the English Classroom*, New York and Berkeley, CA: Teachers College Press and the National Writing Project, 3–35.

Cohen, Margaret (1999) *The Sentimental Education of the Novel*, Princeton, NJ: Princeton University Press.

Colebrook, Claire (2014 [2010]) 'The Linguistic Turn in Continental Philosophy', in Alan D. Schrift, ed., *The History of Continental Philosophy, vol. 6, Poststructuralism and Critical Theory's Second Generation*, London and New York: Routledge, 279–309.

Conroy, Pat (2010) *My Reading Life*, New York: Doubleday.

Conte, Gian Biagio (1986 [1980]) *The Rhetoric of Imitation*, ed. and trans. C. Segal, Ithaca, NY, and London: Cornell University Press.

Coppa, Francesca (2008) 'Women, *Star Trek*, and the early development of fannish vidding', *Transformative Works and Cultures*, 1: n.p. http://journal.transformativeworks.org/index.php/twc/article/view/44. DOI 10.3983/twc.2008.0044.

Cornelius, Janet Duitsman (1991) *When I Can Read My Title Clear: Literacy, Slavery and Religion in the Antebellum South*, Columbia, SC: University of South Carolina Press.

Corner, John (1991) 'Meaning, Genre and Context: the Problematics of "Public Knowledge" in the New Audience Studies', in James Curran and Michael Gurevitch, eds, *Mass Media and Society*, London: Edward Arnold, 267–284.

Cottom, Daniel (2005) *Why Education Is Useless*, Philadelphia, PA: University of Pennsylvania Press.

Cowie, Elizabeth (1997 [1984]) 'Fantasia', in *Representing the Woman: Cinema and Psychoanalysis*, Basingstoke: Macmillan, 123–165.

Crane, Mary Thomas (2009) 'Surface, Depth, and the Spatial Imaginary: A Cognitive Reading of The Political Unconscious', *Representations*, 108(1): 76–97.

Culler, Jonathan D. (1975) *Structuralist Poetics: Structuralism, Linguistics and the Study of Literature*, London: Routledge and Kegan Paul.

Culler, Jonathan D. (1981 [1977]) *The Pursuit of Signs: Semiotics, Literature, Deconstruction*, London: Routledge and Kegan Paul.

Culler, Jonathan D. (1997) *Literature: A Very Short Introduction*, Oxford: Oxford University Press.

Dale, Leigh (1997) *The English Men: Professing Literature in Australian Universities*, Toowoomba, QLD: Association for the Study of Australian Literature.

Dale, Leigh (2013) 'Reading English', *Australian Literary Studies*, 28(1/2): 1–14.

Daly, Mary (1973) *Beyond God the Father: Toward a Philosophy of Women's Liberation*, Boston, MA: Beacon.

D'Arcens, Louise (2016) 'Introduction: medievalism: scope and complexity', in Louise D'Arcens, ed., *The Cambridge Companion to Medievalism*, Cambridge, UK: Cambridge University Press, 1–13.

Darnton, Robert (1982) 'What is the History of Books?', *Daedalus*, 111(3): 65–83.

Darnton, Robert (1984) *The Great Cat Massacre and Other Episodes in French Cultural History*, New York: Basic Books.

Darnton, Robert (1986) 'First Steps Towards a History of Reading', *Australian Journal of French Studies*, 23: 5–30.

Darnton, Robert (2000) 'Extraordinary Commonplaces', in *New York Review of Books*, 82–87.

Davidson, John (1994) 'Sophocles and the *Odyssey*', *Mnemosyne*, 47(3): 375–379.

Davis, Helen (2004) *Understanding Stuart Hall*, London: Sage.

Davis, Todd F., and Womack, Kenneth (2002) *Formalist Criticism and Reader-Response Theory*, Transitions, Basingstoke and New York: Palgrave Macmillan.

de Certeau, Michel (1984 [1980]) *The Practice of Everyday Life*, trans. Steven Randall, Berkeley, CA: University of California Press.

de Certeau, Michel (2003 [1980]) 'The Practice of Everyday Life (Extract)', in Will Brooker and Deborah Jermyn, eds, *The Audience Studies Reader*, London and New York: Routledge, 105–111.

Derrida, Jacques (2001 [1966]) 'Structure, Sign and Play in the Human Sciences', in *Writing and Difference*, trans. Alan Bass, London and New York: Routledge, 351–370.

Derrida, Jacques (1976 [1967]) *Of Grammatology*, trans. Gayatri Chakravorty Spivak, Baltimore: Johns Hopkins University Press.

Derrida, Jacques (1979) 'Living on: Border-Lines', in Harold Bloom, Paul de Man, Jacques Derrida, Geoffrey H. Hartman, and J. Hillis Miller, *Deconstruction and Criticism*, London and Henley: Routledge Kegan Paul, 75–176.

Derrida, Jacques (1982 [1971]) 'Signature – Event – Context', in *Margins of Philosophy*, trans. Alan Bass, Brighton: Harvester Press, 307–330.

Derrida, Jacques (2004 [1968]) 'Plato's Pharmacy', in *Disseminations*, trans. Barbara Johnson, London: Continuum, 66–186.

Derrida, Jacques, and Gadamer, Hans-Georg (1989) *Dialogue and Deconstruction: The Gadamer–Derrida Encounter*, ed. Diane P. Michelfelder and Richard E. Palmer, Albany, NY: State University of New York Press.

Dewey, John (1916) *Democracy and Education*, New York: Macmillan.

Diawara, Manthia (1988) 'Black Spectatorship: Problems of Identification and Resistance', *Screen*, 29(4): 66–79.

Dilling-Hansen, Lise (2015) 'Affective Fan Experiences of Lady Gaga', *Transformative Works and Cultures*, 20: n.p. http://journal.transformative works.org/index.php/twc/article/view/662/543 DOI: http://dx.doi.org/10.3983/twc.2015.0662.

Dimock, Wai Chee (1997) 'A Theory of Resonance', *PMLA*, 112(5): 1060–1071.

Dinshaw, Carolyn (1999) *Getting Medieval: Sexualities and Communities, Pre- and Post-Modern*, Durham, NC: Duke University Press.

Dobinson, Cheryl, and Young, Kevin (2000) 'Popular Cinema and Lesbian Interpretative Strategies', *Journal of Homosexuality*, 40(2): 97–122.

Dorsch, T. S. (1965) *Classical Literary Criticism*, Harmondsworth: Penguin.

Doty, Alexander (1993) *Making It Perfectly Queer: Interpreting Mass Culture*, Minneapolis, MN: University of Minnesota Press.

Douglas, Anne (1980) 'Soft-Porn Culture', *New Republic*, 30: 25–29.

Dowling, Linda (1996) *The Vulgarization of Art: The Victorians and Aesthetic Democracy*, Charlottesville: University Press of Virginia.

Dryden, John (1964 [1668]) 'Defence of an Essay', in *Of Dramatick Poesie: An Essay*, ed. James T. Boulton, London: Oxford University Press, 125–147.

Dubrow, Heather (1982) *Genre*, London: Methuen.

Dyer, Richard (1997) *White: Essays on Race and Culture*, London and New York: Routledge.

Eagleton, Terry (1981) *Walter Benjamin, or, Towards a Revolutionary Criticism*, London: Verso.

Eagleton, Terry (1983) *Literary Theory: An Introduction*, Oxford: Blackwell.

Eco, Umberto (1976) *A Theory of Semiotics*, Bloomington and London: Indiana University Press.

Eco, Umberto (1979a [1959]) 'The Poetics of the Open Work', in *The Role of the Reader: Explorations in the Semiotics of Texts*, Bloomington and London: Indiana University Press, 47–66.

Eco, Umberto (1979b) 'Introduction: The Role of the Reader', in *The Role of the Reader: Explorations in the Semiotics of Texts*, Bloomington and London: Indiana University Press, 1–43.

Eco, Umberto (1986) 'Casablanca: Cult Movies and Intertextual Collage', in *Travels in Hyperreality*, New York: Harcourt and Brace.

Eco, Umberto (1992) 'Overinterpreting Texts', in Umberto Eco, with Richard Rory, Jonathan Culler and Christine Brooke-Rose, *Interpretation and Overinterpretation*, ed. Stefan Collini, Cambridge: UK, Cambridge University Press, 45–66.

Edwards, Derek, and Stokoe, Elizabeth (2004) 'Discursive Psychology, Focus Group Interviews, and Participants' Categories', *British Journal of Developmental Psychology*, 22(4): 499–507.

Egan, Kate, and Barker, Martin (2008) 'The Books, the DVDs, the Extras, and Their Lovers', in Martin Barker and Ernest Mathijs, eds, *Watching the Lord of the Rings: Tolkien's World Audiences*, Peter Lang Publishing, New York, 83–102.

Eisenstein, Elizabeth (1979) *The Printing Press as an Agent of Change*, Cambridge, UK: Cambridge University Press.

Eliot, Simon, and Rose, Jonathan (2009) *A Companion to the History of the Book*, Oxford: Wiley-Blackwood.

Eliot, T. S. (1975 [1919]) 'Tradition and the Individual Talent', in *Selected Prose of T. S. Eliot*, ed. Frank Kermode, London: Faber, 37–44.

Ellis, Samantha (2014) *How to be a Heroine: Or, What I've Learned from Reading Too Much*, London: Chatto & Windus.

Engelsing, Rolf (1974) *Der Bürger als Leser: Lesergeschichte in Deutschland 1500–1800*, Stuttgart: Metzler.

England, Emma (2015) 'Digital Humanities and Reception History; or the Joys and Horrors of Databases', in Emma England and William John Lyons, eds, *Reception History and Biblical Studies: Theory and Practice*, London: Bloomsbury, 169–184.

Erlich, Victor (1980) *Russian Formalism*, fourth edition, The Hague: Mouton Publishers.

Evans, Robert (2014) *Reception History, Tradition and Biblical Interpretation: Gadamer and Jauss in Current Practice*, London: Bloomsbury.

Fabb, Nigel (1988) 'Saussure and Literary Theory: From the Perspective of Linguistics', *Critical Quarterly*, 30(2): 58–72.

Federico, Annette (2016) *Engagements with Close Reading*, London: Routledge.

Felski, Rita (2008) *Uses of Literature*, Malden, MA, and Oxford: Blackwell.

Felski, Rita (2011) 'Context Stinks!', *New Literary History*, 42(4): 573–591.

Felski, Rita (2015) *The Limits of Critique*, Chicago: University of Chicago Press.

Felski, Rita (forthcoming) 'Attunement', n.p.

Ferguson, Kirby (2011) 'Everything Is a Remix', Webseries. http://everything isaremix.info/watch-the-series/.

Fetterley, Judith (1978) *The Resisting Reader: A Feminist Approach to American Fiction*, Bloomington: Indiana University Press.

Finkelstein, David, and McCleery, Alastair (2002) *The Book History Reader*, London and New York: Routledge.

Finkelstein, David, and McCleery, Alastair (2012) *An Introduction to Book History*, second edition, London and New York: Routledge.

Fish, Stanley Eugene (1978) 'Normal Circumstances, Literal Language, Direct Speech Acts, the Ordinary, the Everyday, the Obvious, What Goes without Saying, and Other Special Cases', *Critical Inquiry*, 4(4): 625–644.

Fish, Stanley Eugene (1980a) 'What Makes An Interpretation Acceptable?', in *Is There a Text in This Class? The Authority of Interpretive Communities*, Princeton, NJ: Harvard University Press, 338–355.

Fish, Stanley Eugene (1980b [1970]) 'Literature in the Reader: Affective Stylistics', in Jane Tompkins, ed., *Reader-Response Criticism: From Formalism to Post-Structuralism*, Baltimore: Johns Hopkins University Press.

Fiske, John (1989a) *Understanding Popular Culture*, London: Routledge.

Fiske, John (1989b) 'Moments of Television: Neither the Text nor the Audience', in Ellen Seiter, Hans Borchers, Gabriele Kreutzner, and Eva-Maria Warth, eds, *Remote Control: Television, Audiences and Cultural Power*, London and New York: Routledge, 56–75.

Flint, Kate (1993) *The Woman Reader, 1837–1914*, Oxford: Clarendon Press.

Fortier, Martin (2002) *Theory/Theatre: An Introduction*, second edition, London and New York: Routledge.

Foucault, Michel (2001 [1969]) *The Archaeology of Knowledge*, trans. A. M. Sheridan Smith, London and New York: Routledge.

Fowler, Don (2000 [1997]) 'On the Shoulders of Giants: Intertextuality and Classical Studies', in *Roman Constructions: Readings in Postmodern Latin*, Oxford: Oxford University Press, 115–137.

Freund, Elizabeth (1987) *The Return of the Reader: Reader-Response Criticism*, London: Methuen.

Frow, John (1982) 'The Literary Frame', *Journal of Aesthetic Education*, 16(2): 25–30.

Frow, John (2008) 'Afterlives: Texts as Usage', *Reception* 1: 1–23.

Frow, John (2015) *Genre*, Abingdon and New York: Routledge.

Gadamer, Hans-Georg (1989) 'Reply to Jacques Derrida', *Dialogue and Deconstruction: The Gadamer-Derrida Encounter*, ed, Diane P. Michelfelder and Richard E. Palmer, Albany, NY: State University of New York Press, 55–57.

Gadamer, Hans-Georg (2004 [1960]) *Truth and Method*, trans. J. Weinsheimer and D. G. Marshall, second revised English edition, London and New York: Continuum.

Gaipa, Mark, and Scholes, Robert (1993) 'On the Very Idea of a Literal Meaning', in Reed Way Dasenbrock, ed., *Literary Theory After Davidson*, University Park, PA: Pennsylvania State University Press, 160–179.

Garber, Marjorie (2003) 'The Jane Austen Syndrome', in *Quotation Marks*, London and New York: Routledge, 199–210.

Garvey, Ellen Gruber (2013) *Writing with Scissors: American Scrapbooks from the Civil War to the Harlem Renaissance*, New York: Oxford University Press.

Gates, Henry Louis, Jr (1989) *The Signifying Monkey: A Theory of African-American Literary Criticism*, New York: Oxford University Press.

Gates, Henry Louis, Jr (1992a [1985]) 'Writing, "Race", and the Difference it Makes', in *Loose Canons: Notes on the Culture Wars*, Oxford: Oxford University Press, 43–71.

Gates, Henry Louis, Jr (1992b [1990]) 'The Master's Pieces: On Canon Formation and the African-American Tradition', in *Loose Canons: Notes on the Culture Wars*, New York and Oxford: Oxford University Press, 17–42.

Gates, Henry Louis, Jr (2003) 'Literary Theory and the Black Tradition', in James Machor and Philip Goldstein, eds, *Reception Study: From Literary Theory to Cultural Studies*, London and New York: Routledge, 105–117.

Gaunt, Simon, and Kay, Sarah (2008) 'Introduction', in Simon Gaunt and Sarah Kay, eds, *The Cambridge Companion to Medieval French Literature*, Cambridge, UK: Cambridge University Press, 1–18.

Gavins, Joanna (2007) *Text World Theory: An Introduction*, Edinburgh: Edinburgh University Press.

Genette, Gérard (1997a [1982]) *Palimpsests: Literature in the Second Degree,* trans. Channa Newman and Claude Doubinsky, Stages 8, Lincoln and London: University of Nebraska Press.

Genette, Gérard (1997b [1987]) *Paratexts: Threshholds of Interpretation*, trans. Jane E. Lewin, Cambridge, UK: Cambridge University Press.

Ghosh, Anindita (2006) *Power in Print: Popular Publishing and the Politics of Language and Culture in a Colonial Society, 1778–1905*, Oxford: Oxford University Press.

Gibson, Walter (1980 [1950]) 'Authors, Speakers, Readers and Mock Readers', in Jane Tompkins, ed., *Reader-Response Criticism: From Formalism to Post-Structuralism*, Baltimore and London: Johns Hopkins University Press, 1–6.

Gillespie, Marie (2003 [1995]) 'Television, Ethnicity and Cultural Change', in Will Brooker and Deborah Jermyn, eds, *The Audience Studies Reader*, London and New York: Routledge, 315–321.

Ginzburg, Carlo (1980 [1976]) *The Cheese and the Worms: The Cosmos of a Sixteenth-Century Miller*, trans. John and Anne Tedeschi, London: Routledge and Kegan Paul.

Gitelman, Lisa (2008) *Always Already New: Media, History and the Data of Culture*, Cambridge, MA: Massachusetts Institute of Technology Press.

Goffman, Erving (1974) *Frame Analysis: An Essay on the Organization of Experience*, Cambridge, MA: Harvard University Press.

Gray, Jonathan (2003) 'New Audiences, New Textualities: Anti-Fans and Non-Fans', *International Journal of Cultural Studies*, 6(1): 64–81.

Gray, Jonathan (2006) *Watching with The Simpsons: Television, Parody, and Intertextuality*, New York: Routledge.

Greetham, David (2009) 'What Is Textual Scholarship?', in Simon Eliot and Jonathan Rose, eds, *A Companion to the History of the Book*, Oxford: Wiley-Blackwell, 21–32.

Griffiths, Jane (2014) 'Editorial Glossing and Reader Resistance in a Copy of Robert Crowley's *Piers Plowman*', in Carol Meale and Derek Pearsall, eds, *The Makers and Users of Medieval Books*, Cambridge and Rochester, NY: Boydell & Brewer, 202–214.

Griswold, Charles L. (2016) 'Plato on Rhetoric and Poetry', in Edward N. Zalta, ed., *The Stanford Encyclopedia of Philosophy*, Stanford, CA: Metaphysics Research Lab. https://plato.stanford.edu/archives/fall2016/entries/plato-rhetoric/.

Grossman, Lev (2010) 'Infinite Jest', *Time*. http://entertainment.time.com/2005/10/16/all-time-100-novels/slide/infinite-jest-1996-by-david-foster-wallace/.

Guillory, John (1993) *Cultural Capital: The Problem of Literary Canon Formation*, Chicago: University of Chicago Press.

Guillory, John (2000) 'The Ethical Practice of Modernity: The Example of Reading', in Marjorie B. Garber, Beatrice Hanssen and Rebecca L. Walkowitz, eds, *The Turn to Ethics*, Abingdon: Psychology Press, Taylor and Francis, 29–47.

Güthenke, Constanze (2014) '"Enthusiasm dwells only in specialization": Classical Philology and Disciplinarity in Nineteenth-Century Germany', in Benjamin A. Elman and Sheldon Pollock, eds, *World Philology*, Massachusetts: Harvard University Press, 304–338.

Hall, Stuart (1980 [1973]) 'Encoding/Decoding', in Stuart Hall, Dorothy Hobson, Andrew Lowe and Paul Willis, eds, *Culture, Media, Language: Working Papers in Cultural Studies, 1972–1979*, London: Hutchinson, 128–139.

Hawkes, Terence (1992) *Meaning by Shakespeare*, London and New York: Routledge.

Hawthorne, Nathaniel (1987 [1855]) 'Letter to William D. Ticknor, January 19, 1855', *The Letters*, in Thomas Woodson, L. Neal Smith and Norman Holmes Pearson, eds, Vol. 17, Columbus, OH: Ohio State University Press, 304–305.

Hebdige, Dick (1979) *Subculture: The Meaning of Style*, London: Methuen.

Hélias, Pierre Jakez (1995 [1975]) *Le cheval d'orgeuil: mémoires d'un Breton du pays bigouden*, Paris, France: Plon.

Hensley, Nathan K. (2015) 'In this Dawn to be Alive: Versions of the "Postcritical", 1999, 2015', *Stanford Arcade*, n.p. http://arcade.stanford.edu/content/dawn-be-alive-versions-"postcritical"-1999-2015.

Hexter, Ralph (1996) 'Baswell, Virgil in Medieval England: Figuring the Aeneid from the Twelfth Century to Chaucer', *The Medieval Review*: n.p. https://scholarworks.iu.edu/journals/index.php/tmr/article/view/14384.

Hills, Matt (2002) *Fan Cultures*, London and New York: Routledge.

Hills, Matt (2013) *New Dimensions of Dr Who: Adventures in Space, Time and Television*, London and New York: I. B. Tauris.

Hinds, Stephen (1998) *Allusion and Intertext: Dynamics of Appropriation in Roman Poetry*, Cambridge, UK: Cambridge University Press.

Hirsch, E. D. (1967) *Validity in Interpretation*, New Haven: Yale University Press.

Hochman, Barbara (2011) *'Uncle Tom's Cabin' and the Reading Revolution: Race, Literacy, Childhood, and Fiction, 1851–1911*, Amherst, MA: University of Massachusetts Press.

Hoggart, Richard (1958 [1957]) *The Uses of Literacy: Aspects of Working-Class Life with Special Reference to Publications and Entertainments*, Harmondsworth: Penguin.

Holland, Norman (1968) *The Dynamics of Literary Response*, New York: Norton.

Holub, Robert (1984) *Reception Theory: A Critical Introduction*, London, New York: Methuen.

hooks, bell (1984) *Feminist Theory: From Margin to Center*, Cambridge, MA: South End Press.

hooks, bell (1992) `The Oppositional Gaze: Black Female Spectators', *Black Looks: Race and Representation*, Boston, MA: South End Press, 115–131.

Hopkins, David, and Martindale, Charles (2012), eds, *The Oxford History of Classical Reception in English Literature Volume 3: 1660–1790*, Oxford: Oxford University Press.

Horáček, Josef (2014) 'Pedantry and Play: The Zukofsky Catullus', *Comparative Literature Studies*, 51(1): 106–131.

Howard, Susan M. (1994) 'What Would the Neighbors Say? Social Values in Ramsay Street', *Youth Studies Australia*, 13(4): 13–19.

Howard-Hill, Trevor H. (2009) 'Why Bibliography Matters', in Simon Eliot and Jonathan Rose, eds, *A Companion to the History of the Book*, Oxford: Wiley-Blackwell, 9–20.

Hungerford, Amy (2016) 'Not reading DFW', in *Making Literature Now*, Stanford: Stanford University Press, 141–169.

Hutcheon, Linda (2006) *A Theory of Adaptation*, London and New York: Routledge.

Huyssen, Andreas (1986) 'Mass Culture as Woman: Modernism's Other', in Tania Modleski, ed., *Studies in Entertainment: Critical Approaches to Mass Culture*, Bloomington, IN: Indiana University Press, 188–207.

Ingarden, Roman (1974 [1931]) *The Literary Work of Art*, trans. George G. Grabowicz, Evanston, IL: Northwestern University Press.

Iser, Wolfgang (1972) 'The Reading Process: A Phenomenological Approach', *New Literary History*, 3(2): 279–299.

Iser, Wolfgang (1974 [1972]) *The Implied Reader: Patterns of Communication in Prose Fiction from Bunyan to Beckett*, Baltimore, MD: Johns Hopkins University Press.

Iser, Wolfgang (1978 [1976]) *The Act of Reading: A Theory of Aesthetic Response*, Baltimore, MD: Johns Hopkins University Press.

Iser, Wolfgang (1980) 'Interaction between Text and Reader', in Susan Suleiman and Inge Crosman, eds, *The Reader in the Text: Essays on Audience and Interpretation*, Princeton, NJ: Princeton University Press, 106–119.

Ito, Mizuka (2011) 'Machinima in a Fanvid Ecology', *Journal of Visual Culture*, 10(1): 51–54.

Jackson, H. J. (2001) *Marginalia: Readers Writing in Books*, New Haven, CT: Yale University Press.

Jackson, Leon (2010) 'The Talking Book and the Talking Book Historian: African American Cultures of Print – The State of the Discipline', *Book History*, 13: 251–308.

Jakobson, Roman (1987 [1958: 62–94]) 'Linguistics and Poetics' in Krystyna Pomorska and Stephen Rudy, eds, *Language and Literature*, Cambridge, MA and London: Belknap.

Jameson, Fredric (1981) *The Political Unconscious: Narrative as a Socially Symbolic Act*, Ithaca, NY: Cornell University Press.

Jardine, Lisa, and Grafton, Anthony (1990) '"Studied for Action": How Gabriel Harvey Read His Livy', *Past and Present*, 129: 30–78.

Jauss, Hans Robert (1982) *Toward an Aesthetic of Reception*, trans. Timothy Bahti, Minneapolis, MN: Minnesota Press.

Jauss, Hans Robert (2001 [1985]) 'The Identity of the Poetic Text in the Changing Horizon of Understanding', in James Machor and Philip Goldstein, eds, *Reception Study: From Literary Theory to Cultural Studies*, London and New York, NY: Routledge, 7–28.

Jenkins, Henry (1992) *Textual Poachers: Television Fans and Participatory Culture*, New York, NY: Routledge.

Jenkins, Henry (2000) 'Reception Theory and Audience Research: The Mystery of the Vampire's Kiss', in Christine Gledhill and Linda Williams, eds, *Reinventing Film Studies*, New York, NY, and London: Bloomsbury, 165–183.

Jenkyns, Richard (1989) 'Virgil and Arcadia', *Journal of Roman Studies*, 79: 26–39.

Johnson, William A. (2010) *Readers and Reading Culture in the High Roman Empire: A Study of Elite Communities*, Oxford: Oxford University Press.

Johnston, Freya (2012) 'Samuel Johnson's Classicism', in David Hopkins and Charles Martindale, eds, *The Oxford History of Classical Reception in English* Literature, Oxford: Oxford University Press, 615–647.

Kallendorf, Craig (1984) 'Maffeo Vegio's Book XIII and the *Aeneid* of Early Italian Humanism', in Anne Reynolds, ed., *The Classical Continuum in Italian Thought and Letters*, Altro Polo, Sydney: Frederick May Foundation for Italian Studies, 47–56.

Kirkpatrick, Ellen (2014) 'Toward New Horizons: Cosplay (Re)imagined Through the Superhero Genre, Authenticity, and Transformation', *Transformative Works and Cultures*, 18: n.p. http://journal.trans formativeworks.org/index.php/twc/article/view/613 DOI: http://dx. doi.org/10.3983/twc.2015.0613.

Kittler, Friedrich (1990 [1985]) *Discourse Networks 1800/1900*, trans. Michael Matteer with Chris Cullens, Stanford, CA: Stanford University Press.

Klin, Ami, Jones, Warren, Schultz, Robert, Volkmar, Fred, and Cohen, Donald (2002) 'Defining and Quantifying the Social Phenotype in Autism', *The American Journal of Psychiatry*, 159(6): 895–908.

Kline, Daniel (2016) 'Participatory Medievalism, Role-Playing, and Digital Gaming', in Louise D'Arcens, ed., *The Cambridge Companion to Medievalism*, Cambridge, UK: Cambridge University Press, 60–74.

Kokkola, Lydia (2011) 'Sparkling Vampires: Valorizing Self-Harming Behavior in Stephenie Meyer's *Twilight* Series', *Bookbird*, 49(3): 33–46.

Kolodny, Annette (1985 [1980]) 'Dancing Through the Minefield: Some Observations on the Theory, Practice and Politics of Feminist Literary Criticism', in Elaine Showalter, ed., *The New Feminist Criticism: Essays on Women, Literature and Theory*, New York, NY: Pantheon Books, 144–167.

Kristeva, Julia (1980 [1968]: 36–63) 'The Bounded Text', *Desire in Language*, in Leon Samuel Roudiez, ed., trans. Thomas Gora, Alice Jardine and Leon Samuel Roudiez, Oxford: Basil Blackwell.

Kuhn, Annette (1984) 'Women's Genres', *Screen*, 25(1): 18–28.

Lam, May (1986) *Reading the Sweet Dream: Adolescent Girls and Romance Fiction*, dissertation, M. Ed., University of Melbourne.

Lamond, Julieanne (2014) 'Forgotten Books and Local Readers: Popular Fiction in the Library at the Turn of the Twentieth Century', *Australian Literary Studies*, 29(3): 87–100.

Lang, Anouk (2009) '"Enthralling but at the Same Time Disturbing": Challenging the Readers of *Small Island*', *The Journal of Commonwealth Literature*, 44(2): 123–140.

Lang, Anouk (2012) 'Introduction', in Anouk Lang, ed., *From Codex to Hypertext: Reading at the Turn of the Twenty-first Century*, Amherst and Boston, MA: University of Massachusetts Press, 1–27.

Le Guin, Ursula K. (1992 [1987]) 'Where Do You Get Your Ideas From?', in *Dancing at the Edge of the World: Thoughts on Words, Women, Places*, London: Paladin, 192–200.

Leavis, F. R. (1930) *Mass Civilisation and Minority Culture*, Cambridge: Cambridge University Press.

Leavis, F. R. (1948) *The Great Tradition*, London: Chatto & Windus.

Leavis, Q. D. (2011 [1932]), 'The Book Market', in Shafqat Towheed, Rosalind Crone, and Katie Halsey, eds, *The History of Reading: A Reader*, London and New York, NY: Routledge, 13–22.

Lefevere, André (1992) *Translation, Rewriting and the Manipulation of Literary Fame*, London and New York, NY: Routledge.

Leff, Michael (1997) 'The Idea of Rhetoric as Interpretive Practice: A Humanist's Response to Gaonkar', in Alan Gross and William Keith, eds, *Rhetorical Hermeneutics: Invention and Interpretation in the Age of Science*, Albany, NY: State University of New York Press, 89–100.

Levine, Lawrence A. (1990 [1988]) *Highbrow/Lowbrow: The Emergence of Cultural Hierarchy in America*, Cambridge, MA: Harvard University Press.

Lieb, Michael, Mason, Emma, and Roberts, Jonathan (2011), eds, *The Oxford Handbook of the History of the Reception of the Bible*, Oxford: Oxford University Press.

Littau, Karin (2006) *Theories of Reading: Books, Bodies and Bibliomania*, Cambridge, UK: Polity Press.

Long, Elizabeth (1993) 'Textual Interpretation as Collective Action', in Jonathan Boyarin, ed., *The Ethnography of Reading*, Berkeley, CA: University of California Press, 180–212.

Long, Elizabeth (2003) *Book Clubs: Women and the Uses of Reading in Everyday Life*, Chicago, IL: University of Chicago Press.

Longhurst, Derek (1982) '"Not for All Time, but for an Age": An Approach to Shakespeare Studies', in Peter Widdowson, ed., *Re-Reading English*, London and New York, NY: Methuen, 150–163.

Loomba, Ania (2005) *Colonialism/Postcolonialism*, second edition, London and New York, NY: Routledge.

Lothian, Alexis (2017) 'Sex, Utopia, and the Queer Temporalities of Fannish Love', in Jonathan Gray, Cornel Sandvoss and C. Lee Harrington, eds, *Fandom: Identities and Communities in a Mediated World*, revised second edition, New York, NY: New York University Press, 238–252.

Lynch, Deirdre Shauna (2014) *Loving Literature: A Cultural History*, Chicago, IL, and London: University of Chicago Press.

Lyons, William John (2015a) '"Time to cut him down to size?" A Critical Examination of Depeche Mode's Alternative "John of Patmos"', in Emma England and William John Lyons, eds, *Reception History and Biblical Studies: Theory and Practice*, London: Bloomsbury, 219–230.

Lyons, William John (2015b) 'Some Thoughts on Defining Reception History and the Future of Biblical Studies', *The Bible and Interpretation.* www.bibleinterp.com/articles/2015/08/lyo398005.shtml.

Macherey, Pierre (1978 [1966]) *A Theory of Literary Production*, trans. Geoffrey Wall, London, Henley and Boston, MA: Routledge and Kegan Paul.

Machor, James L. (2011) *Reading Fiction in Antebellum America: Informed Response and Reception Histories 1820–1865*, Baltimore, MD: Johns Hopkins University Press.

Machor, James, and Goldstein, Philip (2001), eds, *Reception Study: From Literary Theory to Cultural Studies*, London and New York, NY: Routledge.

McClary, Susan (1994) 'Constructions of Subjectivity in Schubert's Music', in Philip Brett, Elizabeth Wood, and Gary C. Thomas, eds, *Queering the Pitch: The New Gay and Lesbian Musicology*, London and New York, NY: Routledge, 205–235.

McGann, Jerome J. (1983) *A Critique of Modern Textual Criticism*, Chicago, IL: University of Chicago Press.

McGann, Jerome J. (1991) *The Textual Condition*, Princeton, NJ: Princeton University Press.

McGowan, Todd (2004) 'Lost on Mulholland Drive: Navigating David Lynch's Panegyric to Hollywood', *Cinema Journal*, 43(2): 67–89.

McHenry, Elizabeth (2011 [2007]) '"An Association of Kindred Spirits": Black Readers and Their Reading Rooms', in Shafqat Towheed, Rosalind Crone and Katie Halsey, eds, *The History of Reading: A Reader*, London and New York, NY: Routledge, 310–322.

Macintosh, Fiona, Kenwood, Claire, and Wrobel, Tom (2016) *Medea: A Performance History*, Oxford: Archive of the Performance of Greek and Roman Drama.

McKenzie, D. F. (1984) 'The Sociology of a Text: Orality, Literacy and Print in Early New Zealand', *The Library*, 6(4): 333–365.

McLaughlin, Thomas A. (1996) *Street Smarts and Critical Theory: Listening to the Vernacular*, Madison, WI: University of Wisconsin Press.

McLuhan, Marshall (1964) *The Gutenberg Galaxy: The Making of Typographic Man*, London: Routledge and Kegan Paul.

Mailloux, Steven (1984) *Interpretive Conventions: The Reader in the Study of American Fiction*, Ithaca, NY: Cornell University Press.

Manguel, Alberto (1996) *A History of Reading*, New York, NY: Viking.

Marcus, Sharon (2013) 'The Theatrical Scrapbook', *Theatre Survey*, 54(2): 283–307.

Martindale, Charles (1993) *Redeeming the Text: Latin Poetry and the Hermeneutics of Reception*, Cambridge, UK: Cambridge University Press.

Martindale, Charles (1997) ed., *The Cambridge Companion to Virgil*, Cambridge, UK: Cambridge University Press.

Matzner, Sebastian (2016) 'Queer Unhistoricism, Scholars, Metalepsis, and Interventions of the Unruly Past', in Shane Butler, ed., *Deep Classics: Rethinking Classical Reception*, London: Bloomsbury, 179–203.

Mendelsund, Peter (2014) *What We See When We Read: A Phenomenology, with Illustrations*, New York, NY: Vintage Contemporaries.

Metz, Christian (1974) *Film Language: A Semiotics of the Cinema*, New York, NY: Oxford University Press.

Mignolo, Walter D. (2003) *The Darker Side of the Renaissance: Literacy, Territoriality and Colonization*, Ann Arbor, MI: University of Michigan Press.

Miller, Toby (2008) 'The Reception Deception', in Philip Goldstein and James Machor, eds, *New Directions in American Reception*, New York, NY: Oxford University Press, 353–370.

Millett, Kate (1977 [1970]) *Sexual Politics*, London: Virago.

Mills, Sara (1997) *Discourse*, Abingdon and New York, NY: Routledge.

Minnis, Alastair J., and Scott, A. Brian (1988) *Medieval Literary Theory and Criticism c.1100–c.1375*, Oxford: Clarendon.

Moretti, Franco (2000) 'The Slaughterhouse of Literature', *Modern Language Quarterly*, 61(1): 207–228.

Moretti, Franco (2005) *Graphs, Maps, Trees: Abstract Models for a Literary History*, London and New York, NY: Verso.

Morley, David (1980) *The 'Nationwide' Audience*, London: British Film Institute.

Morrison, Toni (1992) *Playing in the Dark: Whiteness and the Literary Imagination*, Cambridge, MA: Harvard University Press.

Morson, Gary Saul (1989) *Boundaries of Genre: Dostoevsky's Diary of a Writer and the Traditions of Literary Utopia*, Austin, TX: University of Texas Press.

Mowitt, John (1992) *Text: The Genealogy of an Antidisciplinary Object*, Durham, NC: Duke University Press.

Mukherjee, Ankhi (2014) *What is a Classic? Postcolonial Rewriting and Invention of the Canon*, Stanford, CA: Stanford University Press.

Mulhern, Francis (1979) *The Moment of 'Scrutiny'*, London: New Left Books.

Mulvey, Laura (1975) 'Visual Pleasure and Narrative Cinema', *Screen*, 16(3): 6–18.

Muñoz, José Esteban (1996) 'Famous and Dandy Like B. "N" Andy: Race, Pop and Basquiat', in Jennifer Doyle, Jonathan Flatley and José Esteban Munoz, eds, *Pop Out: Queer Warhol*, Durham, NC: Duke University Press, 144–179.

Noyes, Jan M., and Garland, Kate J. (2003) 'VDT versus Paper-Based Text: Reply to Mayes, Sims and Koonce', *International Journal of Industrial Ergonomics*, 31(6): 411–423.

Ong, Walter J. (1982) *Orality and Literacy: The Technologizing of the Word*, New York, NY: Routledge.

Organization for Transformative Works (n.d.) 'What We Believe'. www.transformativeworks.org/what_we_believe/.

Ostriker, Alicia (1985 [1981]) 'The Thieves of Language: Women Poets and Revisionist Mythmaking', in Elaine Showalter, ed., *The New Feminist Criticism: Essays on Women, Literature and Theory*, New York, NY: Pantheon Books, 314–338.

Palmer, Richard E. (1969) *Hermeneutics*, Evanston, IL: Northwestern University Press.

Park, You-me, and Rajan, Rajeswari Sunder (2000), eds, *The Postcolonial Jane Austen*, New York, NY: Routledge.

Parris, David (2009) *Reception Theory and Biblical Hermeneutics*, Eugene, OR: Pickwick Publications.

Paul, Joanna (2007) 'Working with Film: Theories and Methodologies', in Christopher Stray and Lorna Hardwick, eds, *A Companion to Classical Reception*, Oxford: Wiley-Blackwell, 303–314.

Pearce, Lynne (1997) *Feminism and the Politics of Reading*, London: Arnold.

Peirce, Charles Sanders (1931–1958 [1894]) *Collected Writings*, 8 vols., edited by Charles Hartshorne, Paul Weiss and Arthur W. Burks, Cambridge, MA: Harvard University Press.

Penley, Constance (1991) 'Brownian Motion: Women, Tactics and Technology', in Constance Penley and Andrew Ross, eds, *Technoculture*, Minneapolis, MI: University of Minnesota Press, 135–162.

Piper, Andrew (2012) *Book Was There: Reading in Electronic Times*, Chicago, IL, and London: Chicago University Press.

Poletti, Anna, Seaboyer, Judith, Kennedy, Rosanne, Barnett, Tully, and Douglas, Kate (2014) 'The Affects of Not Reading: Hating Characters, Being Bored, Feeling Stupid', *Arts and Humanities in Higher Education*, 15(2): 231–247.

Pollock, Sheldon (2009) 'Future Philology? The Fate of a Soft Science in a Hard World', *Critical Inquiry*, 35(4): 931–961.

Pollock, Sheldon (2014) 'Philology in Three Dimensions', *Postmedieval: A Journal of Medieval Cultural Studies*, 5(4): 398–413.

Potter, Amanda (2009) 'Hell Hath No Fury Like A Dissatisfied Viewer: Audience Responses to the Presentation of the Furies in *Xena: Warrior Princess* and *Charmed*', in Dunstan Lowe and Kim Shahabudin, eds, *Classics for All: Reworking Antiquity in Mass Media*, Newcastle-upon-Tyne: Cambridge Scholars Press, 217–236.

Pratt, Mary Louise (1977) *Toward A Speech Act Theory of Literary Discourse*, Bloomington, IN: Indiana University Press.

Price, Leah (2004) 'Reading: The State of the Discipline', *Book History,* 7(1): 303–320.

Price, Leah (2012) *How to Do Things with Books in Victorian Britain*, Princeton and Oxford: Princeton University Press.

Quine, Willard Van Orman (1980) *From a Logical Point of View: Nine Logico-Philosophical Essays*, second revised edition, Cambridge, MA: Harvard University Press.

Rabinowitz, Peter J. (1987) *Before Reading: Narrative Conventions and the Politics of Interpretation*, Ithaca, NY and London: Cornell University Press.

Radway, Janice (1987 [1984]) *Reading the Romance: Women, Patriarchy and Popular Literature*, London and New York: Verso.

Radway, Janice (2008) 'What's the Matter with Reception Study? Some Thoughts on the Disciplinary Origins, Conceptual Constraints and Persistent Visibility of a Paradigm', in James Machor and Philip Goldstein, eds, *New Directions in American Reception Study*, New York: Oxford University Press, 327–353.

Ranasinha, Ruvani (2007) 'The Fatwa and its Aftermath', in Abdulrasak Gurnah, ed., *The Cambridge Companion to Salman Rushdie*, Cambridge, UK: Cambridge University Press, 45–60.

Rand, E. K. (1926) 'Chaucer in Error', *Speculum,* 1(2): 222–225.

Raven, James, Small, Helen, and Tadmor, Naomi (1996) *The Practice and Representation of Reading in England*, Cambridge, UK and New York: Cambridge University Press.

Reynolds, L. D. and Wilson, N. G. (2013) *Scribes and Scholars: a Guide to the Transmission of Greek and Latin Literature*, fourth edition, Oxford: Oxford University Press.

Reynolds, Suzanne (1996) *Medieval Reading: Grammar, Rhetoric and the Classical Text*, Cambridge, UK: Cambridge University Press.

Rich, Adrienne (1972) 'When We Dead Awaken: Writing as Re-Vision', *College English,* 34(1): 18–30.

Richards, I. A. (2001 [1929]) *Practical Criticism: A Study of Literary Judgement*, Abingdon: Routledge.

Richardson, Edmund (2016) 'Ghostwritten Classics', in Shane Butler, ed., *Deep Classics: Rethinking Classical Reception*, London: Bloomsbury, 221–238.

Richter, David H. (2007) *The Critical Tradition: Classic Texts and Contemporary Trends*, third edition, Boston: St Martin's Press.

Rieu, E. V. (1946) *The Odyssey*, Harmondsworth: Penguin.

Roberts, Jonathan (2011) 'Introduction', in Michael Lieb, Emma Mason and Jonathan Roberts, eds, *The Oxford Handbook to the Reception History of the Bible*, Oxford: Oxford University Press, 1–8.

Rogerson, Anne (2013) 'Vegio's Ascanius: Problems in the Continuation of the *Aeneid*', *Classical Receptions Journal*, 5(1): 105–125.

Rose, Jacqueline (1994 [1984]) *The Case of Peter Pan, or the Impossibility of Children's Fiction*, Basingstoke: Palgrave Macmillan.

Rose, Jonathan (2010) *The Intellectual Life of the British Working Classes*, second edition, New Haven: Yale University Press.

Rosenblatt, Louise (1938) *Literature as Exploration*, first edition, New York and London: Appleton-Century.

Rosenblatt, Louise (1978) *The Reader, the Text, the Poem: The Transactional Theory of the Literary Work*, Carbondale: Southern Illinois University Press.

Rosenblatt, Louise (1995) *Literature as Exploration*, fifth edition, New York: Modern Language Association of America.

Rowling, J. K. (2015) 'Canon: Brown Eyes, Frizzy Hair and Very Clever', Twitter. https://twitter.com/jk_rowling/status/678888094339366914.

Rubin, Joan S. (1992) *The Making of Middlebrow Culture*, Chapel Hill, NC: University of North Carolina Press.

Rudy, Kathryn (2010) 'Dirty Books: Quantifying Patterns of Use in Medieval Manuscripts Using a Densimeter', *Journal of Historians of Netherlandish Art*, 2(1–2): n.p.

Rushdie, Salman (1982) 'The Empire Writes Back with a Vengeance', *Times*, July 3: 8.

Russ, Joanna (1983) *How to Suppress Women's Writing*, Austin, TX: University of Texas Press.

Saenger, Paul (1997) *Space Between Words: The Origin of Silent Reading*, Palo Alto, CA: Stanford University Press.

Saenger, Paul (2011 [1982]) 'Silent Reading: Its Impact on Late Medieval Script and Society', in Shafqat Towheed, Rosalind Crone and Katie Halsey, eds, *The History of Reading: A Reader*, London and New York: Routledge, 114–129.

Said, Edward (1993) *Culture and Imperialism*, New York: Alfred A. Knopf.

Salvatori, Mariolina Rizzi, and Donahue, Patricia (2005) *The Elements (and Pleasures) of Difficulty*, New York: Pearson Longman.

Sanders, Julie (2006) *Adaptation and Appropriation*, London: Routledge.

de Saussure, Ferdinand (2013 [1916]) *A Course in General Linguistics*, trans. Roy Harris, New York: Bloomsbury Academic.

Schein, Seth L. (2016) *Homeric Epic and its Reception: Interpretive Essays*, Oxford: Oxford University Press.

Schmid, Wolf (2013) 'Implied Reader', in Peter Hühn, John Pier, Wolf Schmid and Jörg Schönert, eds, *The Living Handbook of Narratology*, Hamburg: Hamburg University Press. http://wikis.sub.uni-hamburg.de/lhn/index.php/Implied_Reader.

Schweickart, Patrocinio P. (1986) 'Reading Ourselves: Toward a Feminist Theory of Reading', in Elizabeth A. Flynn and Patrocinio P. Schweickart, eds, *Gender and Reading: Essays on Readers, Texts, and Contexts*, Baltimore: Johns Hopkins University Press, 31–63.

Searle, John R. (1975) 'Indirect Speech Acts', in Peter Cole and Jerry Morgan, eds, *Syntax and Semantics Volume 3: Speech Acts*, New York and San Francisco: London Academic Press, 59–82.

Sedgwick, Eve Kosofsky (1994 [1993]) 'Introduction: Queer and Now', in *Tendencies*, London: Routledge, 1–20.

Selbourne, David (1982) *The Making of a Midsummer Night's Dream: An Eye-Witness Account of Peter Brook's Production from First Rehearsal to First Night*, London: Methuen.

Seneca the Younger (1920 [c. 65 CE]) *Ad Lucilium epistulae morales*, vol. 2, trans. Richard M. Gummere, New York: Putnams.

Sherwood, Yvonne (2000) *A Biblical Text and Its Afterlives: The Survival of Jonah in Western Culture*, Cambridge, UK and New York: Cambridge University Press.

Shmoop (2014) '*A Midsummer Night's Dream* Summary', YouTube. www.youtube.com/watch?v=Twz-BuzvBM0.

Showalter, Elaine (1985 [1981]) 'Feminist Criticism in the Wilderness' in Elaine Showalter, ed., *The New Feminist Criticism: Essays on Women, Literature and Theory*, New York: Pantheon Books, 243–270.

Showalter, Elaine (2009) *A Jury of her Peers: American Women Writers from Anne Bradstreet to Annie Proulx*, London: Virago.

Sidney, Philip, Sir (1973 [1595]) *An Apology for Poetry: Or, the Defence of Poesy*, Manchester: Manchester University Press.

Simpson, James (2007) *Burning to Read: English Fundamentalism and Its Reformation Opponents*, Cambridge, MA: Harvard University Press.

Sinfield, Alan (2005) *Cultural Politics – Queer Reading*, second edition, London and New York: Routledge.

Sissa, Guilia (2016) 'Medea's Erotic Jealousy', in Shane Butler, ed., *Deep Classics: Rethinking Classical Reception*, London: Bloomsbury, 203–220.

Slaney, Helen (2016) 'Perceiving (in) Depth: Landscape, Sculpture, Ruins', in Shane Butler, ed., *Deep Classics: Rethinking Classical Reception*, London: Bloomsbury, 87–107.

Slatkin, Laura (1991) *The Power of Thetis: Allusion and Interpretation in the Iliad*, Berkeley and London: California University Press.

Smith, Emma (2016) *Shakespeare's First Folio: Four Centuries of an Iconic Book*, Oxford: Oxford University Press.

Smol, Anna (2004) '"Oh … oh … Frodo!": Readings of Male Intimacy in *The Lord of the Rings*', *Modern Fiction Studies*, 50(4): 949–979.

Sommerstein, Alan H. (1993) ed., *Tragedy, Comedy and the Polis: Papers from the Greek Drama Conference: Nottingham, 18–20 July 1990*, Bari: Levante Editori.

Sontag, Susan (1966) 'Against Interpretation', in *Against Interpretation and Other Essays*, New York: Dell, 3–14.

Spivak, Gayatri Chakravorty (1984) 'Three Women's Texts and a Critique of Imperialism', *Critical Inquiry*, 12(1): 243–361.

Spivak, Gayatri Chakravorty (1990) 'Poststructuralism, Marginality, Postcoloniality, and Value', in Peter Collier and Helga Geyer-Ryan, eds, *Literary Theory Today*, London: Polity Press, 219–244.

Spivak, Gayatri Chakravorty (2012 [1987]) 'Reading the World: Literary Studies in the Eighties', in *In Other Worlds: Essays in Cultural Politics*, Abingdon and New York: Routledge, 127–139.

Stacey, Jackie (2003 [1994]) 'Star Gazing: Hollywood Cinema and Female Spectatorship', in Will Brooker and Deborah Jermyn, eds, *The Audience Studies Reader*, London and New York: Routledge, 150–158.

Staiger, Janet (1992) *Interpreting Films: Studies in the Historical Reception of American Cinema*, Princeton, NJ: Princeton University Press.

Staiger, Janet (2005) *Media Reception Studies*, New York and London: New York University Press.

Staiger, Janet (2008) 'The Revenge of the Film Education Movement: Cult Movies and Fan Interpretive Behaviors', *Reception* 1: 43–69.

Steiner, George (1975) 'Understanding as Translation', in *After Babel: Aspects of Language and Translation*. Oxford: Oxford University Press, 1–31.

Storm, Melvin. 1993. 'The Intertextual Cresseida: Chaucer's Henryson or Henryson's Chaucer?' *Studies in Scottish Literature*, 28: 105–122.

Suleiman, Susan (1976) 'Ideological Dissent from Works of Fiction: Toward a Rhetoric of the *Roman á Thése*', *Neophilologicus,* 60(2): 162–177.

Suleiman, Susan (1980) 'Introduction: Varieties of Audience-Oriented Criticism', in Susan Suleiman and Inge Crosman, eds, *The Reader in the Text: Essays on Audience and Interpretation*, Princeton, NJ: Princeton University Press, 3–45.

Todorov, Tzetvan (1980) 'Reading as Construction', in Susan Suleiman and Inge Crosman, eds, *The Reader in the Text: Essays on Audience and Interpretation*, Princeton, NJ: Princeton University Press, 67–82.

Tompkins, Jane (1980) 'The Reader in History: The Changing Shape of Reader-Response', in Jane Tompkins, ed., *Reader-Response Criticism: From Formalism to Post-structuralism*, Baltimore: Johns Hopkins University Press, 201–232.

Tompkins, Jane (1984) 'Masterpiece Theater: The Politics of Hawthorne's Literary Reputation', *American Quarterly*, 36(5): 617–642.

Tompkins, Jane (1985) *Sensational Designs: The Cultural Work of American Fiction 1790–1860*, New York: Oxford University Press.

Towheed, Shafqat, Crone, Rosalind, and Halsey, Katie (2011), eds, *The History of Reading: A Reader*, London, New York: Routledge.

Traub, Valerie (2013) 'The New Unhistoricism in Queer Studies', *PMLA,* 128(1): 21–39.

Van Toorn, Penny (2006) *Writing Never Arrives Naked: Early Aboriginal Cultures of Writing in Australia*, Canberra: Aboriginal Studies Press.

Vincent, David (2000) *The Rise of Mass Literacy: Reading and Writing in Modern Europe*, Cambridge, UK: Polity Press.

Viswanathan, Gauri (1989) *Masks of Conquests: Literary Study and British Rule in India*, New York: Columbia University Press.

Vodička, Felix (1982 [1941]) 'The Concretization of the Literary Work: Problems of the Reception of Neruda's Works', in Peter Steiner, ed., *The Prague School: Selected Writings, 1929–1946*, trans. John Burbank, Olga Hasty, Manfred Jacobson, Bruce Kochis and Wendy Steiner, Austin, TX: University of Texas Press, 103–135.

Wall, Barbara (1991) *The Narrator's Voice: The Dilemma of Children's Fiction*, Basingstoke and London: Macmillan.

Waquet, Françoise (2001 [1998]) *Latin, or the Empire of the Sign*, trans. John Howe, London: Penguin.

Warhol, Robyn (2002) *Having a Good Cry: Effeminate Feelings and Pop-culture Forms*, Columbia, OH: Ohio State University Press.

Warner, Michael (2002) *Publics and Counterpublics*, New York: Zone.

Warner, Michael (2004) 'Uncritical Reading', in Jane Gallop, ed., *Polemic: Critical or Uncritical?*, New York: Routledge, 11–38.

Wertham, Frederic (1954) *Seduction of the Innocent*, New York: Rinehart and Company.

West, David, and Woodman, Tony (1979) *Creative Imitation and Latin Literature*, Cambridge, UK: Cambridge University Press.

Widdowson, Peter (1999) *Literature*, London, New York: Routledge.

Williams, Raymond (1977) *Marxism and Literature*, Oxford: Oxford University Press.

Williams, Raymond (1985) *Keywords: A Vocabulary of Culture and Society*, second edition, London: Fontana.

Willis, Ika (2006) 'Keeping Promises to Queer Children: Making Space (for Mary-Sue) at Hogwarts', in Karen Hellekson and Kristina Busse, eds, *Fan Fiction and Fan Communities in the Age of the Internet: New Essays*, Jefferson, NC: McFarland, 153–170.

Willis, Ika (2014) 'Philology, or the Art of Befriending the Text', *Postmedieval*, 5(4): 486–501.

Willis, Paul (1990) *Common Culture: Symbolic Work at Play in the Everyday Cultures of the Young*, Milton Keynes: Open University Press.

Wimsatt, W. K., and Beardsley, Monroe (1954) *The Verbal Icon: Studies in the Meaning of Poetry*, Lexington: University of Kentucky Press.

Winkler, John J. (1990) 'Penelope's Cunning, and Homer's', in *The Constraints of Desire: The Anthropology of Sex and Gender in Ancient Greece*, New York: Routledge, 129–161.

Wire, Antoinette Clark (1990) *The Corinthian Women Prophets: A Reconstruction Through Paul's Rhetoric*, Minneapolis, MN: Fortress Press.

Wiseman, T. P. (1992) *Talking to Virgil: A Miscellany*, Exeter: Exeter University Press.

Wittmann, R. (1999) 'Was There a Reading Revolution at the End of the Eighteenth Century?', in Guglielmo Cavallo and Roger Chartier, eds, *A History of Reading in the West*, trans. Lydia G. Cochrane, Amherst, MA: University of Massachusetts Press, 284–312.

Wolf, Maryanne (2016) *Tales of Literacy for the 21st Century: The Literary Agenda*, Oxford: Oxford University Press.

Woolf, Virginia (2010 [1931]) 'The Love of Reading', in Stuart N. Clarke, ed., *The Essays of Virginia Woolf, Vol. 5: 1929–1932*, London: Hogarth, 271–274.

Wu, Yung-Hsing (2013) 'Kindling, Disappearing, Reading', *Digital Humanities* Quarterly, 7(1): n.p. www.digitalhumanities.org.ezproxy.uow.edu.au/dhq/vol/7/1/000115/000115.html.

Zaid, Gabriel (2003) *So Many Books: Reading and Publishing in an Age of Abundance*, trans. Natasha Wimmer, PA: Paul Dry Books.

Zunshine, Lisa (2010) 'Theory of Mind and Michael Fried's *Absorption and Theatricality*: Notes Toward Cognitive Historicism', in Frederick Luis Aldama, ed., *Toward a Cognitive Theory of Narrative Acts*, Austin, TX: University of Texas Press, 179–205.

Zunshine, Lisa (2012) *Getting Inside Your Head: What Cognitive Science Can Tell Us About Popular Culture*, Baltimore: Johns Hopkins University Press.

LITERARY TEXTS

Arnold, Matthew (2013 [1857]) 'Isolation: To Marguerite' in *The Complete Poetic Works of Matthew Arnold*, Hastings: Delphi Classics.

Benchley, Peter (2013 [1974]) *Jaws*, New York: Ballantine.

Brontë, Charlotte (2006 [1847]) *Jane Eyre*, London: Penguin Classics.

Carter, Angela (1995 [1979]) *The Bloody Chamber and Other Stories*, London: Vintage Classics.

Catullus, Gaius Valerius (1969 [c. 55 BCE]) *Poems*, translated by Celia Thaew Zukofsky and Louis Zukofsky, London: Jonathan Cape.

Césaire, Aimé (2002 [1965]) *A Tempest*, translated by Richard Miller, New York: Theatre Communications Group, Inc.

Chaucer, Geoffrey (1900 [c. 1380]) 'Troilus and Criseyde', in Walter W. Skeat, ed., *The Complete Works of Geoffrey Chaucer Volume 2*, Oxford: Clarendon Press.

Chaucer, Geoffrey (1900 [c. 1383]) 'The House of Fame', in Walter W. Skeat, ed., *The Complete Works of Geoffrey Chaucer Volume 3*, Oxford: Clarendon Press.

Dahl, Roald (2013 [1980]) *The Twits*, London: Penguin.

Doyle, Arthur Conan (2001 [1887]) *A Study in Scarlet*, London: Penguin.

Doyle, Arthur Conan (2001 [1890]) *The Sign of Four*, London: Penguin.

Fielding, Henry (1974 [1749]) *The History of Tom Jones, A Foundling*, Volume 1, ed. Fredson Bowers, London: Oxford University Press.

Henryson, Robert (2010 [before 1505]) 'The Testament of Cresseid', in David J. Parkinson, ed., *The Complete Works*, Medieval Institute Publications, Western Michigan University, 102–116.

Hurston, Zora Neale (2001 [1937]) *Their Eyes Were Watching God*, New York: Harper Collins.

Irving, Washington (1996 [1819]), 'Rip Van Winkle', in Susan Manning, ed., *The Sketch-Book of Geoffrey Crayon, Gent*, Oxford: Oxford University Press, 33–49.

Lawrence, D. H. (1995 [1926]) *The Plumed Serpent*, London: Penguin.

Le Carré, John (2011 [1974]) *Tinker Tailor Soldier Spy*, London: Hodder and Stoughton.

Le Guin, Ursula K. (1983 [1974]) 'The Author of the Acacia Seeds, and Other Extracts from the Journal of the Association of Therolinguistics', in *The Compass Rose*, Toronto and New York: Bantam, 3–11.

Lucashenko, Melissa (2013) *Mullumbimby*, Brisbane: University of Queensland Press.

Meyer, Stephenie (2005) *Twilight*, New York: Little, Brown.

Packer, Vin (2004 [1952]) *Spring Fire*, revised edition, Jersey City, NJ: Cleis Press.

Parker, Dorothy (1973 [1928]) 'Penelope', in *The Collected Dorothy Parker*, London: Duckworth.

Rhys, Jean (2000 [1966]) *Wide Sargasso Sea*, Harmondsworth: Penguin.

Rushdie, Salman (2008 [1988]) *The Satanic Verses*, New York: Random House.

Shakespeare, William (2011 [1610–1611]) *The Tempest*, London, New York: Bloomsbury.

Shakespeare, William (2016 [1603]) *Hamlet*, London, New York: Bloomsbury.

Sterne, Laurence (1998 [1760–1767]) *The Life and Opinions of Tristram Shandy*, London: Penguin.

Vegio, Maffeo (2004 [1428]), 'Book XIII of the *Aeneid*', in *Short Epics*, ed. and trans. Michael C. J. Putnam, with James Hankins, Cambridge, MA and London: Harvard University Press, 3–41.

Virgil (Publius Vergilius Maro) (2003 [19 BCE]) *The Aeneid*, translated by David West, London: Penguin.

Virgil (Publius Vergilius Maro) (2006 [29 BCE]) *Georgics*, translated by Peter Fallon. Oxford: Oxford University Press.

Walcott, Derek (2002 [1990]) *Omeros*, London: Faber and Faber.

Walker, Alice (1982) *The Color Purple*, San Diego: Harcourt Brace Jovanovich.

Wallace, David Foster (1996) *Infinite Jest*, New York: Bay Back Books.

Waters, Sarah (2009) *The Little Stranger*, London: Virago.

FILMS

Alfredson, Tomas (2011) dir., *Tinker Tailor Soldier Spy*.

Nichols, Mike (1966) dir., *Who's Afraid of Virginia Woolf?*

Wilder, Billy (1959) dir., *Some Like It Hot*.

INDEX

Abercrombie, Nicholas 104
Aboriginal writing 140–41, 146
active audiences *see* audiences, active
actor-network theory 169
Adaptation and Appropriation 40
Adolphe 148
The Adoption Papers 100
Adorno, Theodor 26, 82
aesthetic disposition 125–7
aesthetic of reception 4, 50
affective fallacy 84
afterlife reception 65
Allen, Graham 40
Allington, Daniel 100–2
alphabetic script 137
Althusser, Louis 26, 29, 79
Altieri, Charles 75–7, 78–9
anachronism as productive 63
Anderson, Benedict 21
annotations 101
Aristotle 8–10
Armstrong, Paul B. 6–7
Arnold, Matthew 14, 18, 26, 75
Ars Poetica 9
art cinema 118
artworks 62
Attridge, Derek 75
attunement 169
audience interpretation 3
audience-oriented criticism 22
audiences: Aboriginal 96; active
    81–4, 93–6, 97–9, 106; of
    cinema 2, 110; as citizens 8;
    effects on 9, 81–2; homosexual
    93; mass 14–15, 83; minority 95;
    social 72, 77; of theatre 8,
    151–2; vulnerable 82, 97
autistic viewers 110

autonomous text, New Critical
    model of 18–20
Averroes (Ibn Rushd) 9, 64

Bal, Mieke 30, 49, 62, 63, 95
Balibar, Etienne 26, 79
Barker, Martin 96
Barthes, Roland 23, 28, 29, 125,
    159–60, 162, 163–5, 168–9
Batstone, William 152–3, 157
Bauschatz, Cathleen 11
Bayard, Pierre 106
Beardsley, Monroe 18, 84
Benjamin, Walter 82
Bennett, Tony 54, 84, 122–3, 156
Benoist, Jean-Marie 28–9
Benwell, Bethan 100–2, 105
Betti, Emilio 97
Bible reading 12, 47
Biblical reception 2, 4, 5, 35, 36, 47,
    49, 50, 53, 145
Biblical translation 47–8
black literary criticism 23–5
black literature 114, 127
black tradition *see* tradition,
    black
black writers 56
Bloom, Harold 40, 51, 60
Bobo, Jacqueline 94, 127–8
Bode, Katherine 86
book groups 100–1, 116
Booth, Wayne 70, 75, 76–7, 99–100,
    107, 113, 125
Bordwell, David 118
Bourdieu, Pierre 125–8, 128
Breed, Brennan 145
Brodhead, Richard 63
Brook, Peter 45
Bulkin, Elly 114

Bury, Rhiannon 98
Butler, Shane 102

Carey, James 103–4
Carrington, André 44
Carter, Angela 55
CCCS (Birmingham Centre for Contemporary Cultural Studies) 29
centered structure 160
Césaire, Aimé 25
Chakrabarty, Dipesh 61–3
Charlie's Angels 92–3
Chaucer, Geoffrey 119
The Cheese and the Worms 123–4
Chomsky, Noam 151
cinema 2–3, 4
citizenship and audience 8
classical music 28
classical reading 162
classical reception 4, 6, 7–9, 35, 36, 43, 49, 50
classical tradition 60
close reading 85
codex 135
coduction 99, 125
cognitive approach 6–7
cognitive fallacy 130, 131
cognitive-interpretative reception 11, 21
Cohen, Margaret 85–6
Colgan, Jenny 122
collaboration and texts 145
collective interpretation 101–2
The Color Purple 59, 94, 100
communication 103–4
communications technology, history of 20–1
concretization 17
Conroy, Pat 102
Constant, Benjamin 148
constraints of circulation 6
Conte, Gian Biagio 39, 60, 68
context-activated reception 152
contexts of judgement 115

Corner, John 148–9
Cottom, Daniel 130–1
A Course in General Linguistics 27
Cowie, Elizabeth 95–6
creation, and reception 41–4
creative imitation 42–4
creativity, basic elements of 41–2
critical reading 90
critical revolution 18
Culler, Jonathan 111–12
cultural capital 119–20
cultural competencies 124–8
culture, high/mass 14–15
Culture and Anarchy 14

Dahl, Roald 71
Dale, Leigh 120, 130
Daly, Mary 55, 57
D'Arcens, Louise 46
Darnton, Robert 34, 87, 88
de Certeau, Michel 51, 84, 92, 97, 103
'The Death of the Author' 23
decoding processes 82–3
deconstruction 157–65
decontextualization 163
Derrida, Jacques 31, 159–61, 163–5
deviant interpretations 51
digital culture 136
digital humanities 86
Dilling-Hansen, Lise 97
Dimock, Wai Chee 155–6, 157, 167
Dinshaw, Carolyn 63
Discourse Networks 20
disidentification/identification 95–6
distant reading 85
Dobinson, Cheryl 93
Doctor Who 52, 92
dominant-hegemonic decoding 83
dominant poetics 47
Douglas, Ann 89
Dryden, John 9
Dubrow, Heather 116–17
Dyer, Richard 135

Eagleton, Terry 26, 79
Early Music 6
Eco, Umberto 68–9, 71, 76
editing as interpretation 145
educational training 90
effective history 50
Eisenstein, Elizabeth 21
Eliot, T.S. 60–1, 63, 64
Ellis, Samantha 130–1
embodied reception 66, 131, 134
emotion, management of 8
encoding processes 82–3
English Literature,
    institutionalization of 19
enunciative relations 151–2
epochal analysis 137–8
Erotic Rearmament Campaign
    130–1
ethical/emotional/embodied
    reception 11
ethnographic research 88–9, 94
Evans, Robert 51
event of reading 98–9
extending the self 75

fan studies 51–3, 97–8
fan writing 91–2
'Fantasia' 95–6
The Fashion System 28
Federico, Annette 77
Felski, Rita 62, 91, 92, 131, 169
female authors 15
feminist literary criticism 23–5
feminist re-writing 55
Ferguson, Kirby 41–2
Fetterley, Judith 78, 79–80, 81, 95,
    108, 114, 122
Fiction and the Reading Public 18
Fielding, Henry 73
Fish, Leslie 52
Fish, Stanley 22, 74, 144, 146–8,
    162
Fiske, John 92–3, 96–7
fixed literal meaning,
    inaccessibility of 33

Flaubert, Gustave 51
Flint, Kate 87
formalism 16–18
Foster, Jodie 93
Foucault, Michel 29, 151
Fowler, Don 41
frame 120–3, 144
Frame Analysis 120
Freud, Sigmund 79, 95
Frow, John 38–9, 116, 121
fusion of horizons 153

Gadamer, Hans-Georg 31, 50,
    153–5, 156, 157, 165
Gaipa, Mark 149
Gates, Henry Louis Jr 24, 25, 59, 60
Gaunt, Simon 43, 138
gender 8, 15, 23–4, 28, 77–8, 128,
    129
Genette, Gérard 29, 37, 41, 54, 57,
    121, 122
genius, Romantic conception of 42
genre 115–20, 144, 164, 167
Gibson, Walter 71–2, 75, 76–7, 107
Gillespie, Marie 103
Ginzburg, Carlo 123–4
Gitelman, Lisa 134, 139–40
Goffman, Erving 120
Goldstein, Philip 163
Grafton, Anthony 87–8
Gramsci, Antonio 25–6, 83
Gray, Jonathan 97, 106
Great Expectations 56
The Great Tradition 18
Greek literature 7–8
Guillory, John 14, 90–1, 119–20
The Gutenberg Galaxy 21
Güthenke, Constanze 91

Hall, Stuart 29, 82–3
haptic imagination 129
Harry Potter 94–5
Hawkes, Terence 2
Hawthorne, Nathaniel 15, 64–5
Hebdige, Dick 29

hegemony 26, 83
Hélias, Pierre Jakez 150, 156–7
Herder, Gottfried 129
hermeneutic approach 5, 22
Hexter, Ralph 119
Hills, Matt 92
historical consciousness 61–3
history of effects 50
Hoggart, Richard 29
Holland, Norman 22
Hollander, John 16
Holub, Robert 4
Homer 44, 47, 56, 61
Homer's Deep 102
homophonic translation 150–1
Hopkins, David 49
Horace 9
Horáček, Josef 151
Howard, Susan 103
human consciousness, and writing 21
Hungerford, Amy 105
Hutcheon, Linda 42
Huyssen, Andreas 15

identification/disidentification 95–6
Imagined Communities 21
imitation 66
implied reader 32, 69–74, 76–7, 83–4, 113
information storage/transmission 13
Ingarden, Roman 17
injection model of reception 82
interactivity in literature 17
internal constraints of circulation 6
interpretation 33, 46–8, 66, 98–102, 109, 111, 130, 145, 155, 167
interpretative conventions 111, 113
intersemiotic translation 44
intertextual relations 142
intertextuality 40–1, 68
Intertextuality 40
intralinguistic translation 44

Iser, Wolfgang 4, 22, 70, 73–4, 88, 106, 109, 111, 121

Jakobson, Roman 16, 44
Jameson, Fredric 79, 96
Jardine, Lisa 87–8
Jauss, Hans Robert 4, 22, 50, 154–5, 156, 157
Jenkins, Henry 51–2
Jenkyns, Richard 49
Johnson, William 132
Jonah, book of 112

Kay, Jackie 100
Kay, Sarah 43, 138
Kindle readers 133
Kirkpatrick, Ellen 66
Kittler, Friedrich 20
Kline, Daniel T. 66
Knight, Jackson 91
Kolodny, Annette 115
Konstanz (Constance) School 4, 19, 22
Korman, Boris 74–5
Kristeva, Julia 40, 159
Kuhn, Annette 72

Lam, May 89
Lamond, Julieanne 86–7, 116
Lang, Anouk 90
language and meaning 33
Lawrence, D.H. 24
lay readers 89–92
Leavis, F.R. 18, 26
Leavis, Q.D. 18, 26
Le Guin, Ursula K. 2, 143
Lefevere, André 46–8, 52, 53, 105–6
Leff, Michael 43
Leisure Learning Group 116
lesbian cinema 93
Lévi-Strauss, Claude 28–9
linguistic analysis 27
linguistic meaning 33, 158–65
linguistic sign 157–8; *see also* semiotics

linguistic turn 20, 26–30
linguistics 157–65
literacy, imposition of 13
literacy, spread of 12–14
literal meaning 146–52
literariness 16
literary criticism 17, 19–20
literary societies 100–1; see also book groups
literary tradition, see tradition
literary-critical readings 90
Literature as Exploration 17
literature as transaction 74
Littau, Karin 10, 130, 136
The Little Stranger 22
Long, Elizabeth 99, 116
Longhurst, Brian 104
The Lord of the Rings 113
Lothian, Alexis 98
Lowell, James Russell 15
Lucashenko, Melissa 69
Luria, Alexander137
Lynch, David 118
Lynch, Deirdre 131
Lyons, William John 36, 167

McClary, Susan 28
McGann, Jerome 145
McHenry, Elizabeth 101
Macheray, Pierre 26, 80, 96
Machor, James 123, 163
McKenzie, D.F. 21, 139–40, 141
McLuhan, Marshall 20–1
McRobbie, Angela 29
macro-historical approaches 85
Mailloux, Steven 109, 111, 116, 163–4
Manguel, Alberto 109
Martindale, Charles 6, 31, 45–6, 49, 167
Marxist theories/criticism 20, 25–6, 29, 79, 83, 122–3
Mass Civilisation and Minority Culture 18
mass communication 12

material constraints of circulation 6
Matzner, Sebastian 91
meaning 142–66; deconstruction 157–65; dialogue 152–7; interface 152–7; linguistics 157–65; literal meaning 146–52; and reception 11; resonance 152–7; semiotics 157–65; stable texts 144–6; three levels of 148–9
meaning-production 109–10
media history 3, 20–1, 133–8
media studies 3, 4, 36, 81–3, 96–7, 152
medieval reception 4, 9–11, 36, 43, 46
Mendelsund, Peter 128–9
Menocchio see Scandella
Metz, Christian 28
Meyer, Stephenie 89
Michaels, Eric 96
A Midsummer Night's Dream 45, 53
Millett, Kate 23–4
mock reader 71–2
Modern Russian Poetry 16
Monroe, Marilyn 72
Montaigne 11
moods 37
More, Thomas 47–8
Moretti, Franco 64, 85, 86
Morley, David 83
Morrison, Toni 80
Morson, Gary Saul 117
Mowitt, John 164, 170
Mulholland Drive 118
Mulvey, Laura 77
Muñoz, José Esteban 95
murder mystery 117
Murray, Gilbert 91
mystery of reading 88

Nagendra, Uma 45
natural selection 64
negotiated decoding 83

Neighbours 103–4
neurological approach 6–7
New Criticism 18, 19–20, 21, 22, 68, 143
Nicholls, Mike J. 39
non-cooperation with text 78
non-reading 32, 106
Not Reading DFW 105
novels, dangers of reading 81

O Brother, Where Art Thou? 3
Omeros 57–9
Ong, Walter 20–1, 137–9
online reading 136
oppositional decoding 83
orality and literacy 137–41
Ostriker, Alicia 55, 56
OTW (Organization for Transformative Works) 42

Packer, Vin 93
palimpsestuous works 41
paratexts 106, 121, 122
Park, You-me 56
Parker, Dorothy 55, 56
paronthocentrism 49
Parris, David 49, 50
participatory medievalism 66
Paul, Joanna 3
Pearce, Lynne 101
Peirce, Charles Sanders 143
Penelope 55, 56
Penley, Constance 51
peritexts *see* paratexts
Phaedrus 160
phenomenological approach 22
Plato 8, 10, 160
Poetics 8–9
poetry 8–10, 16
Poletti, Anna 97
politicized literary criticism 19–20
Pollock, Sheldon 143, 156, 157
popular culture 14–15, 18, 29, 81–3, 84, 86–7, 118–19, 126–7, 129
popular music 2, 36, 37, 45, 82

popular reading practices 90, 98
popular taste 126
The Postcolonial Jane Austen 56
postcolonial literary criticism 23–5
postcolonial rewriting 56–7
post-critical reading 3
post-structuralist theory 20
power of naming 57
Practical Criticism 17
pragmatics 149–50
Prague Structuralists 16–17
Pratt, Mary Louise 118
present-centredness 49
Price, Leah 104–5
Prince, Gerald 22
print literacy 12–15
print-capitalism 21
The Printing Press as an Agent of Change 21
privatization of reading 12, 15, 135
process of creation 42
Procter, James 105
professional readers 89–92
Protestant Reformation 12
Proust, Marcel 51

queer theory 113
queer touch across time 63
queer unhistoricism 63
Quoting Caravaggio 62

Rabinowitz, Peter J. 111, 115, 118
radical staging of works 45
Radway, Janice 44, 88–9, 98–9, 167–8
Rajan, Rajeswari 56
The Reader in the Text 22
reader-activated reception 152
reader-centred approaches 70, 97
reader/implied reader interplay 76–7
readerly hospitality 75
readerly suppositions 111
reader-response criticism 21–3, 81
reader-response theory 4, 9–10, 19

readers 68–107
reader-to-reader dynamics 32
reading 108–41; against the grain
    26, 79; beyond meaning 128–32;
    codes 109–15; cognitive/
    affective dimensions 108; as
    construction 73–4; conventions
    109–15; cultural competencies
    124–8; as culture 15; frames
    120–3; as generalized
    sociocultural system 32–3; genre
    115–20, 144, 164, 167; high/mass
    culture 14–15; as hybrid
    practices 138; and interpretation
    5, 7; literacy 138–41; mass
    readership 12–15; orality
    138–41; privatization of 12;
    reader as passive 10; and
    reception 29–30; rules 109–15;
    as semiotic warfare 97; silent
    reading 12, 138; as social activity
    98–102; as socially framed 99; as
    sociocultural system 108–9; as
    subordination 75–7; talking
    about books 102–7;
    technologies of 132–8; as
    understanding 153; and visual
    art 29–30; see also
    text-to-reader reception
    theories
reading filters 123–4
reading formations 120–3
reading patterns 89–90
reading practices 2, 3, 12–13, 15,
    19, 24, 66, 75–6, 83, 87, 88–92,
    96–8, 108–9, 114, 122, 127, 131,
    136–41, 166, 168, 170
Reading Rembrandt 30
Reading Resilience Project 133
Reading the Romance 88–9, 98, 167
real reader 32, 69–73, 76, 83–9,
    92–107
reception definition 1–2; as
    intertextuality 40–1; its objects
    31–4; prehistories of (1920–1960)
    16–19; prehistories of (classical)
    4, 6, 7–9, 35, 36, 43; prehistories
    of (early modern) 9–11;
    prehistories of (medieval) 4,
    9–11, 36, 43, 46; prehistories of
    (modernity 1700–1900) 11–15;
    usage of word 2–7
reception aesthetics 4, 50
receptive fallacy 85
recipes 122
repentance/penance 47
resistant listening 26
resistant reader 33, 106
retellings 137
re-visioning texts 25, 55
revisionist mythmaking 56
rewriting 36, 37–8, 52, 54, 56–7
Reynolds, Suzanne 101–2
The Rhetoric of Fiction 70–1, 76
Rhys, Jean 57
Rich, Adrienne 25, 55
Richards, I.A. 17, 18
Richardson, Edmund 91
Rieu, E.V. 47
'Rip Van Winkle' 77–8
Roberts, Jonathan 65–6
Robinson, Gemma 105
The Role of the Reader 69, 71
Roman reading 132–3
Rose, Jacqueline 127
Rose, Jonathan 84, 85, 87, 120, 121
Rosenblatt, Louise 17, 74
Rubin, Joan 15
Rudy, Kathryn 146
Rushdie, Salman 57, 105
Russ, Joanna 113–15, 122, 128
Russian Formalists 16–17

Saenger, Paul 135–6, 138
Said, Edward 56–7
Sanders, Julie 40, 52
The Satanic Verses 105
Saussure, Ferdinand de 27–8, 157–8
Scandella, Domenico (Menocchio)
    124

Scholes, Robert 149
Schweickart, Patriciono 76
scriptio continua 132, 135
Searle, John 147–8
second-wave feminism 23
Sedgwick, Eve Kosofsky 113
selective tradition 64
semantics 149–50
semiotic warfare 97
semiotics 28–30, 44, 68–9, 125, 143, 157–65
Seneca the Younger 43
Sexual Politics 23–4
Sherlock Holmes stories 119
Sherwood, Yvonne 50–1, 112
Showalter, Elaine 60
Sidney, Sir Philip 9
sign, interpretation as 143
sign systems 4, 27–9, 44, 107, 108, 125, 144, 148, 157–61, 165
signification 59
silent reading 12, 138
Simpson, James 48
simultaneous order 61
Sissa, Giulia 49–50
Slaney, Helen 129
Slatkin, Laura 44
slaughterhouse of literature 85
Smith, Emma 146
sociocognitive satisfaction 30
sociological research 88–9
Some Like It Hot 72, 110
Sontag, Susan 44, 130
spectatorship 77, 96
Spivak, Gayatri 57, 167
Stacey, Jackie 66
Staiger, Janet 98, 152, 157
Star Trek 52
Star Wars 39
Steiner, George 44
structuralist theory 20
Sulieman, Susan 22, 70, 74, 78
summit-dialogue of authors 50
surface reading 80
symptomatic reading 79–80

technologies of reading 132–8
Tel Quel group 159–60
temporality 61–3
text constructed as consequence of reading 98–9
text, directions given by 111
Text World Theory 6
text-activated reception 152
text-centred approaches 69–70, 152
texts and contexts 2, 5; meaning of 2, 111
text-to-reader reception theories 32, 35, 39, 67–107, 157, 168–9; active audiences (ingenuity and pleasure) 96–8; active audiences (intervention and invention) 92–5; audiences, power and freedom 80–3; identification/disidentification 95–6; mock, implied or real readers 70–5; professional/lay readers 89–92; readers in history 85–8; reading as social activity 98–102; real readers 83–4; resistant readers 77–80; sociological/ethnographic research 88–9; subordinating oneself to the text 75–7; talking about books 102–7; *see also* reading
text-to-text reception theories 32, 35–67, 68; beyond the text 65–7; exemplary or monstrous, high or low 48–54; interpreters 46–8; reception as creation 41–4; reception as interpretation 44–54; reception as intertextuality 40–1; reception as tradition 59–61; temporality 61–3; tradition 59–65; transformation and continuity 38–40; translation and performance 44–6; transmission 63–5; writing back 48, 54–9
textual analysis 142, 144

The Textual Condition 145
textual gamekeeping 98
textuality 29
Tinker Tailor Soldier Spy 39–41
Todorov, Tzvetan 73–4, 148, 149
Tompkins, Jane 9–10, 64–5, 119
tradition 51, 59–65, 102, 119,
    156–7; black 25, 59–60; oral,
    124; selective 64; white, 114–15;
    women's 60
Tradition and the Individual Talent
    60–1
transfocalization 57
transformative rewriting 33
transformative use 42
translation 25, 36, 37, 44–5, 46–8,
    53, 105–6, 139; intralinguistic,
    interlinguistic, intersemiotic 44;
    homophonic 150–1; *see also*
    Biblical translation
transmission 63–5
transposition 54
Traub, Valerie 63
Treaty of Waitangi 139–40
The Twilight Saga 89
Tyndale, William 47

uncritical reading 90
understanding 115, 120, 149–50,
    153–6, 160–1
The Uses of Literacy 29

Van Toorn, Penny 140, 141,
    146
VCR technology 81–2

verbal language 4–5
Virgil 36, 39, 90, 118
Viswanathan, Gauri 57
Vodička, Felix 16
vulnerable audience *see* audience,
    vulnerable

Walcott, Derek 57–9
Walker, Alice 59, 94
Wall, Barbara 71, 76
Warhol, Robyn 129
Warner, Michael 6, 90
Warner, Susan 64–5
Waters, Sarah 22
Who's Afraid of Virginia Woolf?
    110–11
Williams, Raymond 64, 137–8
Wimsatt, W.K. 18, 84
Wire, Antoinette 50–1
Wiseman, T.P. 91
Wolf, Maryanne 136
women-in-pain books 116
women's tradition *see* tradition,
    women's
Woolf, Virginia 76, 78
writing, and human consciousness
    21, 137
writing back 48, 54–9
Wu, Yung-Hsing 133

Young, Kevin 93

Zukofsky, Celia 150–1
Zukofsky, Louis 150–1
Zunshine, Lisa 30